SONS OF ADAM

DAUGHTERS OF EVE

BIBLICAL IMAGES IN ART FROM TULSA COLLECTIONS

WITH INTRODUCTORY MATERIAL BY
ARTHUR M. FELDMAN

ESSAY AND CATALOGUE TEXT BY
KAREN S. YORK, PHD

AN EXHIBITION ORGANIZED BY
THE SHERWIN MILLER MUSEUM OF JEWISH ART
OCTOBER 28, 2007 – JANUARY 20, 2008

The Sherwin Miller Museum of Jewish Art
2021 East 71st Street
Tulsa OK 74136
jewishmuseum.net

EXHIBITION STAFF

Arthur M. Feldman, *Executive Director*
Karen York, *Curator*
Charles Taylor, *Preparator*
Brenda Michael-Haggard, *Development Director*
Sabrina Darby, *Administrative Assistant*
Cathey Wilson, *Volunteer Coordinator*

Design: Carl Brune
Photography: Nathan Harmon

Sons of Adam, Daughters of Eve: Biblical Images in Art from Tulsa Collections

Library of Congress Control No:
20077937207

ISBN 978-0-9799851-0-2

Front Cover Illustration:
Marc Chagall: *The Garden of Eden* (M. 232), from the series *Drawings for the Bible*, original color lithograph, 1960.
Acquired through tribute gifts from family and friends in memory of Cecilia Feldman.

Printed in the United States of America

Funding for this catalogue

Sons of Adam, Daughters of Eve:
Biblical Images in Art from Tulsa Collections

was made possible by these Exhibition Sponsors:

CONTRIBUTING
Ralph and Frances McGill Foundation

SPONSOR
Bezalel Foundation
Jewish Federation of Tulsa Foundation
The Anne and Henry Zarrow Foundation
Maxine and Jack Zarrow Family Foundation

ADVOCATE
The Mervin Bovaird Foundation
Waters Charitable Foundation

FRIEND
Ruth Ann Fate
Tulsa World

Anonymous
Susan Fenster
Hille Foundation
E. P. and R.L. Kirschner Foundation
Rita and Dr. Simon Levit
Jean and Wilfred Sanditen

In-kind donation of banners by
Pearl M. & Julia J. Harmon Foundation

CONTENTS

FOREWORD

The Bible is the word of life. You will find it full of real men and women . . .

—Woodrow Wilson

The Sherwin Miller Museum of Jewish Art, along with generous exhibition sponsors to whom we are most grateful, is pleased to present the exhibition *Sons of Adam, Daughters of Eve: Biblical Images in Art from Tulsa Collections*. This exhibit marks many firsts—the first exhibition organized entirely around Biblical themes; the first exhibition presenting our institutional theme of "common ground" with the greater Tulsa community and the first major publication emanating from the Museum since *Judaic Treasures* of 1973 (a catalogue of the original Fenster Gallery collection).

As a public museum, The Sherwin Miller Museum of Jewish Art is dedicated to the preservation of Jewish history, art and culture through commitment to education, interpretation and scholarship for both Jewish and non-Jewish audiences. The greater audience here in Tulsa is vastly important for us. Non Jews learn who Jews are and Jews think about how we fit into the larger landscape. This exhibition is the tip of an iceberg, where upon we have called on all the intellectual resources of the Museum, presenting in visual terms the philosophies underlying the institution.

We have specifically involved the greater Tulsa community including private collections as well as including a painting from a Tulsa sister art museum. Our exhibit display is designed to be striking and meaningful, a pleasure to the eye and to the mind of the visitor and further, is intended to delight as well as inform the public. Changing exhibitions provide a complimentary and versatile opportunity for eclectic and "edgier" approaches to the presentation of all forms of Judaic material.

Heartfelt thanks extend to the lenders to this exhibition, particularly to those many private collectors who have so generously agreed to part with their objects. Sincerest thanks also to the many patrons whose generosity made this publication possible.

Throughout the months of preparation for this exhibition, staff of various local institutions as well as private individuals, were most cooperative. I would like to commend the Museum's curator and author of this catalogue, Dr. Karen York, for her months of hard work organizing this exhibition and writing this catalogue, and the members of the Museum staff for their support in this effort.

Arthur M. Feldman
Executive Director
The Sherwin Miller Museum of Jewish Art

PREFACE

The history of the Jewish people is inextricably interwoven with the Bible. As literature and a font of moral and religious authority, the Bible has played an integral part in the religious heritage, moral foundation and traditions of many societies. Through the choice of varied media we have attempted to amplify both familiar and lesser-known Biblical personages.

In his 1984 book, *Biblical Images: Men and Women of the Book,* Author Adin Steinsaltz discussed the characters of the Bible as some of the most well-known figures in history. One need not read the Bible regularly nor be versed in the Scriptures to know at least some of the names of the major personalities. Directly or indirectly we encounter them repeatedly in speech, literature, folklore and in art. Biblical personae are so familiar or "famous" very often they are stereotyped. The Biblical narrative provides more than life portraits; the characters are not ordinary historical figures but archetypes that live and function long after their deaths. Their images have continued throughout the generations, expanded through Talmud, Kabbalah, and folk tales and historically have become part of the collective personality of the Jewish nation. *Sons of Adam, Daughters of Eve* is intended to reacquaint the audience with the men and woman of the Bible and perhaps to enable and encourage our audience to rediscover and reread the stories as a map not only of the past but perhaps become a guide for the present and future. Further, we recognize that art and culture have emerged as a path to Jewish identity and as a museum, we are transforming ourselves into a center of continuity, multiculturalism and outreach for Jewish and non-Jewish audiences—young and old, tourists and locals. We are here to convey an authentic message, while reaching to our own community and at the same time are reaching to a larger cultural context not bounded by religion or ethnicity.

Vast and wide as the world, rooted in the abysses of creation, and towering up behind the blue secrets of heaven! Sunrise and sunset, promise and fulfillment, birth and death, the whole drama of humanity, are all in this book.

—Heinrich Heine*

Arthur M. Feldman
Executive Director
The Sherwin Miller Museum of Jewish Art

*Steinsaltz, Adin. *Biblical Images: Men and Women of the Book.* New York: Basic Books, Inc., 1984.

ACKNOWLEDGEMENTS

This project, catalogue and exhibition, presenting biblical images borrowed from our community in Tulsa, Oklahoma, would never have been possible without the support and cooperation of so many Museum board members, volunteers and staff members. Having only five months to conceptualize, borrow, photograph and write a catalogue, then create an exhibition, finding funding for this near impossible task was taken on by Brenda Michael-Haggard. Sabrina Darby has been a great help in coordinating all the efforts of the staff to organize the exhibition. Borrowing the works from private collections was orchestrated by Sallye Mann and Museum Director Arthur Feldman, whose tireless work helped gather the wonderful variety of objects in the exhibition. Catalogue designer Carl Brune patiently accepted having to design the catalogue as it was written, all in six weeks. Without the help of volunteer copy editors Katherine Frame, Gay and Dr. William Clarkson, Laurie Berman, and Fred Strauss, the catalogue would not have made it to press. Finally, without the Museum's preparator, Charles Taylor, who worked tirelessly over five months to build, design and supervise the gallery installation, the exhibition would never have been possible.

BIBLICAL IMAGES IN ART

The history of art is also the history of religion. Since the moment G-d appointed Bezalel—the first artist of the Israelite nation, designer of the ark and the tabernacle in the wilderness—the Bible and the art of western civilization have been linked. Ancient sites where biblical frescoes and mosaics are found have been excavated throughout the twentieth century, providing a more accurate picture of the artistic ancestry of such images in Christian and Jewish art. Early Christian wall paintings, circa 350 CE, found in catacombs in Rome, and carved sarcophagi from the same period exemplify the building blocks from which Byzantine Christian art would be formed. Jewish art, however, was slow to catch up to the explosion of Christian painting. Scholars argue that Jewish creativity was constrained by the directives of the Second Commandment: the covenant between G-d and the Israelites forbidding the creation of graven images. This anti-idolatry restriction, reinforced by rabbinic directives over the centuries, was held by nineteenth century art historians as the reason the Jewish people were not prolific producers of fine art. However, twentieth century discoveries such as the second synagogue excavated at Dura-Europus in the 1920s belie that theory with hard evidence; the Jewish frescoes from the Late Antique period illustrated people and events from the five books of Moses.

Christian, Judaic, and Islamic traditions share a common cultural history told in these five books—the history of the biblical patriarchs. During the Middle Ages both Jewish and Christian artists illustrated these stories. Byzantine craftsmen told the stories in mosaics, Greeks and Italians used painting on plaster to make church frescoes, and monks toiled over illuminated manuscripts. Christian artists illustrated the Bible in painting and sculpture to educate the illiterate lower classes. Although Jewish tradition forbade the representation of the image of G-d, scribes illustrated the stories of the Bible in illuminated scrolls such as the Esther Megillah and the Passover Haggadah.

Until the fifteenth century most biblical art was the product of artists and guild craftsmen commissioned by the Church and nobility. Not until the advent of the first printing presses did reproductions of woodblock prints make biblical art available to the middle and lower classes. Tiny black and white prints were made for prayer books and were purchased at market stalls to pin up in the homes of average people throughout Europe. This new market opened the door for an explosion of artistic interpretation of the Bible. Although the greatest market was still the Church and nobility, the availability of printed Bibles, prayer books, and Haggadot allowed, for the first time, artists to choose and interpret scenes from the Bible without being commissioned to paint a particular subject. For example, when the book of Esther was included in an edition printed in the Netherlands in the early sixteenth century, it became a favorite subject of Rembrandt van Rijn who painted scenes from the story many times. These paintings were available for purchase by wealthy merchants to display in their homes. Illustrations from the Old Testament, or Tanakh, were favorites of seventeenth century Dutch artists, since the people of Holland, a small nation who had been oppressed by the Spanish, identified with the Israelites, also an oppressed group who had freed themselves from bondage.

Biblical images created for the mass market have exploded in popularity since the sixteenth century. Learning the arts of printmaking, painters and engravers from all over Europe traveled to Italy to copy the biblical paintings of the Renaissance and interpret them in woodcuts, etchings, and engravings. Thus began the distribution of the images we know today of Bible stories: Adam and Eve in the Garden, the Binding of Isaac, Moses and the Exodus of the Israelites from Egypt, the Parting of the Red Sea, David and Goliath, Esther, and Daniel in the Lions' Den.

As the printed Bible became more widely available for artists to study and interpret, the images became more commonly produced. Biblical images appeared in every medium; they were painted, etched and printed in books, engraved or hammered into silver trays, cups, or boxes. Sculptures of wood, stone and metal illustrated the Binding of Isaac, or Rebekah at the Well. Christian and Jewish textiles were woven or embroidered with scenes from the Bible, and ceramics for use during Jewish holidays were painted with scenes from the Exodus or the Book of Esther.

Stylistic changes in biblical paintings occurred during the nineteenth century. In Christian art the popularity of history painting led European academic artists to include biblical scenes of both major and minor characters in their oeuvres. Romanticized versions of the Queen of Sheba or Salome titillated attendees of the French Salon openings from the mid-nineteenth century on. Rather than finding the freedom to romanticize Biblical scenes, Jewish artists emerged into the fine arts during this period with genre-based paintings. The cultural climate was changing to an appreciation of genre scenes (scenes of everyday life and of everyday people). The combination of enlightened attitudes toward Jewish occupations in Germany and the rising popularity of genre painting may have created the milieu in which the first Jewish painters, such as Daniel Moritz Oppenheim (1799–1882), began their careers. Over the course of the centuries the restrictions of the Second Commandment began to slip away from Jewish art as they had from Christian art. Scholars discuss different ways in which Jewish artists began to interpret the restriction against making graven images.

In his 2001 book, *Idolizing Pictures: Idolatry, Iconoclasm, and Jewish Art,* Anthony Julius describes the different interpretations and their distinctions. First, he points out that modern Jewish artists bypassed the religious restriction by creating abstract art. But his more important statement discusses the Second Commandment's new interpretation as a call to combat idolatry, by either reducing the image to one of illustration or 'witness,' or by attacking the idol in a form of iconoclastic art. Most of the art in this exhibition falls into the category of witness or illustrative art, as it portrays the characters and events of the Bible. It is in this genre that Jewish painting emerged from the ghettos of Germany and Poland during the late nineteenth century. Jews portrayed their homes and holidays, and began the work of finding their artistic voices.

At the turn of the twentieth century, as Jewish painters found their way into the mainstream of European art, nationalism in art was of great importance in their countries of origin (Germany, Russia and the Netherlands). A portion of the artists left behind the genre scenes of Jewish life and culture to embrace modernistic movements: Cubism, Expressionism, and Surrealism. Others who trained in that atmosphere of nationalistic symbolism joined the Zionist movement, immigrated to Palestine, and sought their own national art—that of the nation of Israel. The ancient land of the Israelites inspired them to return to biblical subjects.

In 1901, Russian-born artist Boris Schatz proposed founding the Bezalel School of Arts and Crafts in Jerusalem. His mission was not only to prove Jews had inherent artistic ability, but also to find a true Jewish art in the combination of biblical history and Near Eastern classical design. The result was stylistic combination of biblical subject matter, Palestinian settings, oriental influences, and a touch of the Art Nouveau influence of the Jugendstil Arts and Crafts movement. European Jews flocked to the Bezalel School, and over the next thirty years helped formulate an Israeli national art. Reuven Rubin's lithographs are examples of this training and influence. Over the course of his life, Rubin created numerous paintings and suites of prints of biblical subjects. Other European Jewish artists, such as Marc Chagall, spent time in Palestine and, taking their photographs and sketches, also created series of images from the Bible. For the first time, a mainstream Jewish biblical art was created that did not reside in a book or scroll. This trend, continuing throughout the twentieth century attracted Americans such as Phillip Ratner and Laszlo Ispanky.

Most American art, however, lacks biblical references. Scholars theorize that the cause is the pluralism of religion in America. At a time when countries such as England, Italy, or Palestine had populations who mostly followed one religion (whether Protestant, Catholic, or Jewish), religious subject matter became a part of the mainstream artistic language of the nation. America, a polyglot populace of Protestant, Catholic, Jewish, Muslim, Buddhist, transcendental, and spiritual religions, had not produced a national art whose subject was religion. Rather, our artists of the nineteenth century turned to nature as an expression of spirituality. Modernists such as Mark Rothko alluded to religion in abstract expressionist works. In mainstream American art, most religious works are either commissioned by specific congregations or produced in the commercial sector. Hence, we have a profusion of material produced for the celebration of religious holidays, but very little American religious art can be found in museums.

This exhibition, *Sons of Adam, Daughters of Eve: Biblical Images in Art from Tulsa Collections*, contains many examples of aforementioned biblical images. The focus of the exhibit is objects from our Museum collection, and art our community members chose to purchase—art which occupies pride of place in Tulsa homes, in our institutions, museum, schools, temple, and synagogue. The fact that our fellow Tulsans live with these objects explains the diversity found in the exhibition. Collected for personal enjoyment, it ranges from bronze or porcelain sculptures to large quilts and tapestries; from Kosta Boda crystal to Chagall lithographs. Collectors found the lithographs of Reuven Rubin, Marc Chagall, Salvador Dali, and Phillip Ratner suited their desire to live with characters from the Bible. Sculpture by the Israeli artist Aharon Bezalel and American artists Phillip Ratner and Laszlo Ispanky also portrays patriarchs and biblical heroes. Women of the Bible, Esther, Rebekah, and Ruth are well-represented. The Sherwin Miller Museum collections contribute examples of biblical subjects in seventeenth century Dutch panel painting, Persian Bible illustration, European and Near Eastern metalwork, and European and Israeli textiles. In all, the scope of this exhibit encompasses a variety of both the fine and decorative arts collected by our unique community in Tulsa.

KAREN S. YORK, PHD
Curator
The Sherwin Miller Museum of Jewish Art

SELECTED BIBLIOGRAPHY

Arthurs, Alberta and Glenn Wallach, eds. *Crossroads: Art and Religion in American Life*. New York: New Press: Distributed by W.W. Norton, 2001.

Grossman, Grace Cohen. *Jewish Art*. New York: Hugh Lauter Levin Associates, 1995.

Julius, Anthony. *Idolizing Pictures: Idolatry, Iconoclasm and Jewish Art*. London: Thames & Hudson, 2001.

Olin, Margaret *The Nation without Art: Examining Modern Discourses on Jewish Art*. Lincoln: University of Nebraska Press, 2001.

Sed-Rajna, Gabrielle. *Jewish Art*; with essays by Ziva Amishai-Maisels ... [et al.]; translated from the French by Sara Friedman and Mira Reich. New York: H.N. Abrams, 1997.

Schapiro, Meyer. *Modern Art: 19th & 20th Centuries*, Selected Papers. New York: G. Braziller, 1978.

Ungerleider-Mayerson, Joy. *Jewish Folk Art: From Biblical Days to Modern Times*. New York: Summit Books, 1986.

Webberley, Helen. "The Book of Esther in 17th Century Dutch Art." ttp://www.artgallery.nsw.gov.au/aaanz_2002/__data/page/2345/helen_webberley.pdf

THE EXHIBITION

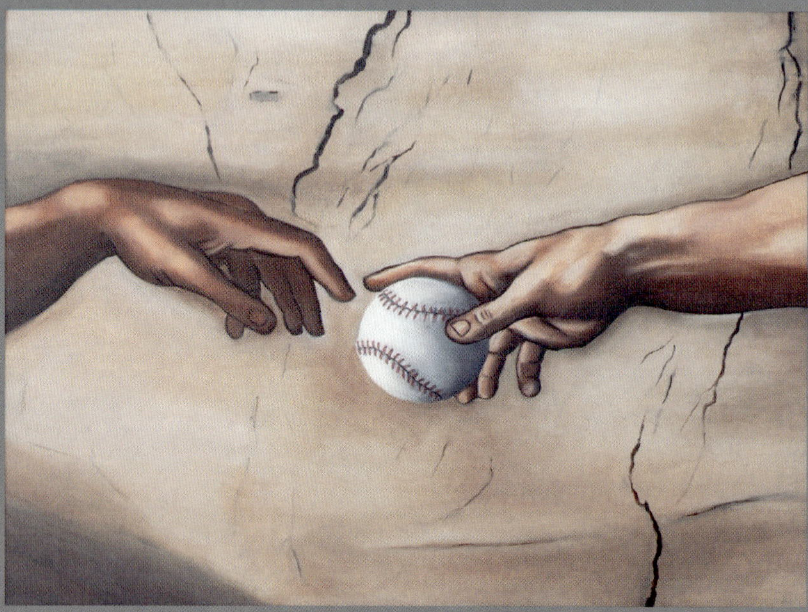

Michael Langenstein, currently Assistant Professor of Music and Art at the Borough of Manhattan Community College, is an active participant in New York City arts events and exhibitions. This image was first created for a postcard that Michael Langenstein did for the exhibition "Artists and Letters" in 1982.

Play Ball, 1984
Michael Langenstein
American, born 1947
Oil on canvas
Loan from a private collection, Tulsa, Oklahoma

opposite: This 28-inch bronze sculpture, *Let There Be Light*, is one of few copies of the sculpture which Ispanky produced on commission for former Egyptian President Anwar Sadat. A long-haired male figure, G-d, levitates above a circle which represents the heavens. In his right hand he holds Earth, and in his left hand he holds the Sun. His art has come to encompass the myths, legends, and religious stories of the Western world.

Born in Budapest in 1919, Laszlo Ispanky found his artistic talents as a boy. He studied at Hungarian Fine Art Academy, but found life as an artist difficult under Communist rule, and made his way to America in 1956. Ispanky began his American career as a designer for Cybis Porcelains. In 1966, he established his own studio in Pennington, New Jersey and since 1976, has worked for Goebel of North America. He works in stone, wood, or metal, as well as porcelain.

Mr. Ispanky's work also can be seen at the Smithsonian Institution in Washington, D.C., The Cincinnati Children's Zoo, The Basketball Hall of Fame in Springfield, Massachusetts, as well as a piece on exhibit at the New Jersey State Museum in Trenton.

Let There Be Light, ca. 1980
Laszlo Ispanky
Hungarian, born 1919
Bronze
28½ x 28 x 21½ in.
Loan from Jennifer and Bruce Fadem

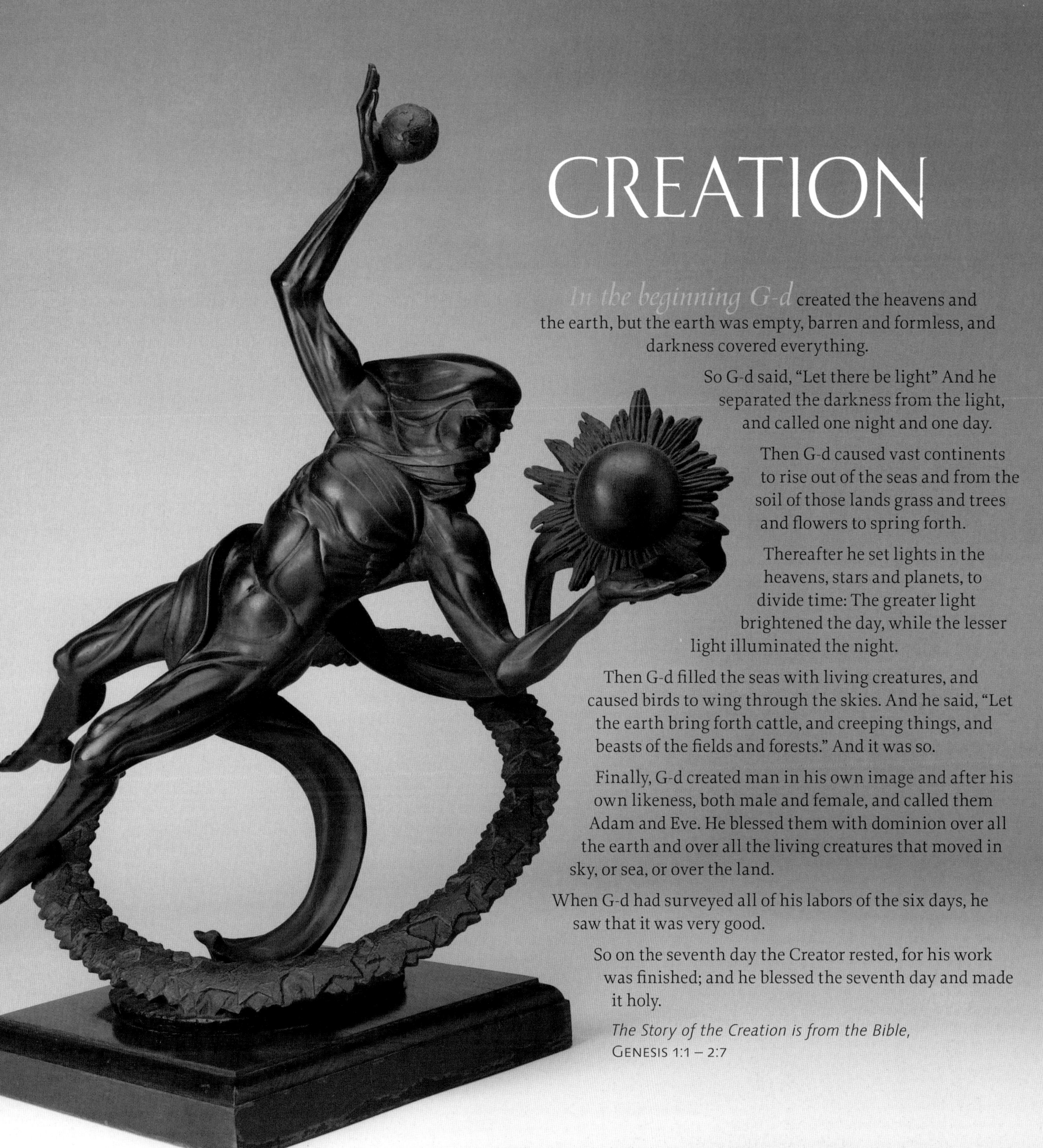

CREATION

In the beginning G-d created the heavens and the earth, but the earth was empty, barren and formless, and darkness covered everything.

So G-d said, “Let there be light” And he separated the darkness from the light, and called one night and one day.

Then G-d caused vast continents to rise out of the seas and from the soil of those lands grass and trees and flowers to spring forth.

Thereafter he set lights in the heavens, stars and planets, to divide time: The greater light brightened the day, while the lesser light illuminated the night.

Then G-d filled the seas with living creatures, and caused birds to wing through the skies. And he said, “Let the earth bring forth cattle, and creeping things, and beasts of the fields and forests.” And it was so.

Finally, G-d created man in his own image and after his own likeness, both male and female, and called them Adam and Eve. He blessed them with dominion over all the earth and over all the living creatures that moved in sky, or sea, or over the land.

When G-d had surveyed all of his labors of the six days, he saw that it was very good.

So on the seventh day the Creator rested, for his work was finished; and he blessed the seventh day and made it holy.

The Story of the Creation is from the Bible,
GENESIS 1:1 – 2:7

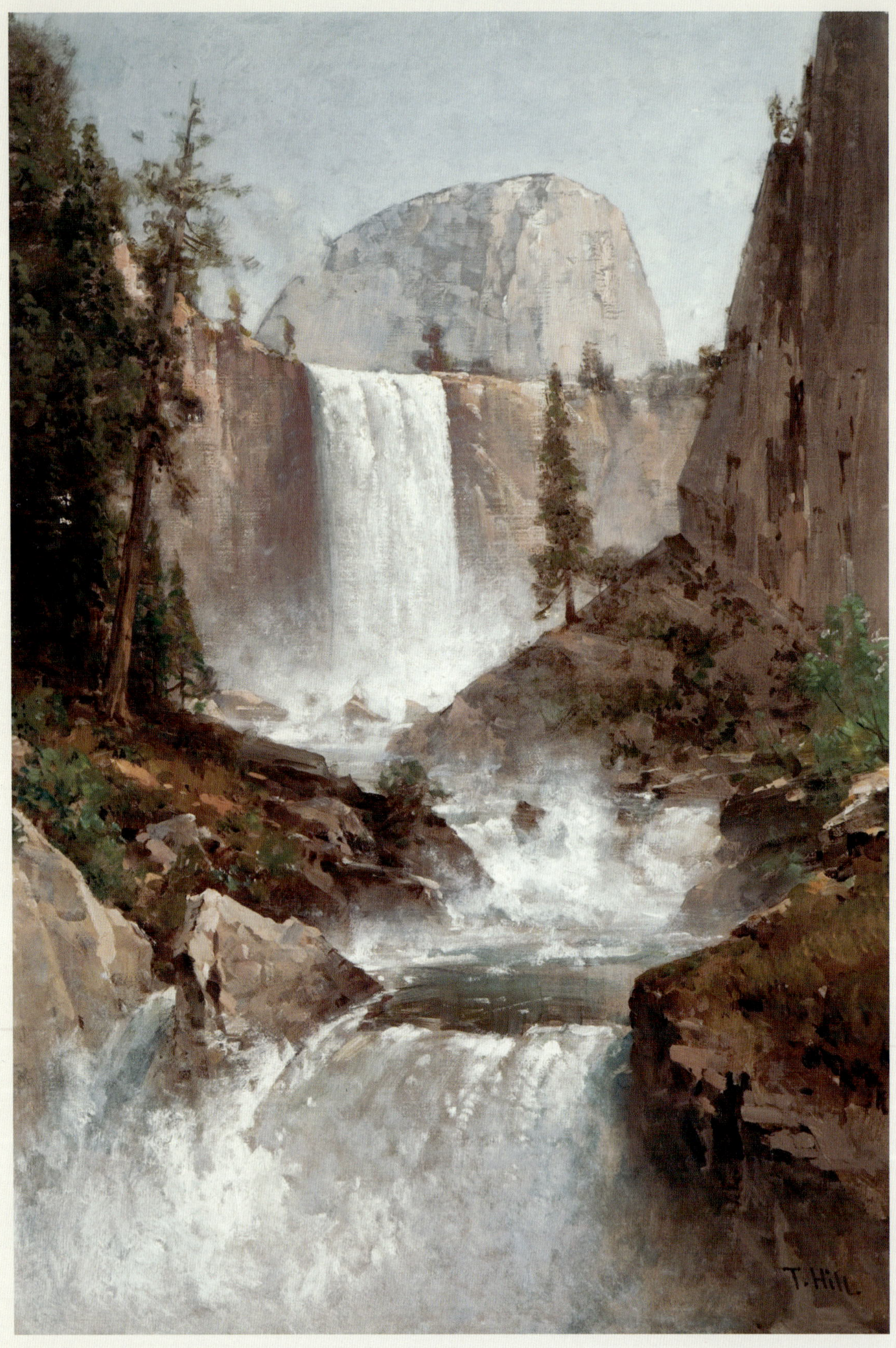

Thomas Hill came to America from England in 1841. Although he studied art at the Pennsylvania Academy of Fine Arts, he was primarily self-taught. Beginning as a carriage painter, Hill moved around from San Francisco to Boston and then to New England from 1850 to 1880. He helped found the San Francisco School of Design in 1874, and was commissioned by John Muir to paint in Alaska in 1887. Hill produced nineteen illustrations for Muir's *Picturesque California* in 1888, and is best known for his majestic landscapes of California, especially Yosemite.

Hill exhibited at the Art Union of San Francisco, the 1876 Philadelphia Centennial Expo, and The Pennsylvania Academy of the Fine Arts. His work is in the collections of the Denver Art Museum, the Los Angeles Museum of Art, the Worcester Museum of Art, the Oakland Museum of Art, and the Gilcrease Museum of Art.

Yosemite Valley No. 2, ca. 1880s
Thomas Hill
American, 1829–1908
Oil on canvas, 30 x 20 in.
0116.1581
Loan from The Gilcrease Museum, Tulsa, OK

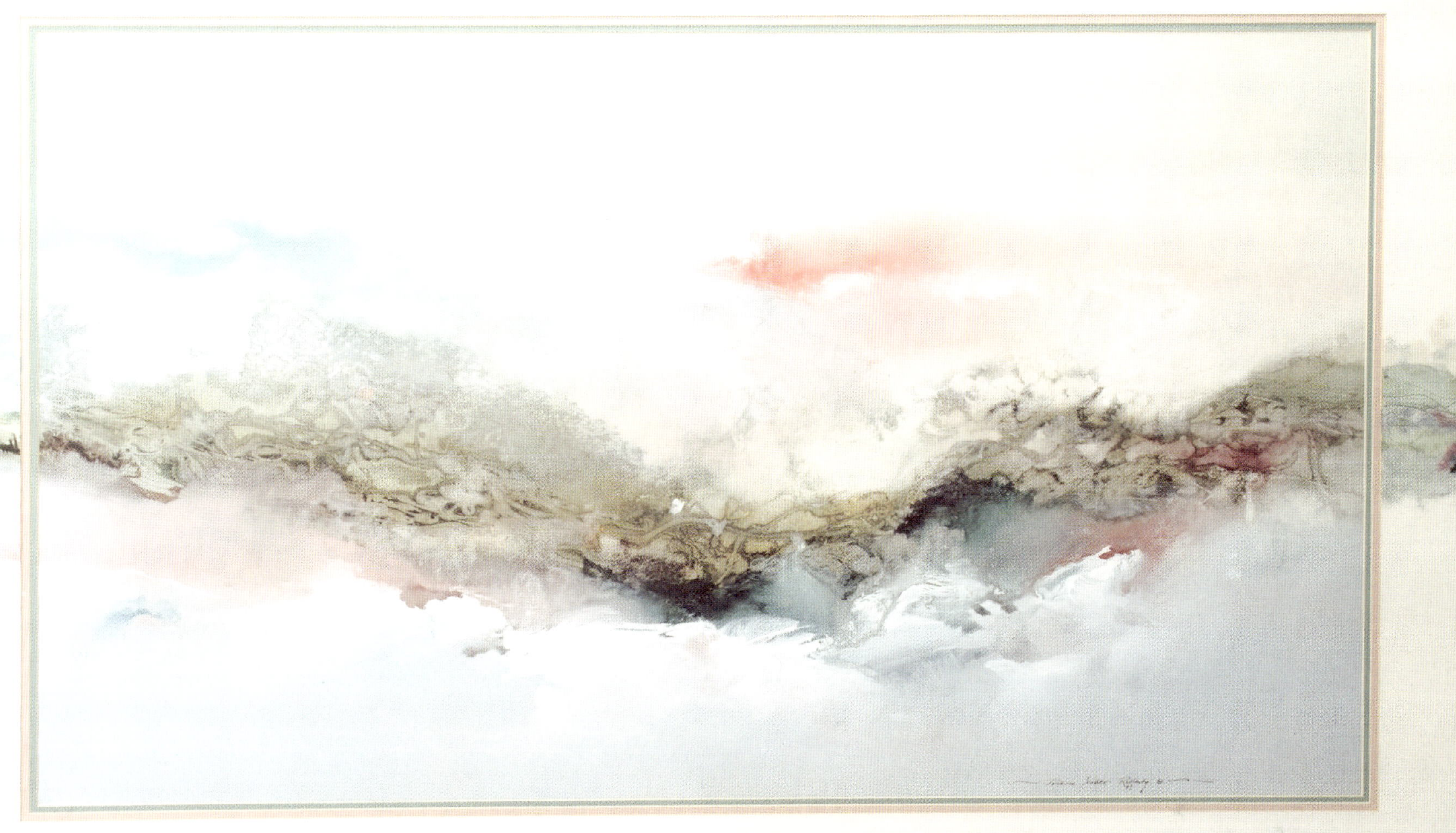

Joanne Miller Rafferty's contemporary paintings are composed of splashes of vibrant color and quick line that convey her lively style along with her love of land, sky and sea. *Tranquil Light* typifies her horizontal composition that creates an abstract mood.

Joanne writes, "Painting is a continual journey, an eternal act of energy. Sometimes the creative process is finely controlled: sometimes it is frenetic and wildly abstracted. More times than not, it is a combination of both and a phenomenal experience."

Joanne holds a Bachelor's Degree in Art Education from Daemen College and Graduate Certification in Art Education from the State University of New York at Buffalo. During her thirty-year artistic career she has received awards in numerous juried exhibitions, and has participated in exhibitions at the Hickory Art Museum, the Monmouth Museum, the Montclair Museum, the Cayuga Museum of Art, the Members Gallery of the Albright Knox, the Noyes Museum and the Museum of the Great Plains. Her original works are held in public and private collections including Exxon Corporation, IBM, Marriott Hotels, MasterCard International and American Express. She is listed in *Who's Who in American Art*, *Strathmore Who's Who*, *Mantle Fielding's Dictionary of American Painters, Sculptures* and *Engravers 2001*, and is a member of the National Association of Women Artists.

Tranquil Light
Joanne Miller Rafferty
American, born 1948
Watercolor and acrylic on paper
Loan from Estelle Finer

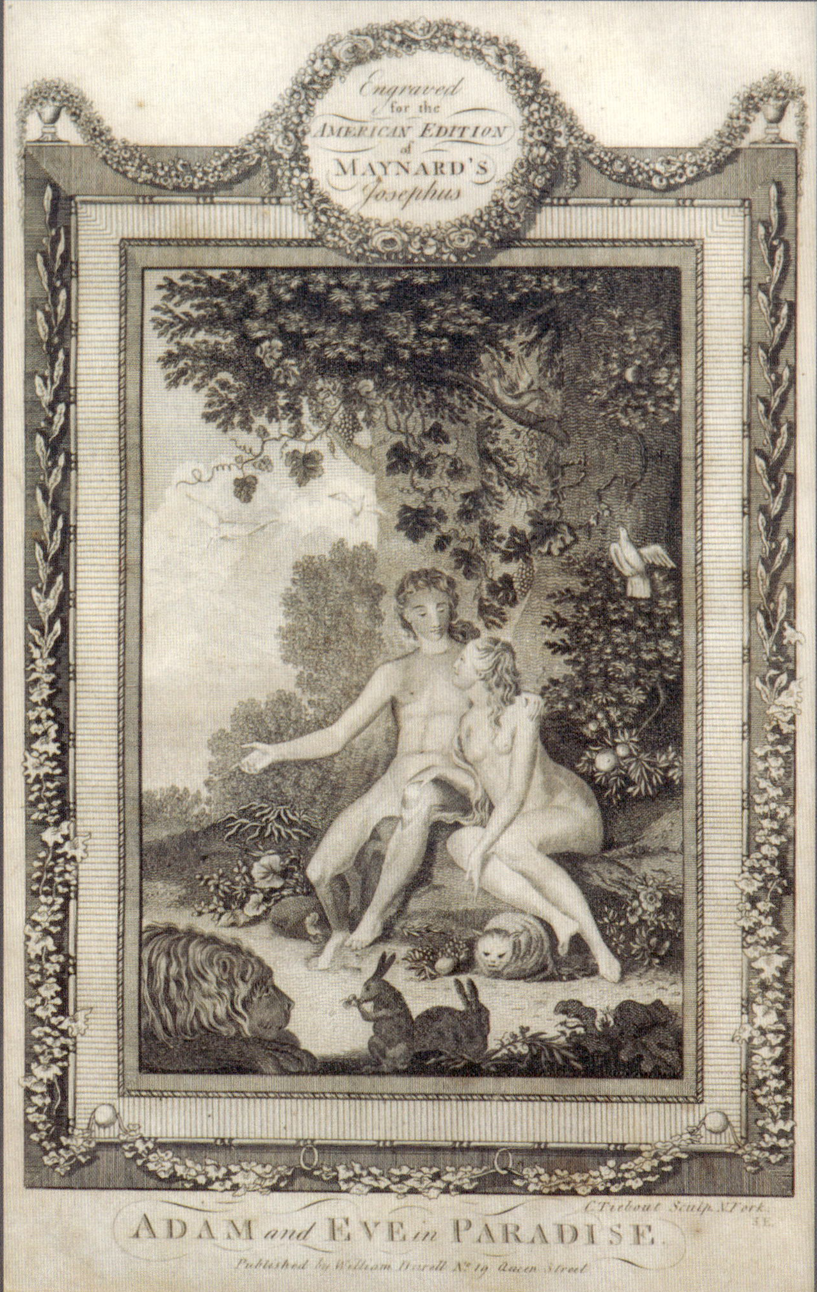

This work was engraved to illustrate the 1791 edition of *The Whole Genuine and Complete Works of Flavius Josephus, The Learned and Authentic Jewish Historian, Celebrated Warrior*, translated from the original in the Greek language and edited by George Henry Maynard and the Rev. Edward Kimpton. New York: William Durrell, 1792. It is embellished with 60 engraved plates, including two maps and a folding plan of Jerusalem.

This is one of the great illustrated books printed in the new United States of America during the 18th century. Almost by necessity, the roster of "American artists" responsible for these large engravings forms a Who's Who of early American craftsmen. Seven of these plates were executed by Alexander Andersen, who is generally considered America's first professional book illustrator. There are fourteen plates each by Amos Doolittle and Cornelius Thiebout. William Rollinson made six, J. Allen five, and two are the work of Benjamin Tanner.

Adam & Eve, 1792
Copperplate engraving
10 x 8 in.
1973.3

OPPOSITE: Born in Afghanistan as a son of a Kabbalist rabbi, Aharon Bezalel grew up on bible stories. During the 1950s, in the form of small wood sculptures, he began to tell the stories he knew so well. At the time, modern Israeli artists were exploring Israel's connection to its biblical roots, and Bezalel's small sculptures touched the heart of that effort, helping Bezalel find his place in Israeli art. Although the semi-abstract influences of Giacometti and Henry Moore are evident in Bezalel's early wood and bronze figures, the underlying biblical narrative is told without representing each character as metaphor.

This small bronze, created in the 1970s, is an excellent example of Bezalel's move from wood to bronze sculpture. In this piece, he retained the simple subject, an episode form the story of a biblical character, while this work shows his trend toward related couples, begun in the late 1960s. The influence of ancient archeological figures is evident in the eye slits and two-dimensionality of these figures, while the tension and interdependence between two figures reveals the progression of Bezalel's sculptural language.

Aharon Bezalel has lived, worked, and taught art in Jerusalem for many years. He works primarily in bronze and wood, and has shown all over the world. His works are included in museums and galleries world-wide.

The Meeting, 1971–1972
Aharon Bezalel
Israeli, born Afghanistan 1926
Bronze, 6 in.
Loan from Susan Fenster

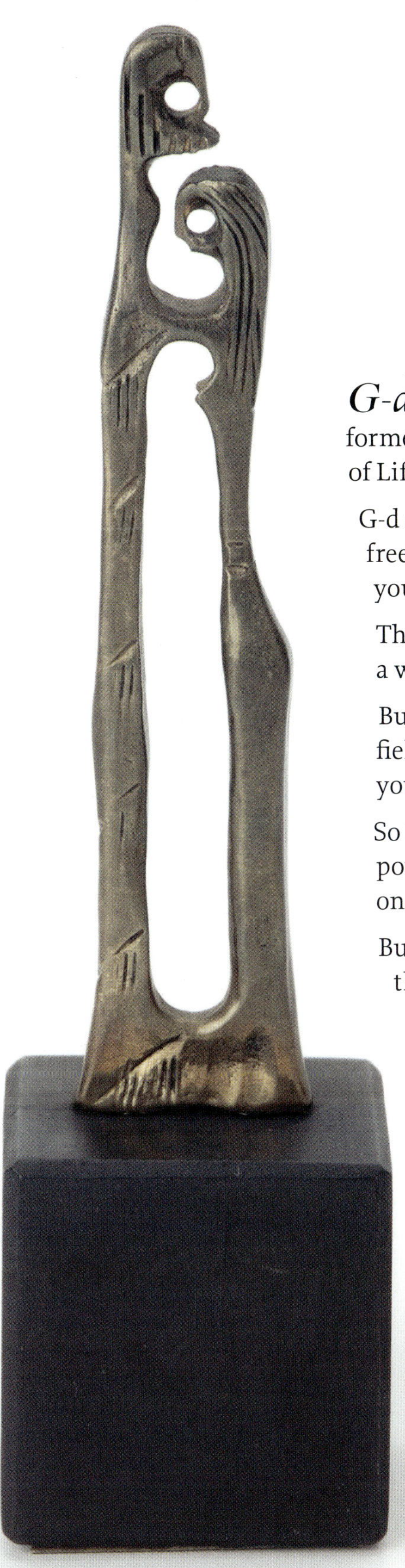

ADAM & EVE

G-d planted a Garden in Eden and he put there the man he had formed, to till it and to keep it. In the midst of the Garden He placed the Tree of Life and the Tree of the Knowledge of Good and Evil.

G-d commanded the man, saying, "Of every tree in the Garden you may freely eat, except the Tree of the Knowledge of Good and Evil; for on the day you eat of it you will surely die."

Then G-d caused Adam to sleep and, taking a rib from Adam's side, formed a woman, Eve, to become Adam's wife.

But the serpent of the Garden was more subtle than any other beast of the field, and he tempted Eve, "If you should eat of the fruit of the Tree of Life, you would become as G-d, knowing good and evil."

So Eve looked with longing at the beautiful fruit of the tree, which held the power to make one wise, and she picked an apple and ate it, and also gave one to Adam.

But even as their eyes were opened, they knew they were naked, they hid themselves.

They heard G-d walking through the Garden in the cool of the day calling, "Where art thou?" Adam replied, "I was afraid, because I am naked, and I hid myself."

And so G-d knew that they had eaten of the fruit of the Tree of Life, and he was angered. And Adam blamed on Eve, and Eve blamed the serpent.

Then G-d told the serpent, "Because you have done this, you shall be cursed more than any beast of the field, and you shall crawl on your belly and eat dust for the rest of your days." To Adam and Eve he said, "Now is this ground cursed because of your disobedience," and G-d banished Adam and Eve forever from the Garden of Eden.

The Story of Adam and Eve is from the Bible, GENESIS 2:11 – 3:24

Adam and Eve are traditional characters found in decorative Persian and early Israeli carpets. Moses and Abraham also can be found in figurative weavings from the near east. Scenes that picture people and animals are not common in near-eastern weavings; more often carpet designs are based on organic or architectural forms.

Pictorial designs based on scenes taken from life, history, or mythology are originated in workshops from Persia, in particular, Kerman, Tabriz and Kashan. Sometimes they comprise a single identifiable scene or group of figures and differ from other designs showing human and animal forms by the prominence of the figures and the narrative quality of the scene.

The beginning of the carpet weaving in Kerman goes back only to shortly after the First World War. Many fine rugs based on historical and legendary images were created during this period, including images such as The Garden of Paradise or Adam and Eve. The Sunnite Muslims forbid the depiction of living forms, whereas the Shiite Muslims of Persia are not bound by such doctrinal restraints.

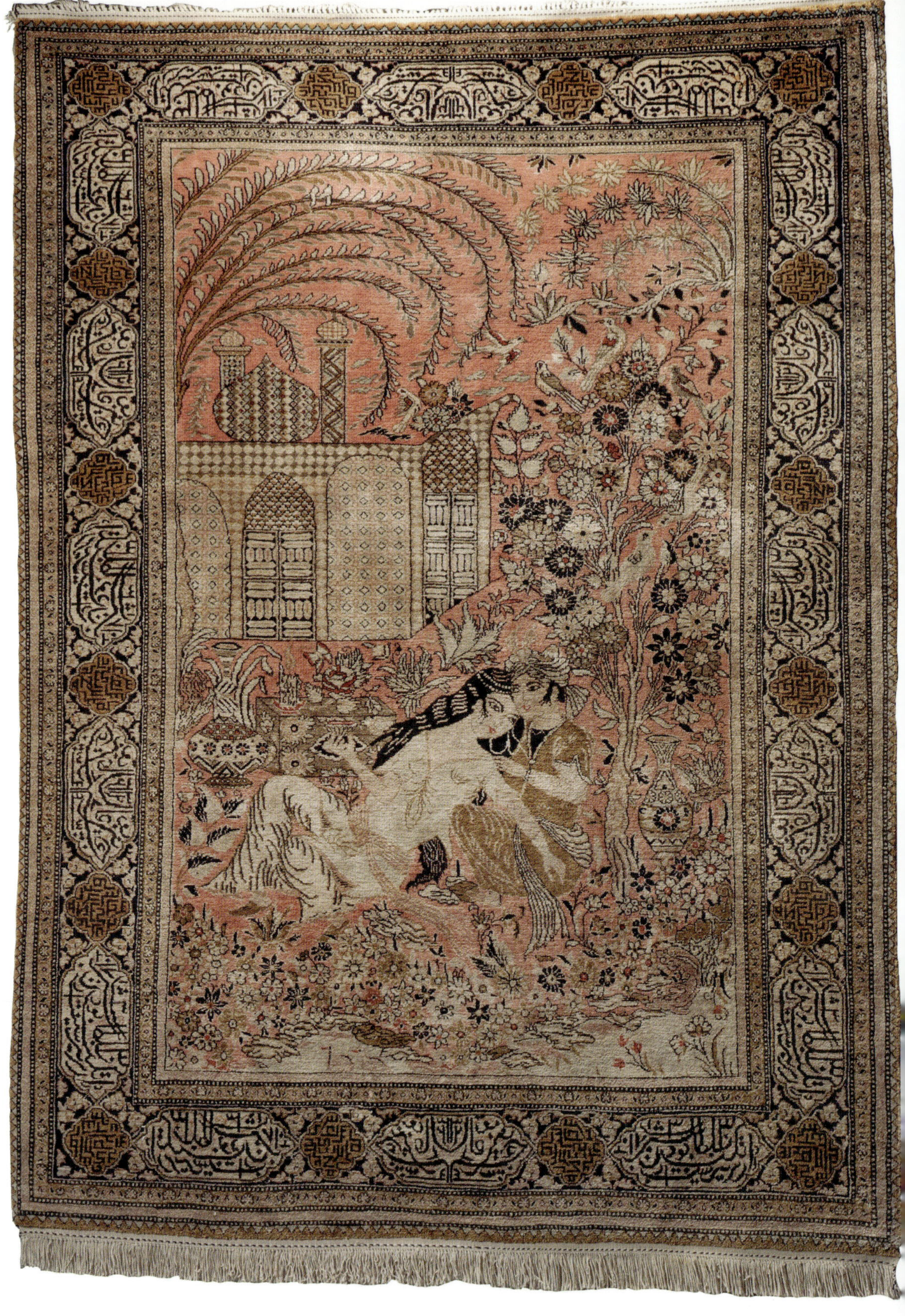

ADAM AND EVE IN THE GARDEN
Persian carpet, ca. 1920
Wool, 3 x 5 ft.
Loan from Temple Israel

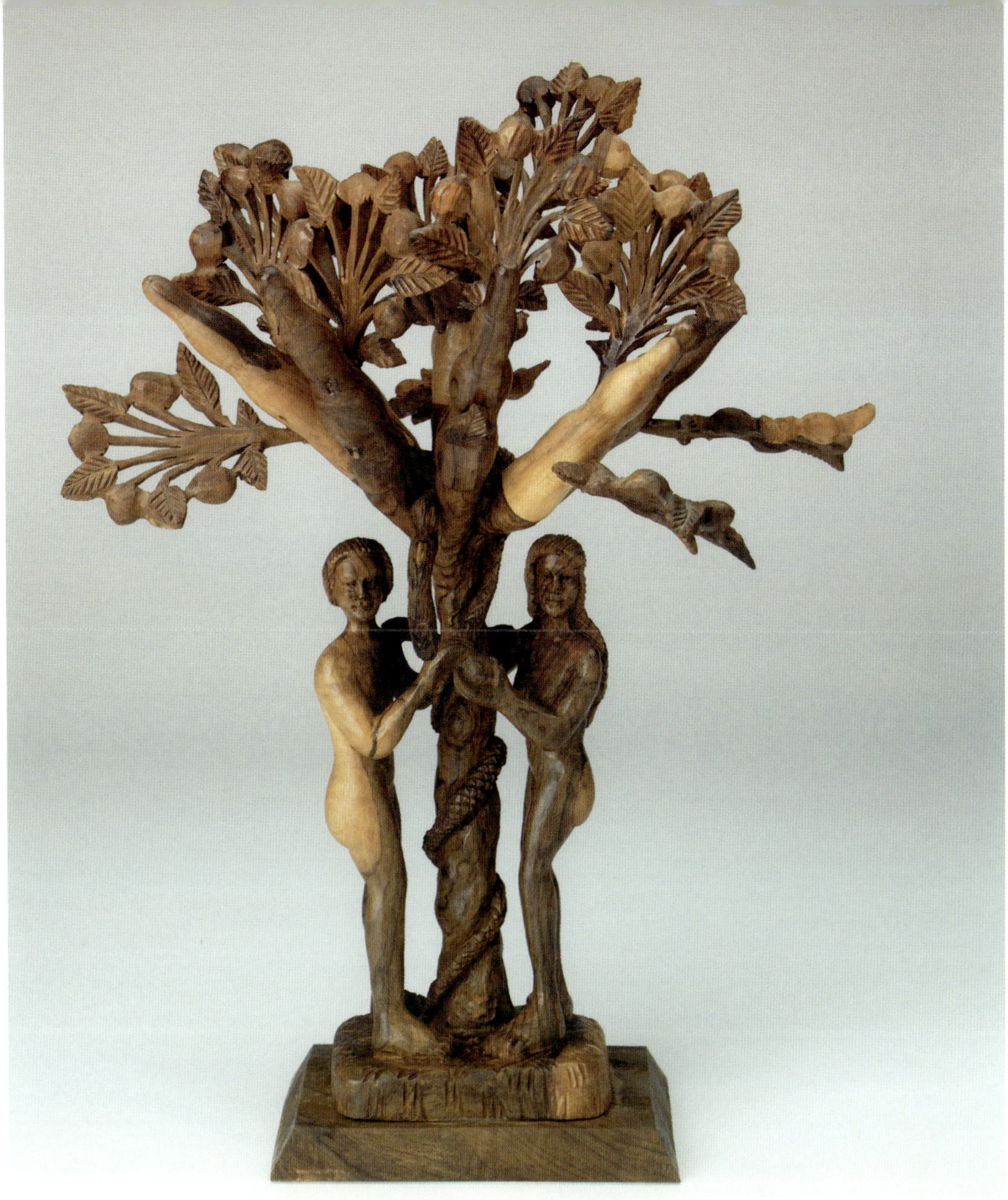

This charming representation of Adam and Eve standing at the Tree of the Knowledge of Good and Evil depicts the moment when Eve handed Adam the apple and admonished him to eat. Purchased in Israel, it was carved from a traditional material, olivewood. Carving religious and artistic artifacts from olivewood is a tradition among the natives of Bethlehem, where it is a local material.

The olivewood carving industry started in the 15th century when Franciscan fathers introduced it to regional craftsmen. Families have passed this profession down from generation to generation, a tradition that is continued in modern-day Israel. The olive tree is an evergreen tree that grows in the Holy Land. It has numerous branches and can survive up to 2000 years. In addition to the handmade quality of the carvings, the grain of the wood gives each piece a special character.

Adam and Eve
Israel, 20th century
Olivewood, 16½ x 12 x 11 in.
Loan from Carolyn and Ron Kriegsman

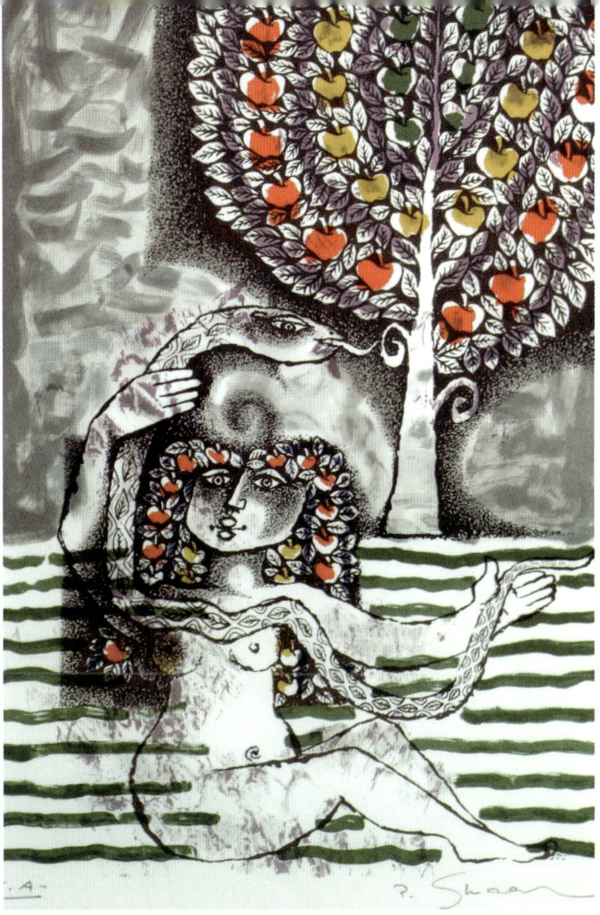

Pinchas Shaar's vision of Eve presents his characteristic color, animated design and whimsical depiction of fables, myths and biblical subjects. She sits, innocent eyes wide, admiring the beauty of the serpent as it tempts her to eat of the Tree of Knowledge. Shaar's graphic style and use of color highlight the garden and the apples in this lithograph.

Born in Poland, Shaar immigrated to Israel in 1956, and finally settled in New York in 1975. His paintings and lithographs are populated with lions, lambs, birds, horses, unicorns, and people with stylized features and enormous eyes. After his studies at the Munich Art Academy and the Academie des Beaux-Arts in Paris, Shaar emerged from his childhood in the Lodz ghetto to express his Jewish conciousness in both biblical and cultural subjects such as his silkscreen prints of Jewish Holidays, created in1977.

Eve, 1965
Pinchas Shaar
Israeli (1923 –1996)
Lithograph, Edition Artiste
Loan from Estelle Finer

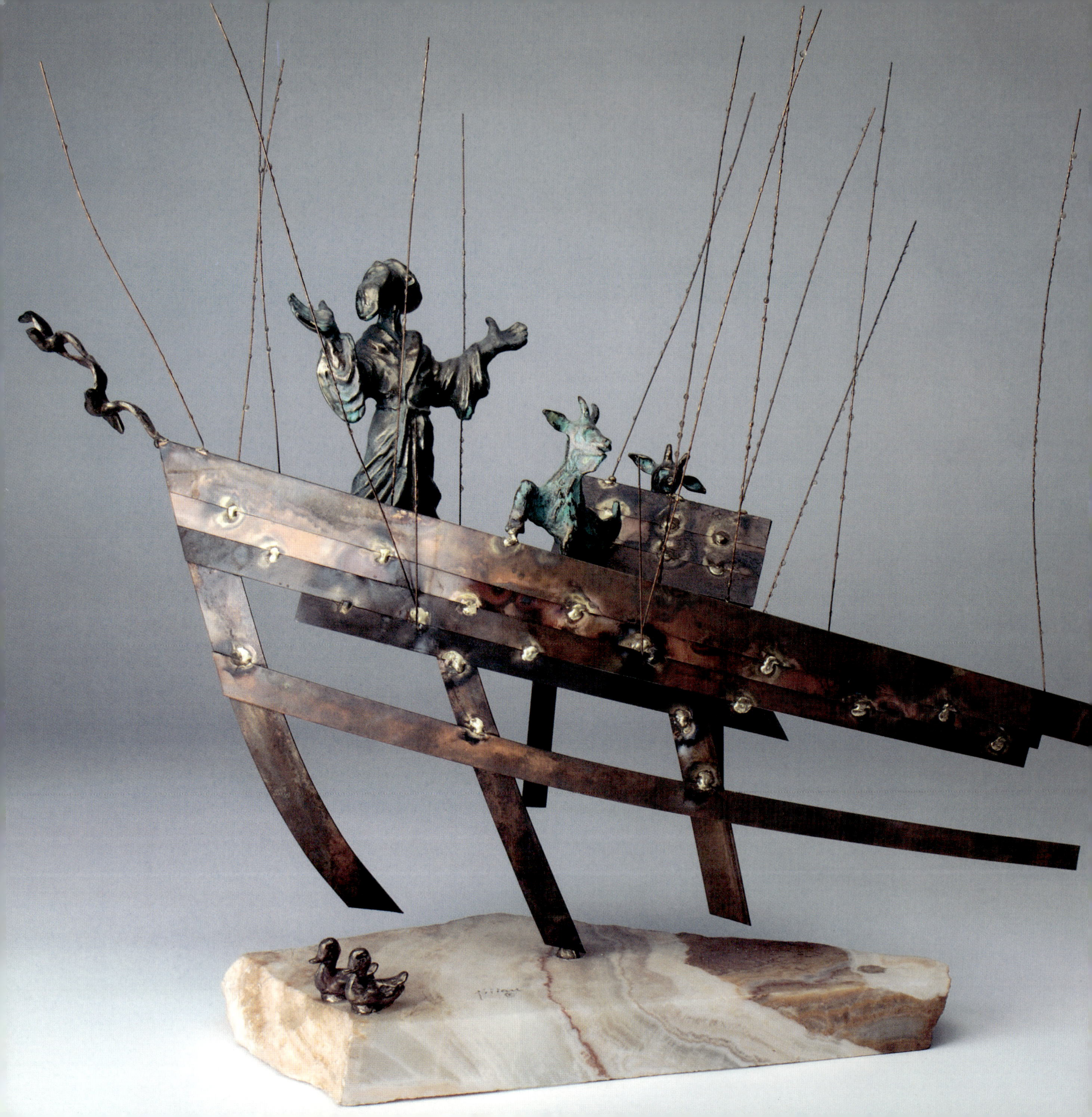

NOAH AND THE GREAT FLOOD

As people multiplied upon the earth, and their wickedness grew swiftly, G-d was grieved and regretted that he had ever created them.

But there was one man, Noah, whose goodness won him the Favor of G-d.

G-d commanded Noah to build a great ark of gopher-wood, made water-tight with pitch, into which should be placed every living creature on the earth: one male and one female of all the birds, beasts, reptiles, and insects upon His earth.

So Noah and his three sons, Shem, Ham and Japheth, built the ark, according to G-ds design. Then, as it began to rain, Noah and his family herded all of the creatures they had gathered, two by two, into the ark.

For forty days and forty nights, the rain poured down. The ark was lifted from the ground and floated upon the sea of waters. Nothing remained but sea and sky, and all of the creatures of the earth, save those in the ark, perished.

Finally the torrents of rain ceased, and after 150 days, the waters began to recede. Then Noah opened the window of the ark and sent forth a dove. Soon the dove returned, bearing an olive branch in its beak, and Noah knew that the waters were abating from the earth.

A week later, as a beautiful rainbow arched the heavens, Noah, his family, and all the creatures from the ark came out upon the green earth. G-d blessed them all and gave them the rainbow as a token of his promise never to flood the earth again.

The Story of Noah's Ark is from the Bible, GENESIS 6:9 – 9:17

Bijan J. Bijan, educated in his native Persia (Iran) came to the United States in 1958 to pursue his career in the arts. His early style combined his training in near-eastern design and sculpture with modern western techniques to produce modernistic works which used traditional Persian materials, such as copper. Bijan's sculptural techniques were developed while designing architectural sculptures, murals, and fountains, including the fountain for the "Tournament of Roses" headquarters in Pasadena, California.

Bijan's works have been collected by people from every walk of life. Over the course of his career, he designed and sold more than three million bronze sculptures and ten thousand functional and decorative products for established national companies. He is considered a pioneer in the field of metal sculpture, working mainly in copper and bronze, and also teaches sculpture and designs and fabricates his works.

NOAH AND THE ARK, ca. 1970
Bijan J. Bijan
American, born Persia 1935
Oxidized copper, travertine marble base
19¼ x 20 x 11 in.
Gift of Sara Kahan
94.19d

America's oldest existing art porcelain studio, Cybis is recognized as one of the world's foremost creators of fine porcelain art. The first page of the Biblical Figures in the wonderful Cybis Book is a full page picture of Noah, with the following written, "We begin with a Cybis Noah, at the moment of the dove's returning to the ark with a leaf, showing that the waters of the earth have begun to recede."

Boleslaw Cybis, founder of the Cybis Studio, came from Wilno, Lithuania with his wife in 1939. Cybis, who studied at the St. Petersburg Academy of Fine Arts and the Academy of Fine Arts in Warsaw, was selected to paint murals for the Polish Pavilion at the 1939 New York World's Fair. He finished his commission, enjoyed the fair, and then he and his wife headed for home. After they sailed for Poland word came that Germany had invaded their homeland. The ship immediately returned to the United States, and the couple was stranded. They formed a small company, Cybis Art Productions, and sold their porcelain figures to stores in New York City. A larger studio was established in Trenton, New Jersey—still in business today—where, for more than 55 years the Cybis studio has produced outstanding art porcelain figurines. Examples of those figures can be found in many museums and private collections throughout the United States.

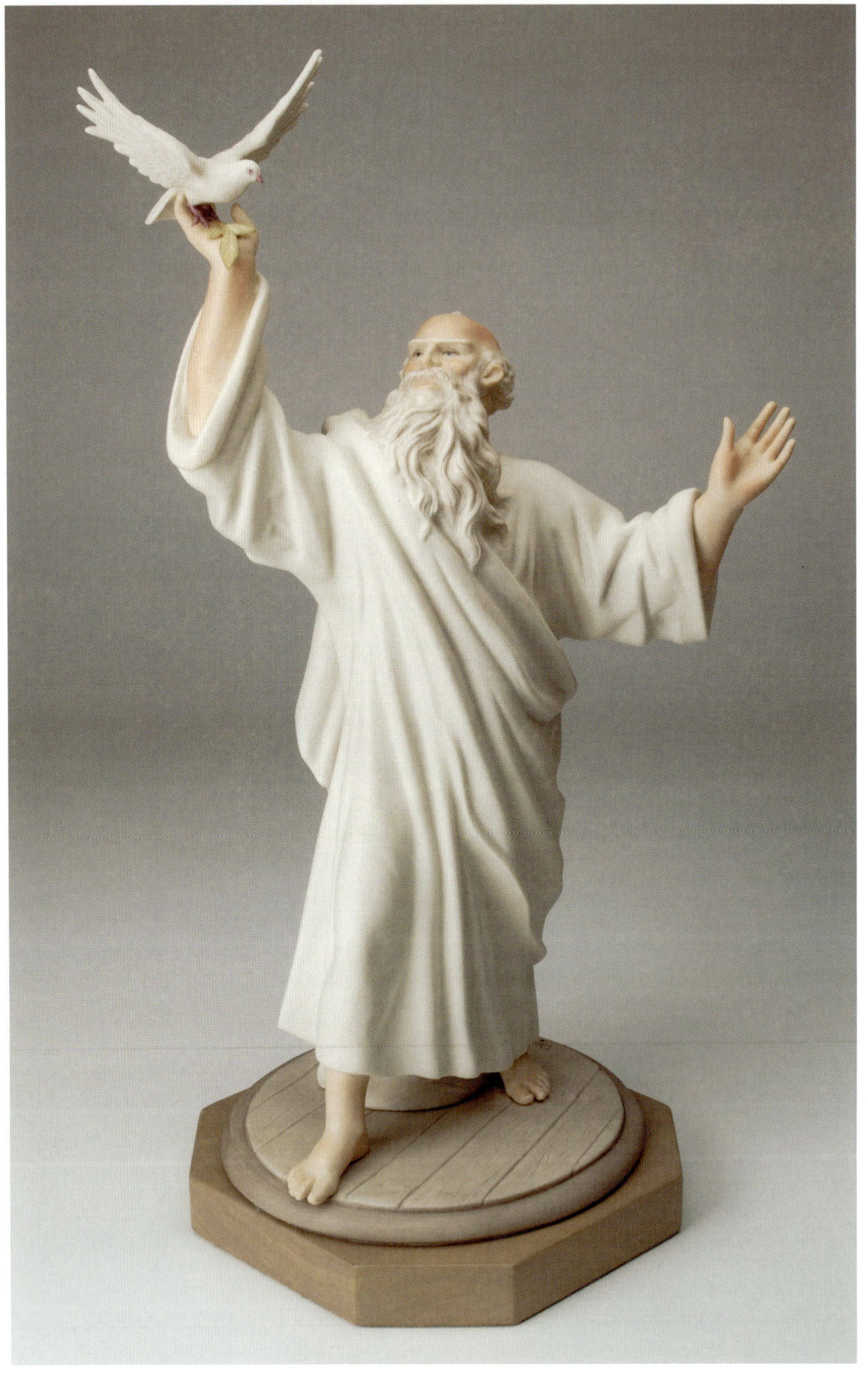

Noah
Cybis Porcelain, Closed Limited Edition of 500, 20th century
Porcelain, Hand-painted, 19 x 11 in.
SMMJA Collections

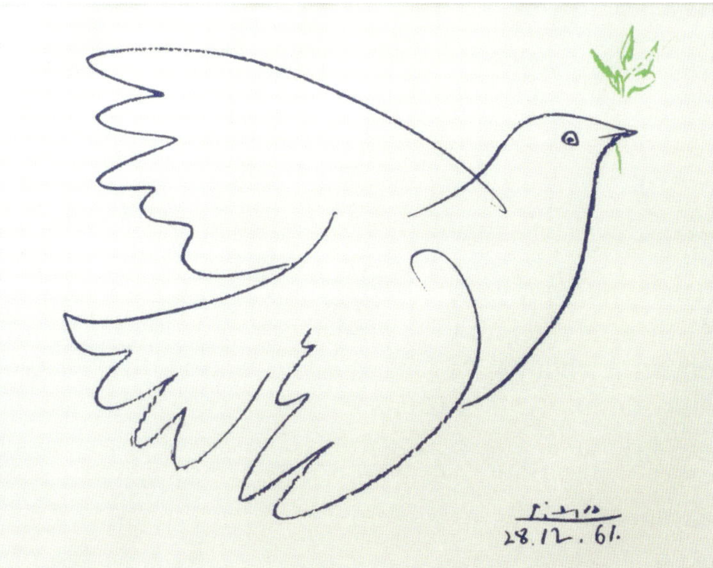

ABOVE: In the Hebrew Bible, a dove was released by Noah after the Great Flood in order to find land. The dove came back carrying an olive branch in its beak, telling Noah that the Great Flood had receded and there was land once again for Man. (Genesis 8:11). This symbolized that G-d was ending his "war" with mankind. The appearance of the rainbow (Genesis 9:12–17) at the end of the Flood story represents G-d's promise that He will never again destroy the earth with a flood.

Pablo Picasso, a painter and printmaker who revolutionized western art, lived and worked in Spain and France during the 20th century. He studied art in Paris and began to paint there in 1901. Over the course of his lifetime he developed and participated in revolutionary concepts in art such as Cubism and Surrealism, designed opera sets, worked in the graphic arts and did lithographs, etchings, woodcuts, aquatints and sometimes combinations. He also explored the mediums of sculpture and ceramics. In 1944 he became an active participant in the Paris Peace Movement, a Communist organization active during the Cold War. Picasso, who was always supportive of Humanistic movements, was a Communist sympathizer. He designed and donated the *Peace Dove*, an original drawing, to the Peace Movement and gave them the authority to print it in a limited edition. Once printed, Picasso signed them and the Peace Movement was free to sell them. This was his way to contribute to the Peace Movement in lieu of money.

PEACE DOVE, 1961
Pablo Picasso
Spanish, 1881-1973
Lithograph
19½ x 25½ in
Loan from Estelle Finer

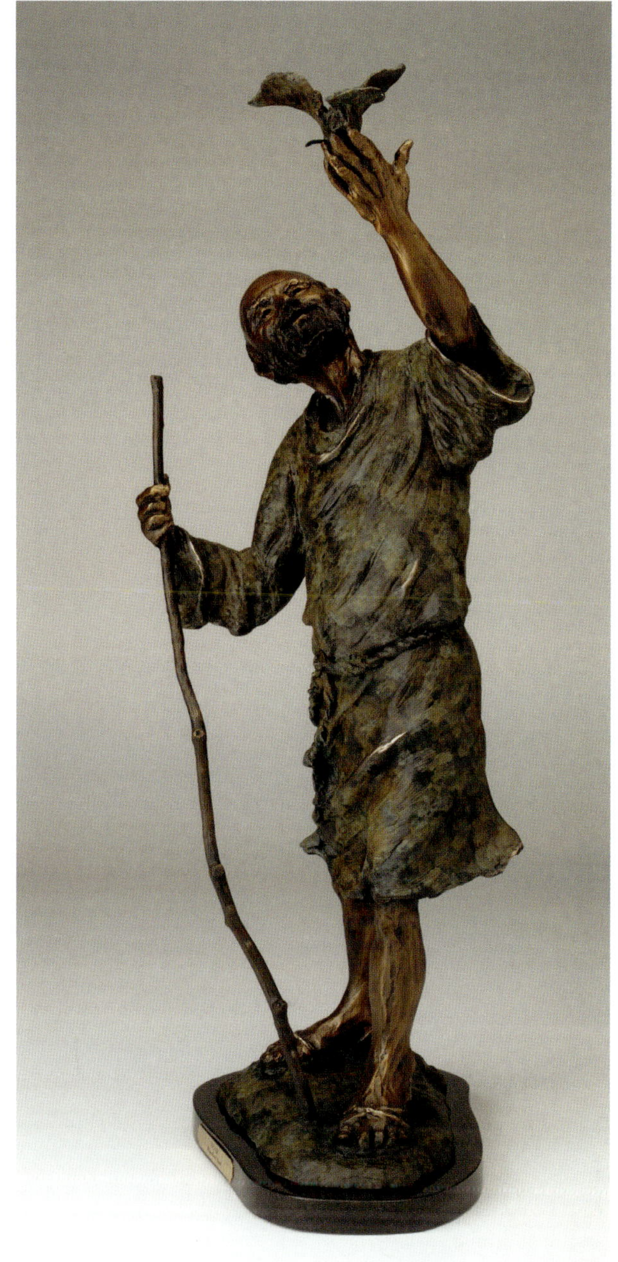

RIGHT: Rosalind Cook's contemporary bronze portrays an elder Noah joyfully leaning on his staff, other hand outstretched to welcome a dove with an olive branch. Second in a series of Noah figures, it captures the biblical promise of land for mankind. Rosalind Cook, was born in Lima, Peru in 1946. Living in the Andes until the age of seven fostered an appreciation for the myths of diverse cultures and people, which is evident in her bronze sculptures.

She began sculpting as a hobby, but soon turned to sculpture as a career. Veteran of numerous exhibitions, Cook's figurative sculptures grace hospitals, parks, libraries, and corporate headquarters as well as private homes across the country.

She teaches annual classes for Tulsa's Gilcrease Museum, in the lost-wax casting process. As a sculptor, she remains in awe of the great skills of this ancient art. Children, religious figures, peoples of varied cultures and races are prominent subjects of her bronze sculptures, which range in size from eight inches to monumental.

NOAH II, ca. 2006
Rosalind Cook
American, Born Lima, Peru, 1946
Bronze, 26¾ x 13 x 10 in.
Loan from the artist

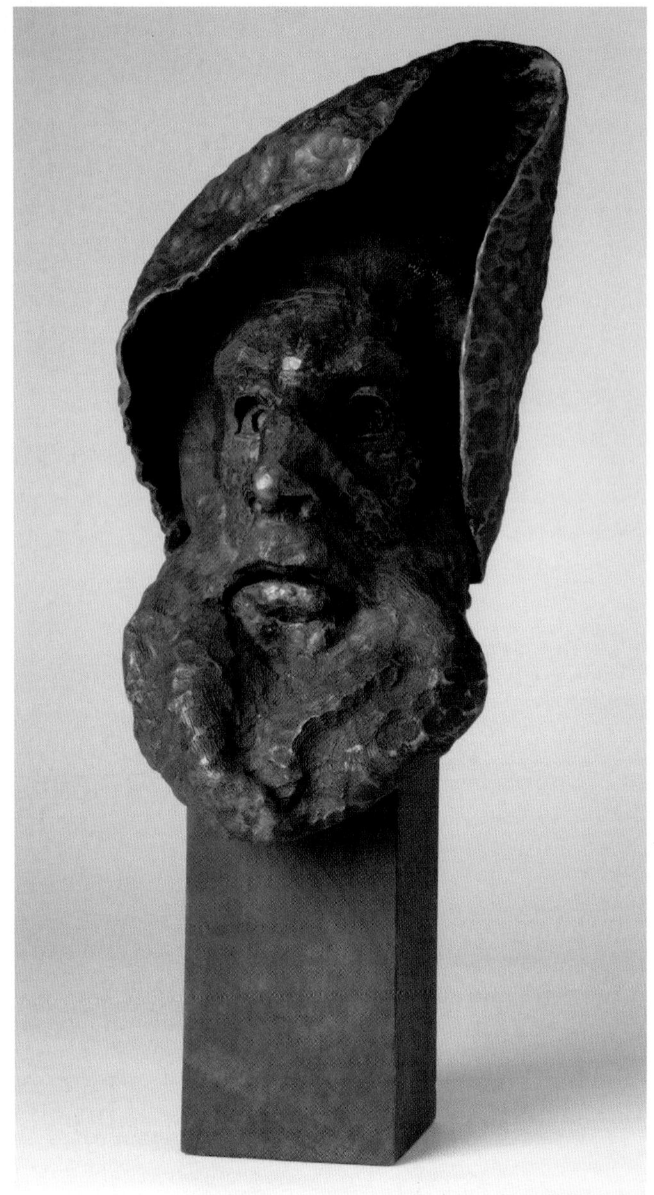

ABRAHAM

The voice of G-d came to Abraham, a descendant of Noah, and said to him, "Take your wife Sarah and your nephew Lot, and go forth from your father's house into a far country where I will create a great nation from your children." And Abraham obeyed and set out, knowing not where he was going, but trusting the voice of G-d. They journeyed many days toward the South until they reached a fertile valley in the land of Shechem. They continued on to Egypt, but returned to settle in Canaan.

Lot and Abraham both owned many animals, and their herdsmen began to quarrel over the pastureland. Abraham suggested they choose different areas to settle so Lot chose to camp near Sodom, and Abraham set out for the land of Canaan.

There the voice of G-d told him that the lands as far as the eye could see would belong to him and his descendants, who would be as numerous as the stars of heaven.

This prophecy seemed impossible to fulfill to Abraham, for Sarah, his wife, had no children. But he trusted the word of G-d. One day as he rested in his tent from the midday heat, three strangers approached. And as he arose to entertain and refresh them, they said that Sarah would bear him a son.

Sarah laughed because Abraham was a hundred years old, and Sarah was ninety, but the prophecy was fulfilled, and when the child was born, they called him Isaac.

The Story of Abraham and Sarah is from the Bible, GENESIS 12:1 – 21:8

Created by Tulsa artist Robert Wilson, this sculpture follows a movement during the early 1970s of a small group of American artists, led by John Cavanaugh who experimented with producing sculpture in "hammered", "beaten" or "pounded" lead. Saul Bazierman, Jose de Creeft, Ellie Nadleman, and Dorothea Greenbaum, among numerous others, were known to produce lead sculpture.

The history of lead in art begins in Greece with statues and relief sculpture. As an early cast metal, lead has been found in votive figures from Sparta in the 6th Century B.C., and in English and French Romanesque art and architecture. Lead has been used in art for centuries, falling in and out of favor with the artistic community, until its resurgence in the 20th century Arts and Crafts movement.

Lead is soft and easily worked compared to other metals. However, lead requires considerable care when hammering, not to stretch it too much, rendering it thin and breakable. Lead is now considered a hazardous material, and some artists who worked with lead in the 1970s developed cancer from the day-to-day contact.

ABRAHAM, ca. 1980-85
Robert Burns Wilson
Beaten lead. 20¼ x 8 x 6½ in.
87.6

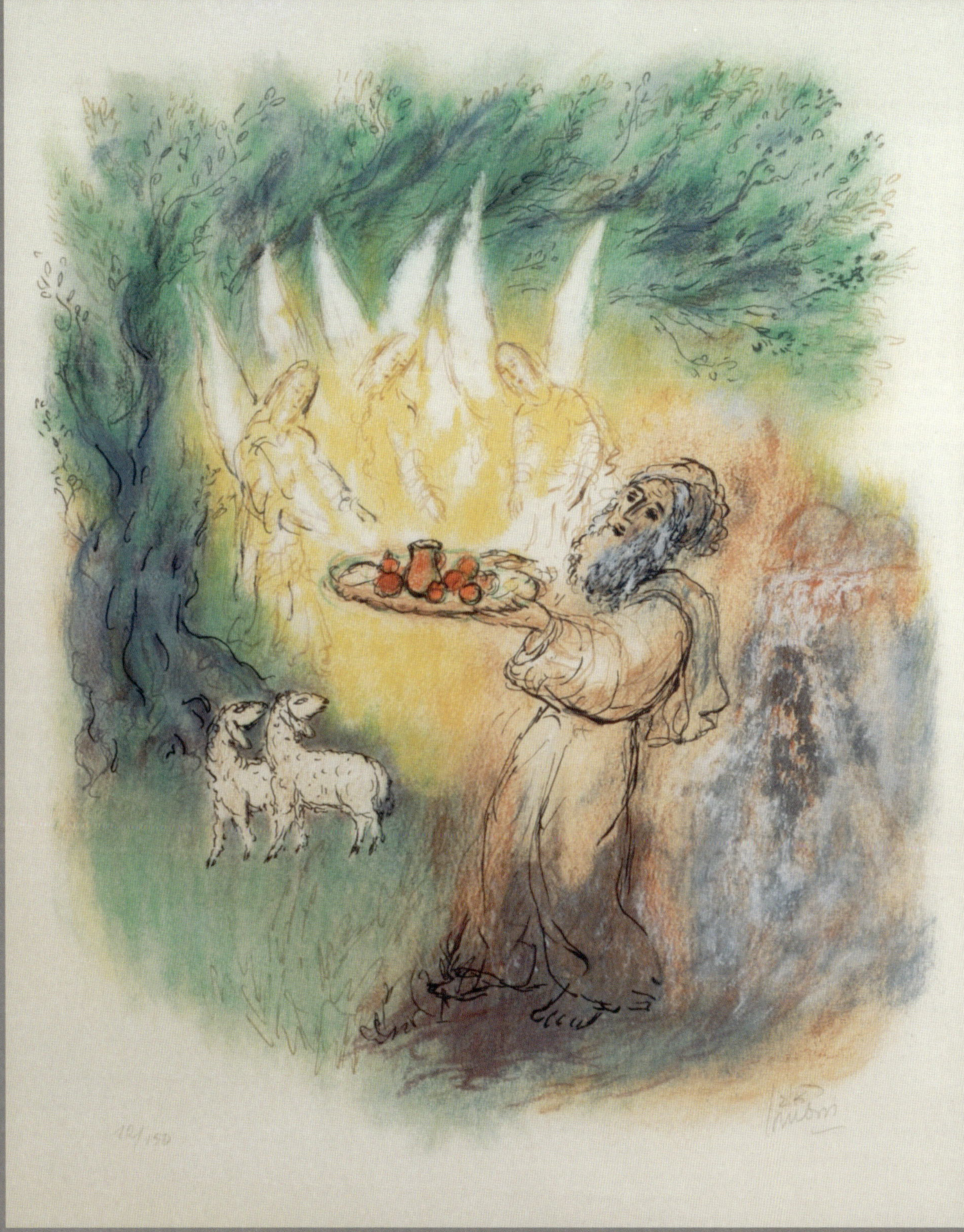

This color lithograph is part of a folio printed in 1972 by Abrams titled *Visions of the Bible*. An edition of 150, the set of twelve lithographs were presented in a large folio with its own slipcase.

Born in Romania in 1893, as a young man Rubin visited Palestine to paint the ancient sites of Galilee and Judea. He studied painting in Paris at the École des Beaux-Arts, but returned to study briefly at the Bezalel School and then settled in Tel Aviv. Rubin, working to develop an indigenous style of art, began signing his paintings with his name, Rubin, in both Hebrew and English. Rubin's work remained focused on the Palestinian landscape, its folklore, and its population, but included in his search for an art connected to the ancient land of Israel were the recurring Biblical images and themes found in much of his later works. From Abraham to Moses, Rubin illustrated the stories of the Bible in paintings and lithographs. He first exhibited his work in New York, and since then, has exhibited many times in New York, Paris, Los Angeles, London, Venice, Geneva, Tel Aviv, and Jerusalem. Recognized as one of the most significant artists in the history of Israeli art, Rubin was a significant contributor to Israeli artistic culture.

Abraham and the Three Angels, 1972
Reuven Rubin
Israeli, 1893 – 1974
Lithograph, 29 x 23 in.
From the series *Visions of the Bible*
Loan from Irene and Irving Fenster

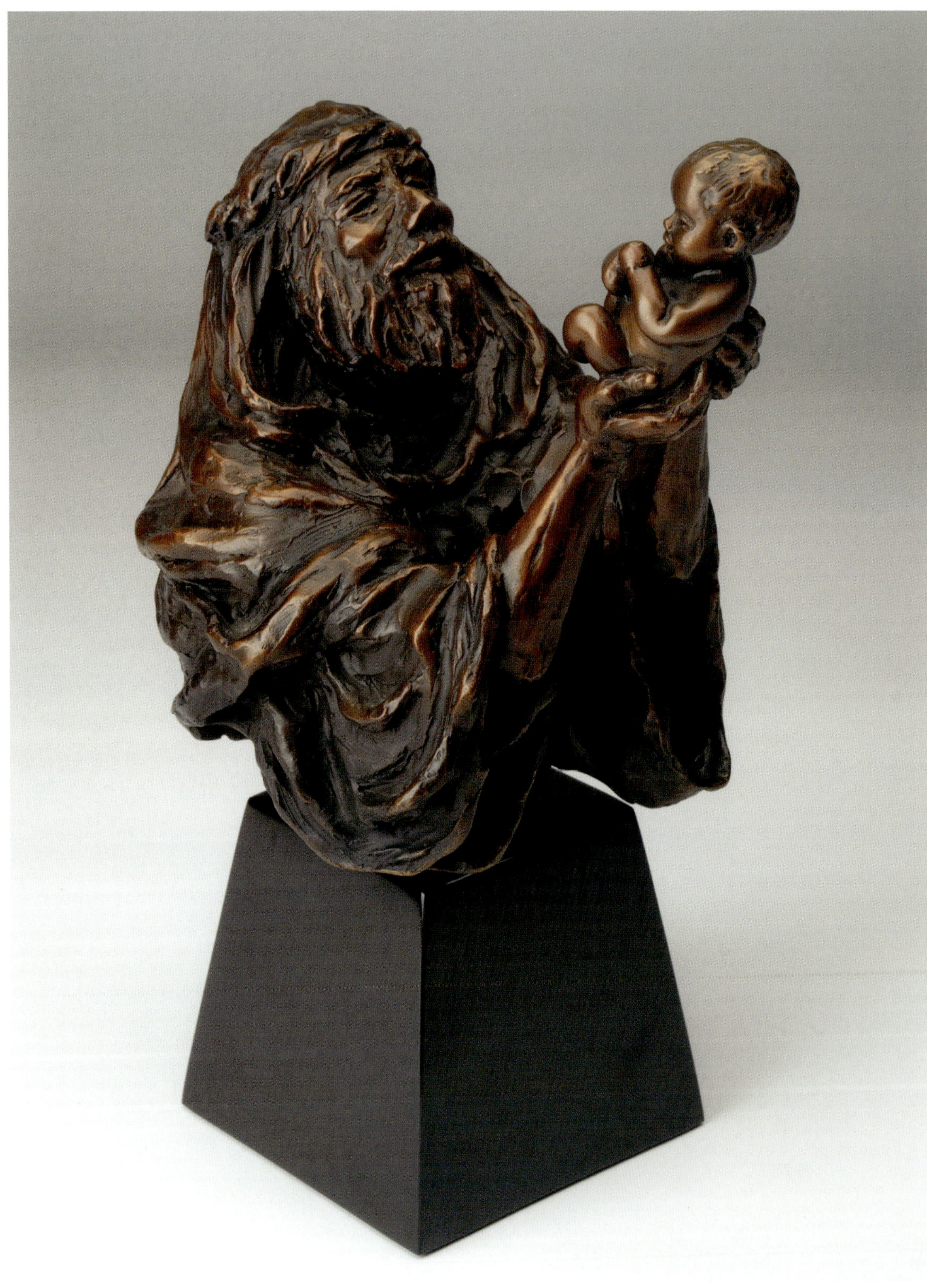

This second contemporary bronze from artist Rosalind Cook represents a promise fulfilled: that of the birth of Isaac to Abraham. G-d is faithful to fulfill His promises.

Promise Fulfilled (The Birth of Isaac to Abraham), 2006
Rosalind Cook
American, born Lima, Peru, 1946
12½ x 6 x 7¾ in.
Edition Size: 40
Loan from the artist

OPPOSITE: Born in Poland in 1904, Perlman immigrated to the United States with his parents in 1914. He moved to Washington, D.C. in 1924 to study art at the Maryland Institute College of Art in Baltimore and the Corcoran Art School. He became an artist for The Washington Post, where he did caricatures of political and show business personalities in the 1920s and 1930s. He began working in glass in 1949, creating carved glass murals for some of the Washington's most prominent institutions. He created the giant glass seal of President James Madison that was displayed in the headquarters of the old Madison National Bank in Washington, murals for Howard University, and a memorial wall for the Washington Hebrew Congregation. In the mid-1960s, he created a series of glassworks that were exhibited at the B'nai B'rith's Klutznick Museum. The works depicted Abraham Lincoln and historic personalities from Jewish history. Many of Mr. Perlman's works have a religious or historical theme and can be found in area galleries and government buildings and in more than 100 synagogues across the country.

The Patriarchs: Abraham, Isaac, and Jacob, ca. 1960–70
Herman Perlman
American, (Born Poland) 1904–1995
Glass sculpture, carved and sandblasted
12¾ x 12¼ x ¾ in.
Loan from Sallye and Donald Mann

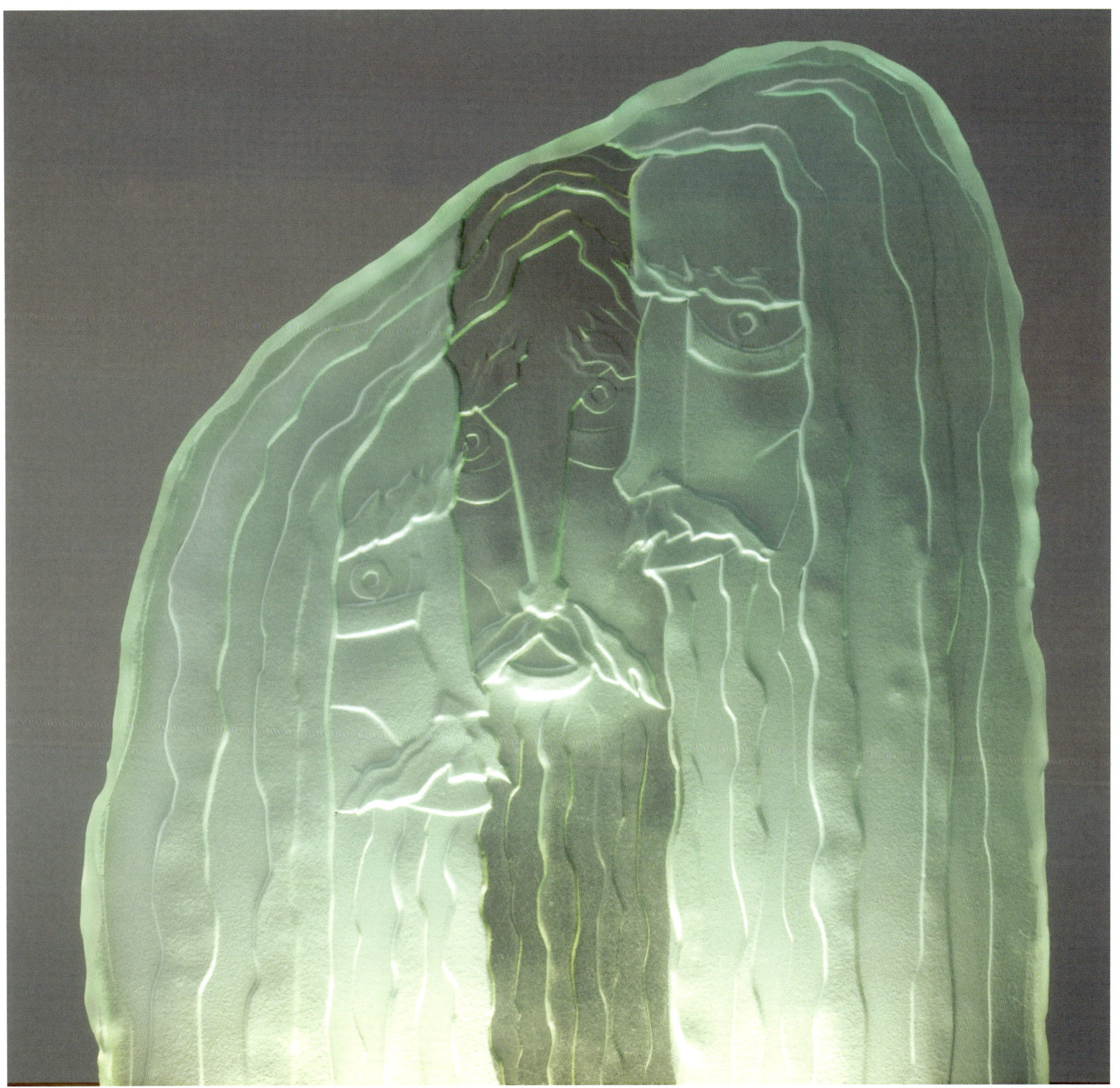

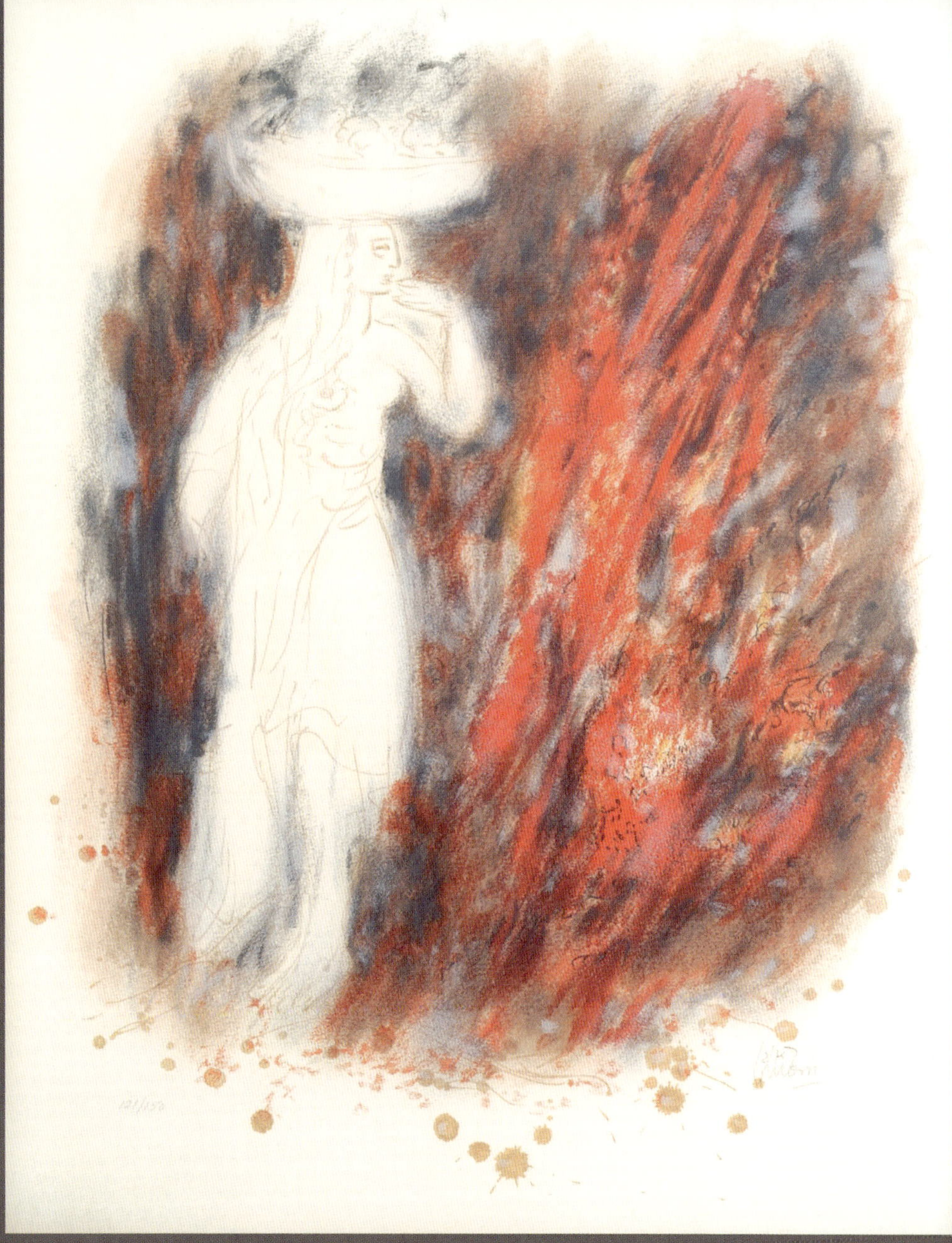

Born in Romania in 1893, as a young man Rubin visited Palestine to paint the ancient sites of Galilee and Judea. He studied painting in Paris at the École des Beaux-Arts, but returned to study briefly at the Bezalel School and then settled in Tel Aviv. Rubin, working to develop an indigenous style of art, began signing his paintings with his name, Rubin, in both Hebrew and English. Rubin's work remained focused on the Palestinian landscape, its folklore, and its population, but included in his search for an art connected to the ancient land of Israel were the recurring Biblical images and themes found in much of his later works. From Abraham to Moses, Rubin illustrated the stories of the Bible in paintings and lithographs. He first exhibited his work in New York, and since then, has exhibited many times in New York, Paris, Los Angeles, London, Venice, Geneva, Tel Aviv, and Jerusalem. Recognized as one of the most significant artists in the history of Israeli art, Rubin was a significant contributor to Israeli artistic culture.

Lot's Wife, 1972
Reuven Rubin
Israeli, 1893–1974
Lithograph
Loan from Estelle Finer

LOT AND HIS WIFE

The cities of Sodom and Gomorrah, where Lot, the nephew of Abraham, and his wife lived, were so wicked that they drew down upon them the curse of G-d.

One evening two angels came to Sodom and sat by the city gate. Lot welcomed them to his house, giving them food and lodging for the night. But his sinful neighbors, knowing that he harbored two strangers, came to his door, clamoring to see his guests, that they might abuse and humiliate them. Lot begged them to go away, but they began to batter down the door. Then the angels of G-d blinded them, so they could not see the door, and they went away.

In the morning the angels said to Lot, "Take your family, and get out of Sodom, for tomorrow G-d will destroy the city. But as you go, make sure that no onc looks back, or turns in his flight." Lot, with his wife and his two daughters, obeyed the angels' command and hurried from the city and across the plain. But as they ran, Lot's wife, forgetting the warning, turned back for one more look at the city that had been her home, and she was changed into a pillar of salt. Then fire and brimstone fell on Sodom and Gomorrah, and they were destroyed.

The Story of Lot and his wife is from the Bible,
Genesis 19:1 – 30

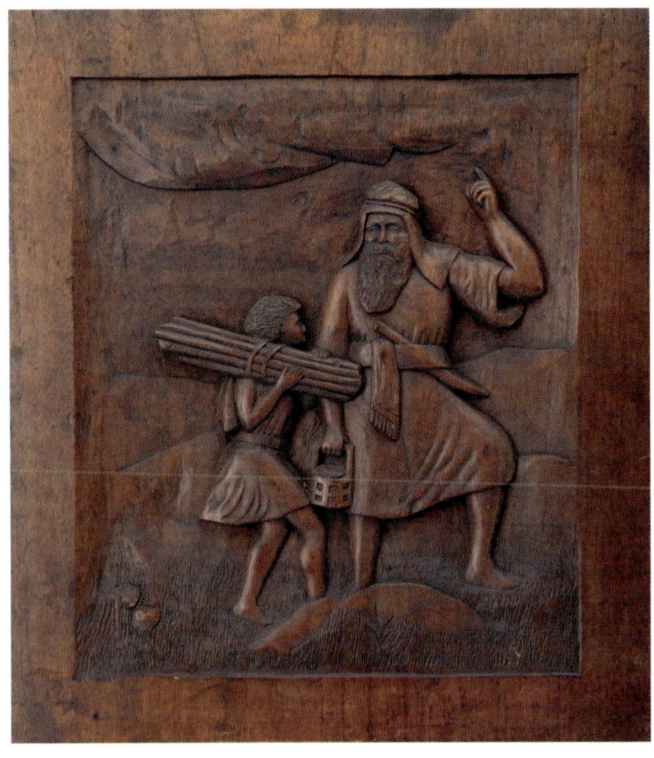

This wood panel carved in low relief depicts the journey of Abraham and Isaac up Mount Moriah after they left the servants and the donkey to wait for them at the bottom. Abraham carries the fire and Isaac carries the wood to build the altar. Panels of this type were traditionally carved as parts of an altar or screen placed in a sanctuary. By the nineteenth century, however, this panel might have been made for a home, or may have been intended as part of a series done for a set of doors. In Christian liturgy, the ascent of Mount Moriah is sometimes conflated with Christ's ascent of Calvary, including the symbolism of Isaac carrying the wood for the altar compared to Christ carrying the wooden cross.

ABRAHAM AND ISAAC
Relief carving, Italy, 1850
Wood, 19 x 16¼ in.
Gift of Mr. and Mrs. Julius Sanditen in memory of her father Nathan Taichert
65.37

ISAAC

The boy Isaac grew sturdy and straight, and he was the joy of Abraham's life. But there came a day when G-d decided to test his servant Abraham, and he commanded, "Take your only son, whom you dearly love, and offer him for a burnt offering upon a mountain where I shall lead you."

Early the next morning, Abraham saddled an ass and taking two servants and his son Isaac, set forth. When then reached the mountain that G-d had designated, Abraham asked the servants to wait with the ass, and he picked up the knife and a torch. He handed the wood to his son Isaac and they climbed upward alone.

And as they went Isaac asked, "My father, here are the fire and the wood, but where is the lamb for the burnt offering?"

Abraham answered, "My son, G-d himself will provide a lamb." When they reached the summit, Abraham laid the wood for the fire, bound Isaac, and placed him upon the altar. Then he picked up the knife wherewith to kill his son. But at that moment the angel of G-d called out, saying, "Lay not your hand upon the lad, for I know now that you love G-d, since you have not refused to sacrifice your only son."

Then Abraham looked up and saw a ram caught by his horns in a thicket. Unbinding Isaac, he laid the ram, instead, upon the altar, and he called that place *Adonai-yireh*, which means "G-d shall provide."

The Story of Isaac is from the Bible, GENESIS 22:1 – 19

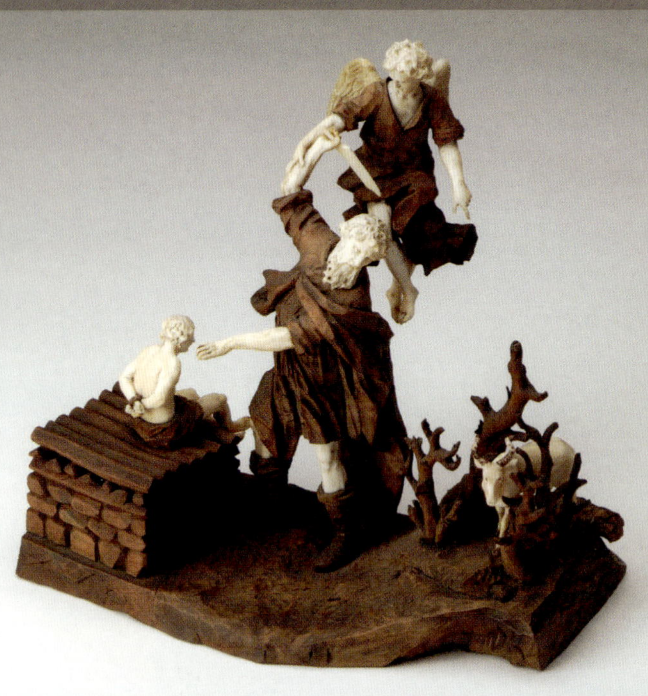

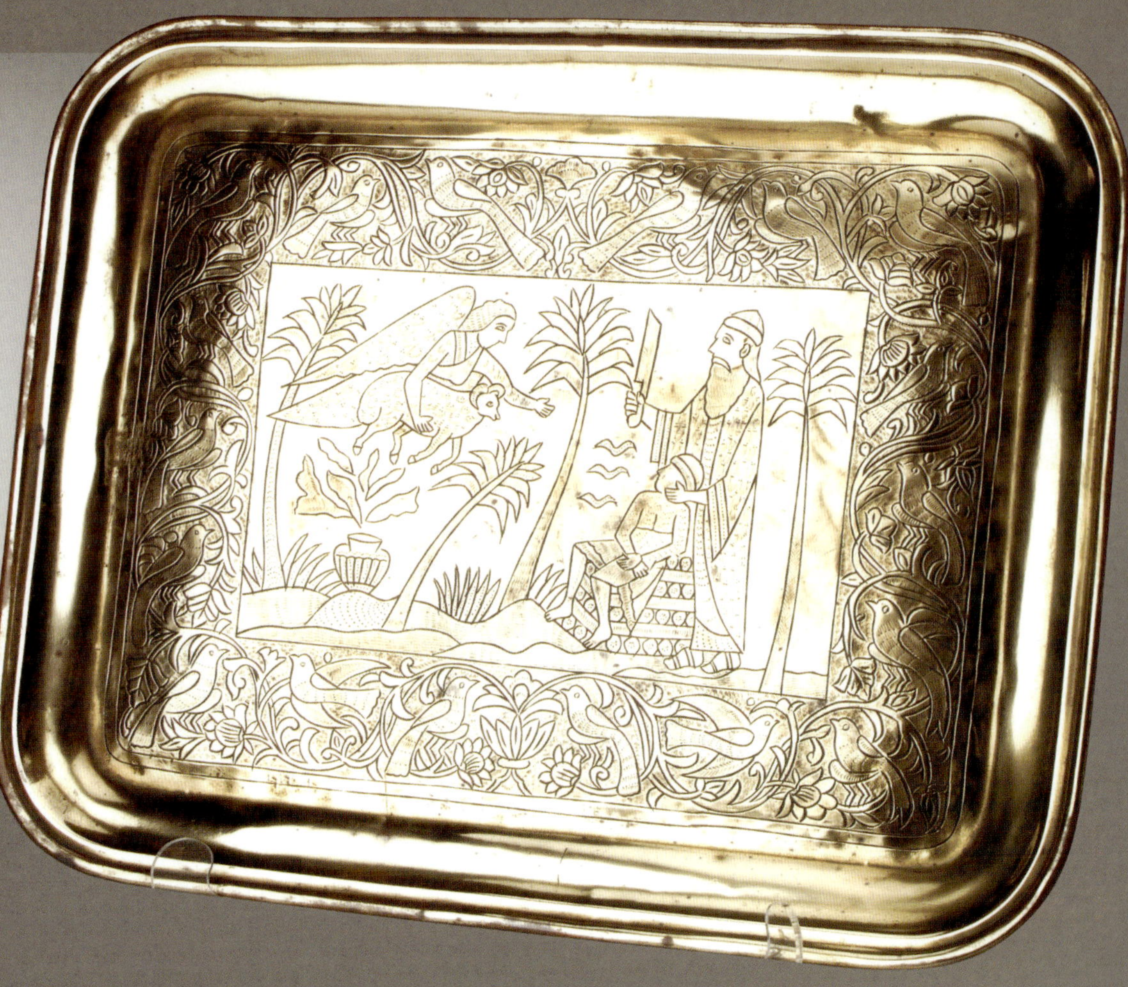

This boxwood and ivory sculpture, most likely made in Northern Italy in the 18th century, also captures the scene of the Binding of Isaac at the moment of the angel's intervention.

Boxwood, native to Southern Europe, has a fine grain that takes a high polish and ages to a warm bronze patina, is prized for its ability to take fine detail in carving. It is a shrub whose wood can only be used in small sculptures. Although the sixteenth century was the high point of boxwood carving, it was used by later Baroque sculptors in combination with ivory. Ivory carving was a staple of religious sculpture through the Middle Ages, and was revived between 1600 and the mid-eighteenth century as new sources of material became available in Africa. Central European court patrons employed ivory carvers, and supported workshops whose traditions influenced generations of sculptors. Noble patrons amassed collections of small ivory and boxwood sculptures and princes of the church commissioned small-scale devotional sculptures and reliquaries for religious collections.

The Sacrifice of Isaac
Sculpture
Southern Germany/Northern Italy, 18th century
Carved wood & ivory , 9¼ w. x 8¾ h. x 6¾ in.
Dedicated by Mr. and Mrs. S.M. Kantor in honor of Joseph S. Kantor 66.41

This highly decorative, bright cut engraved, 20th Century Persian brass tray has a flared edge surrounding an inner, wide border featuring a floral and avian motif. The inner field is decorated with figures depicting the Binding of Isaac. In this scene, Isaac is seen bound on the altar while Abraham raises his knife as G-d instructed. To the left an angel, messenger of G-d, brings the ram to substitute for Isaac as an offering to G-d.

Scenes of the Binding of Isaac, the Sacrifice of Isaac, and the Journey of Abraham and Isaac up Mount Moriah can be found in Hebrew, Christian, and Muslim artistic traditions from the late Middle Ages through the 21st century.

There are differences in the representation of these events that stem from the religious context. Called the *Akedah*, or the Binding of Isaac in the Hebrew tradition, the scene as portrayed by a Hebrew craftsman highlights the willingness of Abraham to obey G-d and offer his son Isaac as a sacrifice, and represents the covenant between Abraham and G-d. In contrast, the same scene in the Christian tradition is seen as a foreshadowing of the sacrifice of Christ on the cross. By the early 3rd century Christian art emphasizes the connection between Abraham's sacrifice and the remembrance of Christ's sacrifice. While Persian or Islamic artists seem to depict the events of the story using the same composition as a Judaic representation, in Islam there is a belief that Ishmael, not Isaac was the son Abraham offered for sacrifice.

The Sacrifice of Isaac
Brass tray
Persia, 20th century
14¼ x 18 in.
67.23

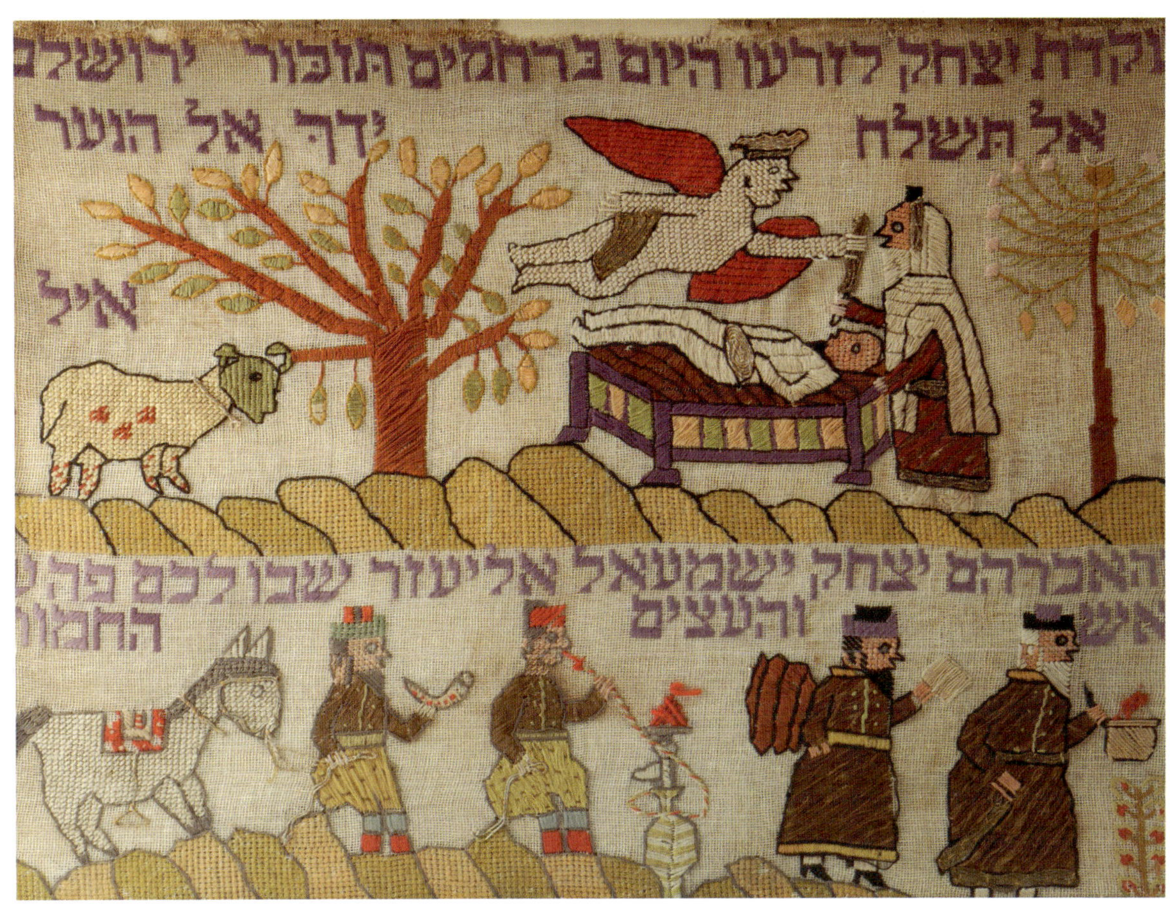

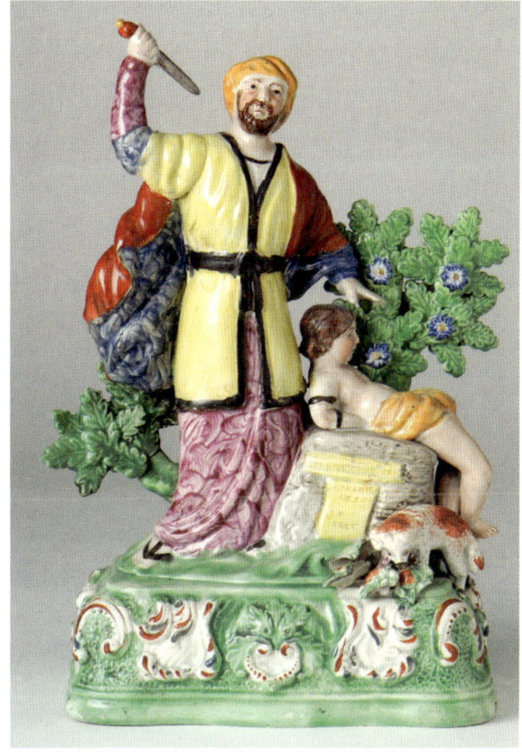

ABOVE: The upper panel of this embroidery, picturing the *Akedah*, or the Binding of Isaac, shows the moment in which Abraham's hand is stopped from carrying out the sacrifice by angel. The ram, Isaac's substitute, is tied to the tree on the left side of the textile. The lower panel depicts the journey up Mount Moriah. Abraham leads the group followed by Isaac carrying the wood for the sacrifice, behind them come Ishmael, Eliezer, and one donkey.

The embroidered Hebrew inscriptions on the panels read:

> (Top) Binding of Isaac for generations today with mercy, Remember Jerusalem, Do not stab the boy. (The ram is labeled "ram").
> (Bottom) Here Abraham, Isaac, Ishmael, and Eliezer return with the fire, wood, and the donkey.

THE SACRIFICE OF ISAAC
Pictorial embroidery
Israel, Jerusalem ca. 1900
Loan from an anonymous lender

RIGHT: Staffordshire figures were created to satisfy the desire of English working-class families for images of 18th and 19th century celebrities. These pearl glazed earthenware figures covered every possible topic from the Royal Family to politicians, murderers, sportsmen, soldiers, religious figures, and famous explorers. Early Staffordshire figures have a plinth base, and are made from pearlware. The clay was hand pressed into two molds, joined, painted and fired. Made by potters such as Obadiah Sherratt and Isaac Walton, many are called *bocage* figures. A *bocage* figure is one in its own setting, with a tree from which leaves and flowers hung.

Figures depicting scenes from the Old Testament were in great demand, and were created in the round from engravings of religious paintings. At least three versions of the Binding of Isaac were made, a dozen Rebekah's, and other familiar figures: Jacob meeting Rachel; Joseph sold into captivity in Egypt; Moses; Ruth and Boaz; Samuel and Eli; Saul and David; Daniel in the lions' den; and Balaam and his ass.

ABRAHAM AND ISAAC
Staffordshire figure, ca. 1835
English pearlware, Obadiah Sherratt type
Height 11¼ in.
Loan from an anonymous lender

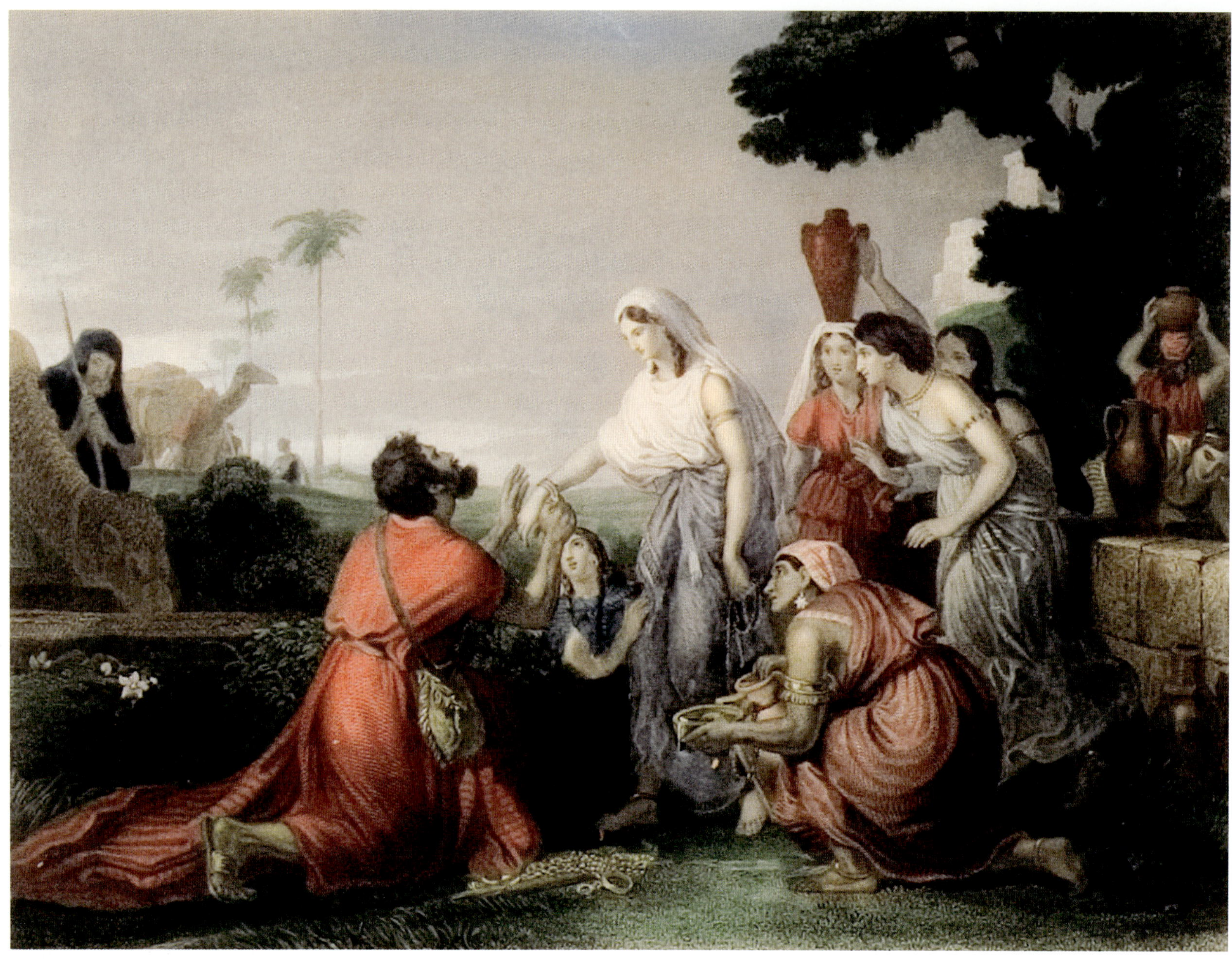

William Hilton was born in Lincoln, son of a portrait-painter. He apprenticed with an engraver, John Raphael Smith, while studying at the Royal Academy in London.

Like many young English painters, he toured Italy as a young man, painting scenes from antiquity. Upon his return he enjoyed a successful career producing paintings of both biblical and historical figures. His works can be seen in the collections of the National Gallery and the Tate Gallery in London. The National Gallery now owns *Rebecca and Abraham's Servant* (1829), the original painting from which this was engraved. Engraving was a historically important method of producing images for commercial reproductions and illustrations for books and magazines.

The passages in Scripture illustrated are in Genesis, chap. xxiv., verses 22 and 47:

> And it came to pass, as the camels had done drinking, that the man took a golden ear-ring of half a shekel weight, and two bracelets for her hands of ten shekels weight of gold, "and he put the ear-ring upon her face, and the bracelets upon her hands.

Rebekah at the Well, 1851
William Hilton, RA
English, 1786–1839
Copperplate engraving, C. Rolls, engraver
7½ x 10½ in.
Loan from Rebecca Kantor

REBEKAH

When Abraham was very old and much blessed by G-d, he had only one last wish. He wanted to see his son Isaac married. He called a faithful servant to him and said, "Swear a solemn oath that you will go back to the land whence I came and bring out a wife for my son from my own people."

The servant loaded ten camels with expensive gifts from Abraham, and traveled many days till he came to a well near Nachor, where Abraham had lived.

There he prayed, "O G-d, here I stand by a well where the daughters; of the city come to draw water. When I ask for a drink, let there be one who answers. 'Drink and I will give drink to your camels also.' Then I shall know that she is the chosen wife for Isaac."

Even before he had finished his prayer, there came a lovely maiden, Rebekah, along the path from the city, with her pitcher on her shoulder. The servant said, "May I have a drink from your pitcher?" And Rebekah answered, "Drink, my lord,and I will draw water for your camels also."

Then the servant knew he had found the wife for Isaac, and he took out a golden earring and two bracelets, and adorned the maiden. The servant followed her to her father's house and spoke to her family. When he had stated his errand, the father and brother of Rebekah said she could marry Isaac in a year and a day. When the servant protested, Rebekah's parents allowed her to decide, and soon afterward Rebekah and her servants accompanied Abraham's servant back to Canaan. Isaac met them coming on the road home, and he loved Rebekah, and she became his wife.

The Story of Rebekah at the Well is from the Bible, GENESIS 24.

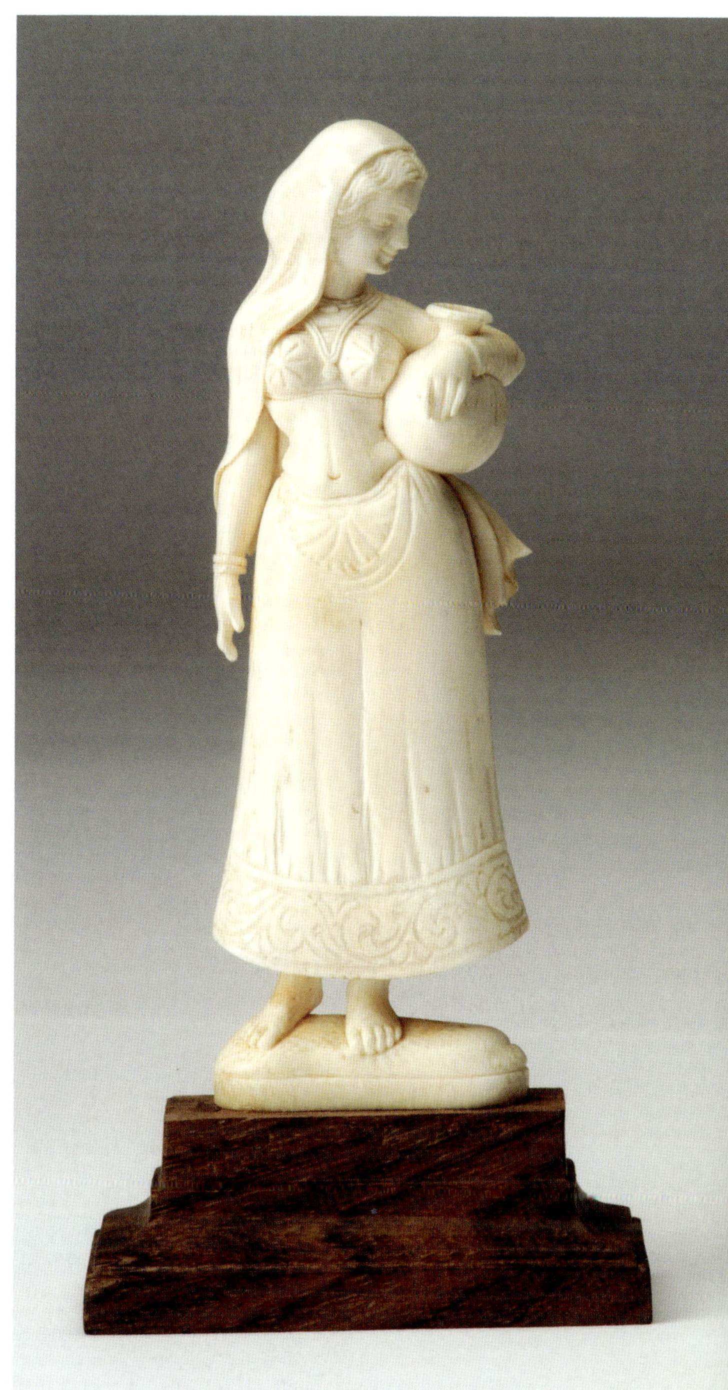

REBEKAH AT THE WELL
Ivory figurine
European
10 x 3 in.
Loan from Joe Degen

A traditional rendition of the figure of *Rebekah at the Well*, Rebekah is shown with her water jar as she offers to draw water for Abraham's servant and his camels. This contemporary rendition has simplified lines and a lyrical rendition of Rebekah's pose.

REBEKAH AT THE WELL, ca. 1970
Unknown artist
Ceramic figure, 11 in.
Loan from Cynthia and Yohanan Zomer

Copper has been worked in the Middle East since before the Bronze Age, and the tribes of Israel have been coppersmiths since the production of the first tabernacle.

Copper trays have been a staple of daily life in Persia/Iran and Morocco since the Middle Ages, and the centers of production still exist in Isfahan and Marrakesh. This tray was produced in Israel, and can be identified as such by the figural scene from the Bible and the lack of floral, foliate and Arabic inscription in the decoration.

To produce a copper tray, the metal must first be hammered out into a sheet. The design is engraved onto the back and the tray is laid face-down onto a large block of hardened tar, which supports the tray while the design is hammered out from the back. When it is nearing completion the tray is plated with tin to give it its silver color and coal dust is rubbed into the engraving to heighten the contrast.

Rebekah at the Well
Copper platter, Israel, 19th – 20th century
Silver over copper
8 in. diameter
Gift of Frimi Apt
86.7.2

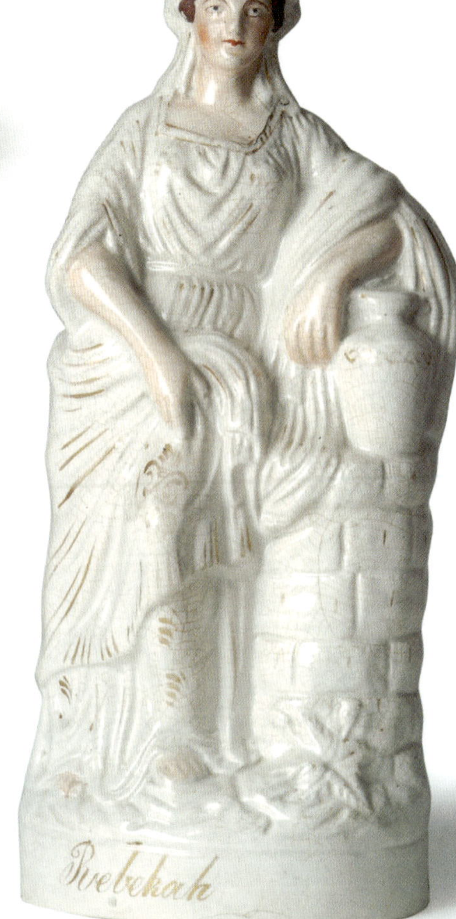

RIGHT: Staffordshire figures were created to satisfy the desire of English working-class families for images of 18th and 19th century celebrities. These pearl glazed earthenware figures covered every possible topic from the Royal Family to politicians, murderers, sportsmen, soldiers, religious figures, and famous explorers. Early Staffordshire figures have a plinth base, and are made from pearlware. The clay was hand pressed into two molds, joined, painted and fired. Made by potters such as Obadiah Sherratt and Isaac Walton, many are called *bocage* figures. A *bocage* figure is one in its own setting, with a tree from which leaves and flowers hung.

Figures depicting scenes from the Old Testament were in great demand, and were created in the round from engravings of religious paintings. At least three versions of the Binding of Isaac were made, a dozen Rebekah's, and other familiar figures: Jacob meeting Rachel; Joseph sold into captivity in Egypt; Moses; Ruth and Boaz; Samuel and Eli; Saul and David; Daniel in the lions' den; and Balaam and his ass..

Rebekah
Staffordshire figure, ca. 1820
Glazed pottery
Loan from an anonymous lender

JACOB AND ESAU

Soon after her marriage to Isaac, Rebekah bore twin sons, Esau and Jacob. Esau, the first-born, became a great hunter, and was Isaac's favorite. But Rebekah preferred Jacob, the younger, because he was quiet. Jacob, however, tricked his brother into selling Jacob his birthright as firstborn for a bowl of stew. Years later, Jacob tricked Isaac into giving him the blessing reserved for the firstborn son, Esau. As Isaac neared death he asked Esau to go hunting and prepare him a savory meal. When Esau left, Rebekah helped Jacob disguise himself as Esau, cook the meal, and trick Isaac into giving Jacob-disguised-as-Esau the blessing.

When Esau discovered he had been tricked out of the blessing he was furious, and swore revenge. Rebekah feared Esau would kill Jacob, so she convinced Jacob to flee for safety to the house of her brother, Laban. On his journey Jacob camped one night near Haran. Jacob lay down to sleep in the fields with a stone for a pillow and dreamed of a great ladder stretching from earth to heaven on which angels of G-d were ascending and descending. A voice said, "I am the G-d of your fathers. This land where you sleep shall be for you and your descendants. Wherever you go, I will be with you to guard you and to bring you safe again to this place." Jacob awoke, filled with awe. He thought, this is the house of G-d and here is the gate of heaven. He got up, and, taking the stone that had been his pillow, he set it up as a pillar, and named the place Bethel (House of G-d). Jacob journeyed on to the house of his uncle Laban, where he worked for fourteen years, marrying both Laban's daughters, Leah and Rachel. After twenty years, Jacob wanted to go home, but he was afraid of Esau's reaction. He set out and sent word ahead that he was coming. The messenger came back to tell Jacob that Esau was coming to meet him with four hundred men. Jacob was afraid Esau would attack him, and that night, he wrestled all night with an angel. Neither was winning, and Jacob would not let go of the angel until the angel blessed him. As day broke, the angel asked his name and then told him that hereafter his name would be Israel, meaning Prince of G-d. The next day Esau welcomed Jacob home with joy, and all was right between the brothers.

The Story of Jacob and Esau is from the Bible, GENESIS 25 – GENESIS 33

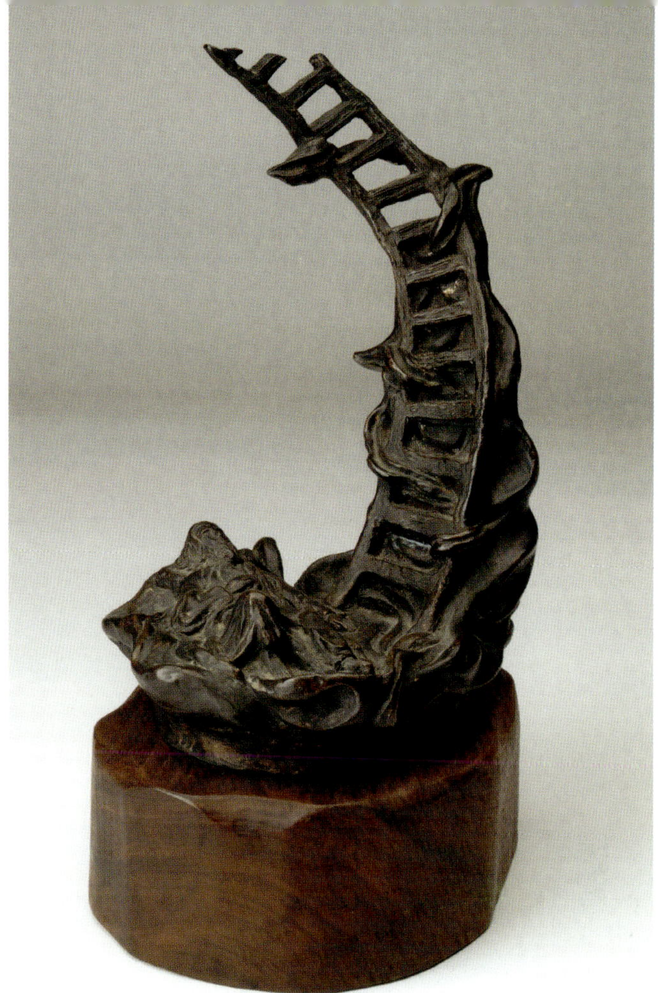

This small original bronze sculpture by Tulsa Jewish community member Allan Avery illustrates the vision in Jacob's dream of a great ladder stretching from earth to heaven, on which angels of G-d were ascending. This sculpture is one of a series of three biblical sculptures, all included in the *Sons of Adam* exhibition.

Avery, Curator of the Arkansas River Historical Society and The Tulsa Port of Catoosa, studied art growing up in Tulsa. He took private art instruction with Maggie Gough, studied at the Philbrook Museum School of Art, and studied with Inez Henson, an Oklahoma artist. His interest in sculpture developed as a young man during his artistic training, and some early works include a biblical series of clay busts of the Prophets. Allan's work has been included in many regional exhibitions, and this work, *And He Dreamed*, won a sculpture competition in Tulsa.

AND HE DREAMED, ca. 1975
Allan Avery (Avrum Ben-Yakov)
American, born 1945
Bronze, 12¾ h x 10 w x 6 d
Gift of the artist 02.58

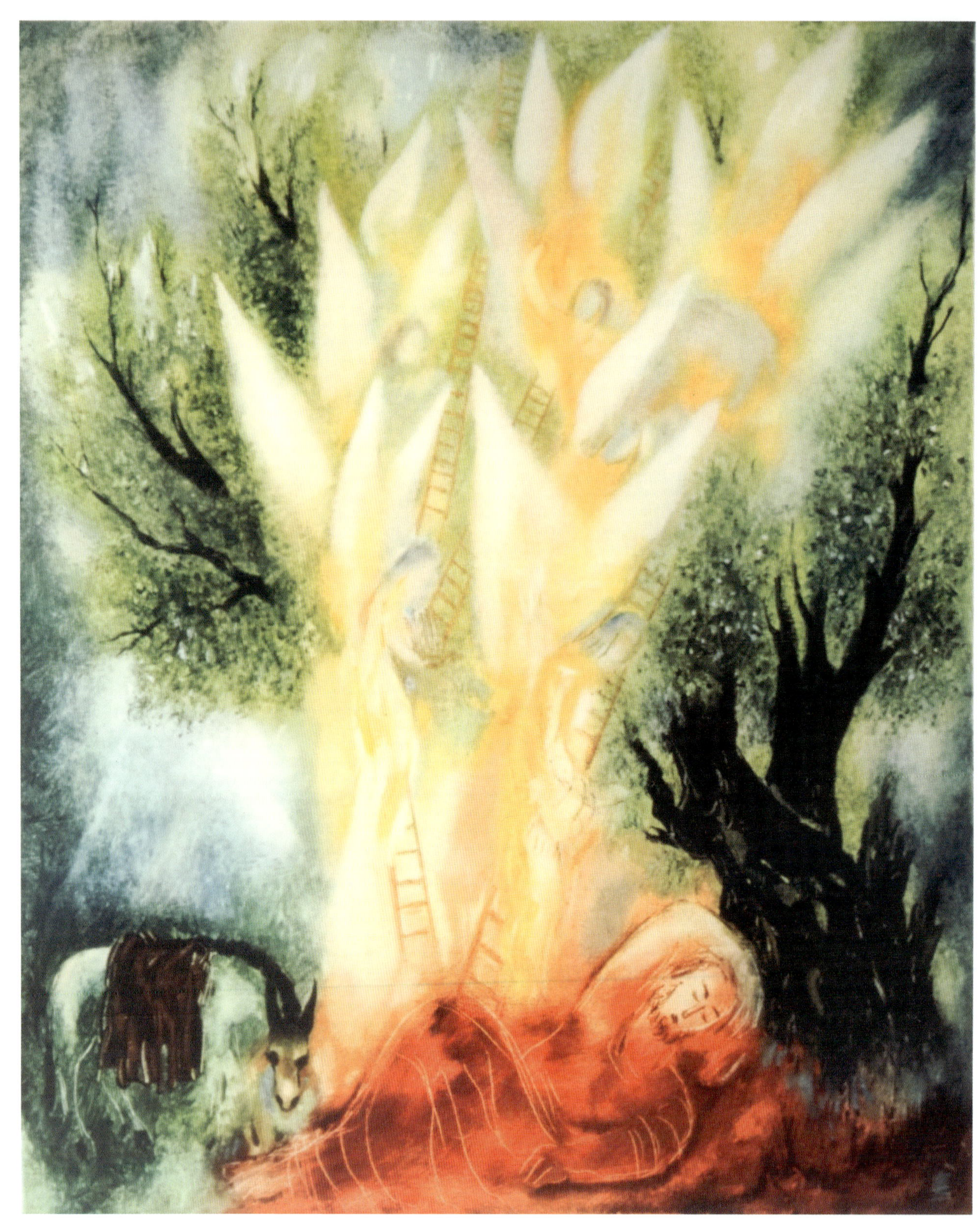

JACOB'S DREAM, 1970
Reuven Rubin
Israeli, 1893–1974
Lithograph
23 x 15 in.
Loan from an
anonymous lender

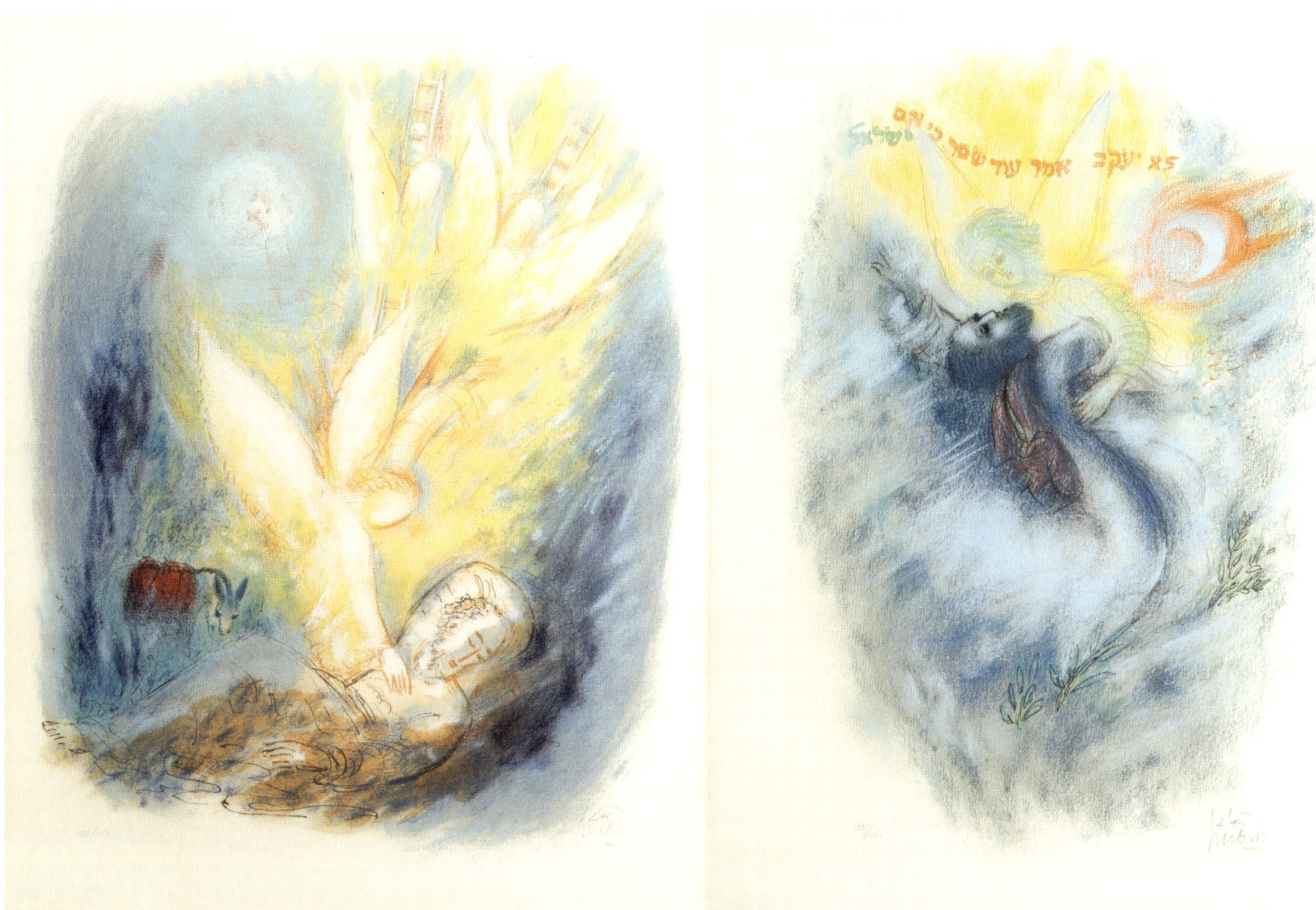

Born in Romania in 1893, as a young man Rubin visited Palestine to paint the ancient sites of Galilee and Judea. He studied painting in Paris at the École des Beaux-Arts, but returned to study briefly at the Bezalel School and then settled in Tel Aviv. Rubin, working to develop an indigenous style of art, began signing his paintings with his name, Rubin, in both Hebrew and English. Rubin's work remained focused on the Palestinian landscape, its folklore, and its population, but included in his search for an art connected to the ancient land of Israel were the recurring Biblical images and themes found in much of his later works. From Abraham to Moses, Rubin illustrated the stories of the Bible in paintings and lithographs. He first exhibited his work in New York, and since then, has exhibited many times in New York, Paris, Los Angeles, London, Venice, Geneva, Tel Aviv, and Jerusalem. Recognized as one of the most significant artists in the history of Israeli art, Rubin was a significant contributor to Israeli artistic culture.

ABOVE LEFT:
JACOB'S DREAM, 1972
Reuven Rubin
Israeli, 1893–1974
Lithograph, 29 x 23 in.
Loan from Estelle Finer

ABOVE RIGHT:
JACOB AND THE ANGEL, 1972
Reuven Rubin
Israeli, 1893– 974
Lithograph, 29 x 23 in.
Loan from Estelle Finer

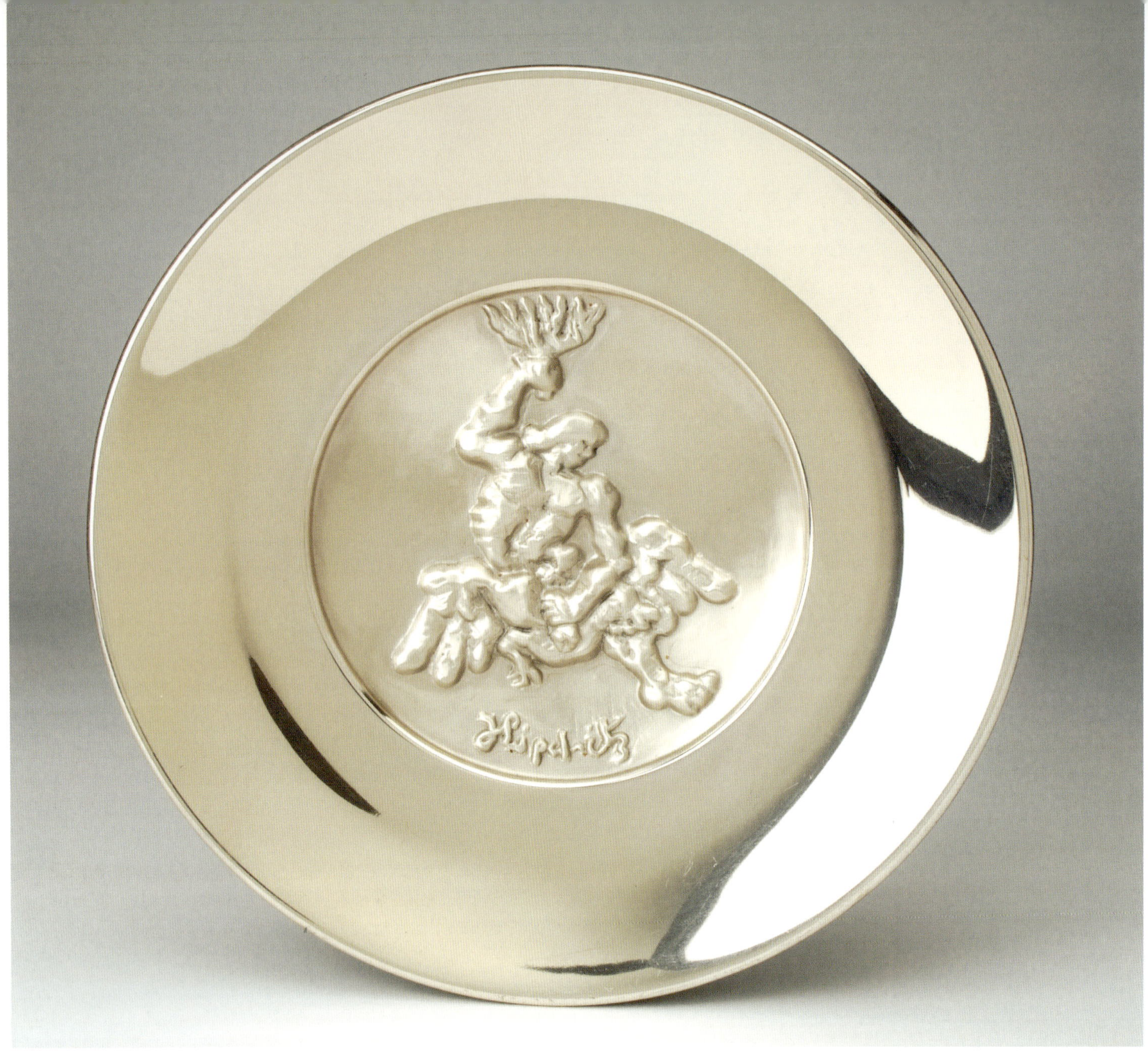

Jacques Lipchitz grew up in Russian Lithuania, son of a Jewish building contractor who opposed his son's desire to become a sculptor. Fortunately, Lipchitz's mother was sympathetic and arranged for him to go to Paris in 1909. He arrived with no formal academic training and studied briefly at the École des Beaux-Arts before transferring to the Académie Julian. From 1915 to 1930 Lipchitz was widely recognized as an important cubist sculptor, and in 1930 had his first large retrospective exhibition. After 1930 his work took on a symbolic quality, using biblical and mythological themes related to his anxiety over political events in Europe. An early example of this is the work *The Return of the Prodigal Son*, completed in 1930. Lipchitz continued to explore biblical themes of struggle in works such as *Jacob and the Angel* (1932) and *David and Goliath* (1933). He fled Paris in May 1940, when France was invaded by Germany, temporarily stopped in Toulouse, and finally reached New York City in June 1941, where he re-established his career. Lipchitz was honored with many commissions and retrospective exhibitions during the later years of his career.

The Struggle, ca. 1973
Jacques Lipchitz
American, born Lithuania, 1891–1973
Sterling plate, 8 in. dia.
Loan from Joe Degen

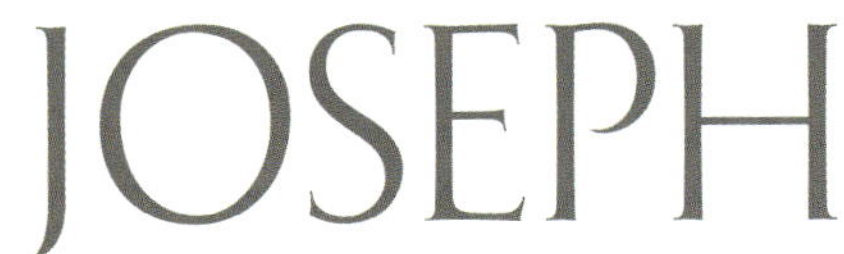

JOSEPH

Joseph, eleventh of Jacob's twelve sons, was the favorite. Joseph's father gave him a coat of many colors, and his brothers were consumed with jealousy. One day as young Joseph was helping tend the sheep, his brothers seized him. They tore off his coat and dipped it in goat's blood, to fake his death. Then they sold Joseph as a slave to a company of Ishmaelite traders on their way to Egypt. That evening the brothers showed the bloodied coat to Jacob, their father, who believed an evil beast had killed Joseph, and Jacob mourned for many days. Soon the traders arrived in Egypt, and sold Joseph to Potiphar, a Captain in Pharaoh's guard.

Joseph became an important member of that household, but Potiphar's wife, who wanted to have an affair with Joseph and was rebuffed, falsely accused Joseph of a crime, and he was sent to prison. Joseph was assigned to serve two men of Pharaoh's household, his baker and his cupbearer, who were also imprisoned. One night both men had strange dreams, which Joseph interpreted correctly. Although the baker was released from prison, he forgot about Joseph until two years later when Pharaoh had a strange dream. Joseph was brought to Pharaoh to hear his dream. In Pharaoh's dream seven fat cattle were grazing when suddenly seven weak, scrawny cattle appeared and devoured them. Joseph told Pharaoh it was a warning that after seven years of plenty would come seven years of famine. He advised Pharaoh to prepare by selecting a wise man to collect grain during the seven fat years. Pharaoh, pleased by Joseph's interpretation, appointed Joseph viceroy of Egypt. Joseph stored abundant amounts of corn and grain, and when famine came Egypt had food to sell. Jacob sent all his sons but Benjamin to Egypt to buy grain, because Canaan also suffered from famine. When the brothers arrived, Joseph recognized them, and made them bow down to him. He accused them of spying, and threw them in prison, where the brothers cried that this was punishment for their past crimes against their brother Joseph. After three days Joseph released them, and sent them home with their grain, but he wanted them to return with Benjamin to prove they were not spies. They went back to Egypt, taking Benjamin as Joseph had requested. On their return Joseph was overcome with emotion and revealed himself, saying, "I am your brother Joseph, whom you sold into bondage. But be not dismayed. You have truly repented. Return once more to Canaan and bring the entire family to Egypt where you shall live prosperous lives." And Pharaoh welcomed the family of Joseph, and gave them the province of Goshen as their home. They lived there for many years, and from them sprang the twelve tribes of Israel.

The Story of Joseph and his brothers is from the Bible, GENESIS 37:1 – GENESIS 50

This nineteenth century box, created to recall Gothic architecture in German towns such as Nuremberg, features as decoration the elements of a Gothic secular building: an arcade on each side in which are hammered figures of Moses and Aaron at each end. In the arcades on each side are scenes of Joseph being lowered into pit by his brothers and Joseph being sold to a company of Ishmaelite traders.

From the middle to the end of the nineteenth century copies of old silver and decorative items designed in a combination of historic styles were in demand by collectors in both America and Western Europe. To fulfill this demand many firms in Europe and in the United States produced this type of silver. In Germany, towns such as Hanau were home to thriving antique silver workshops who created new works in silver from antique forms, and this Gothic casket form could have been made in one of those workshops.

SILVER ALMS BOX FEATURING VIGNETTES OF MOSES AND AARON, AND JOSEPH.
Nuremberg, Germany, late 19th century
German 800 silver
5½ x 3 x 5½ in.
Gift of Mr. and Mrs. Charles Miller in memory of Mr. and Mrs. Michael Green, 65.23

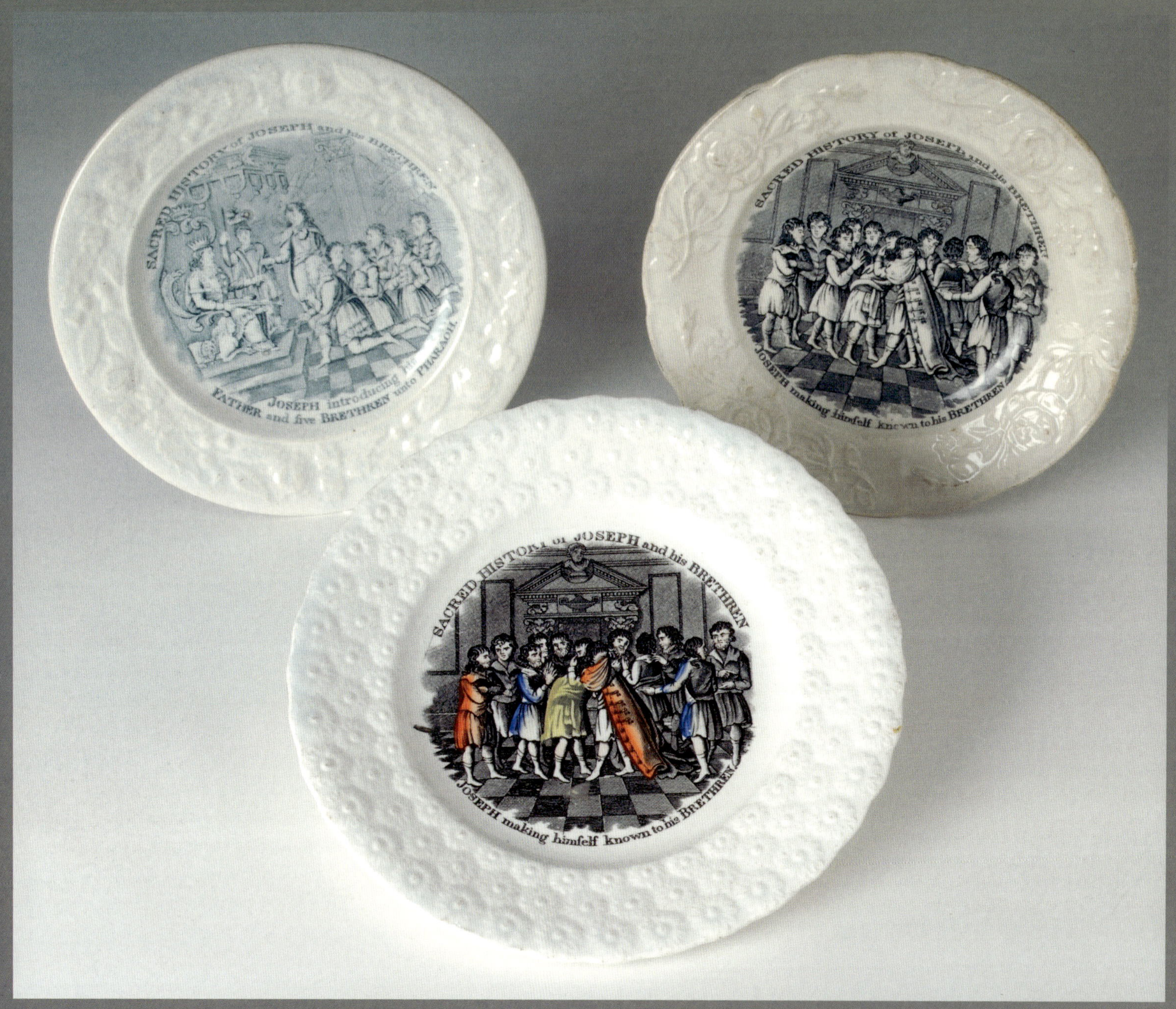

These Staffordshire children's plates were transfer printed and hand-colored in the early nineteenth century. Children's plates and mugs were made in large numbers during the 19th century but few survive today. They were typically decorated with animals, birds, games or morals and proverbs, making them educational as well as amusing. They were made in Staffordshire, Sunderland and Wales, but few were marked. The trend grew as interest in children's products and books began to grow in the 1790s, and were produced for the children of the nobility and upper classes. There were as many as sixty workshops and small factories around Staffordshire, sometimes employing child labor and some lasting for only a very short period.

This well-known series was made, with a cauliflower border, by the company J. & G. Meakin.

The Sacred History of Joseph and his Brethren, ca. 1830
England, Staffordshire soft paste child's plates
Series of three plates:
Joseph Making Himself Known to His Brethren (center front)
Joseph Introducing His Father and Five Brethren to the Pharaoh (upper left)
Joseph Making Himself Known to His Brethren (upper right)
Loan from an anonymous lender

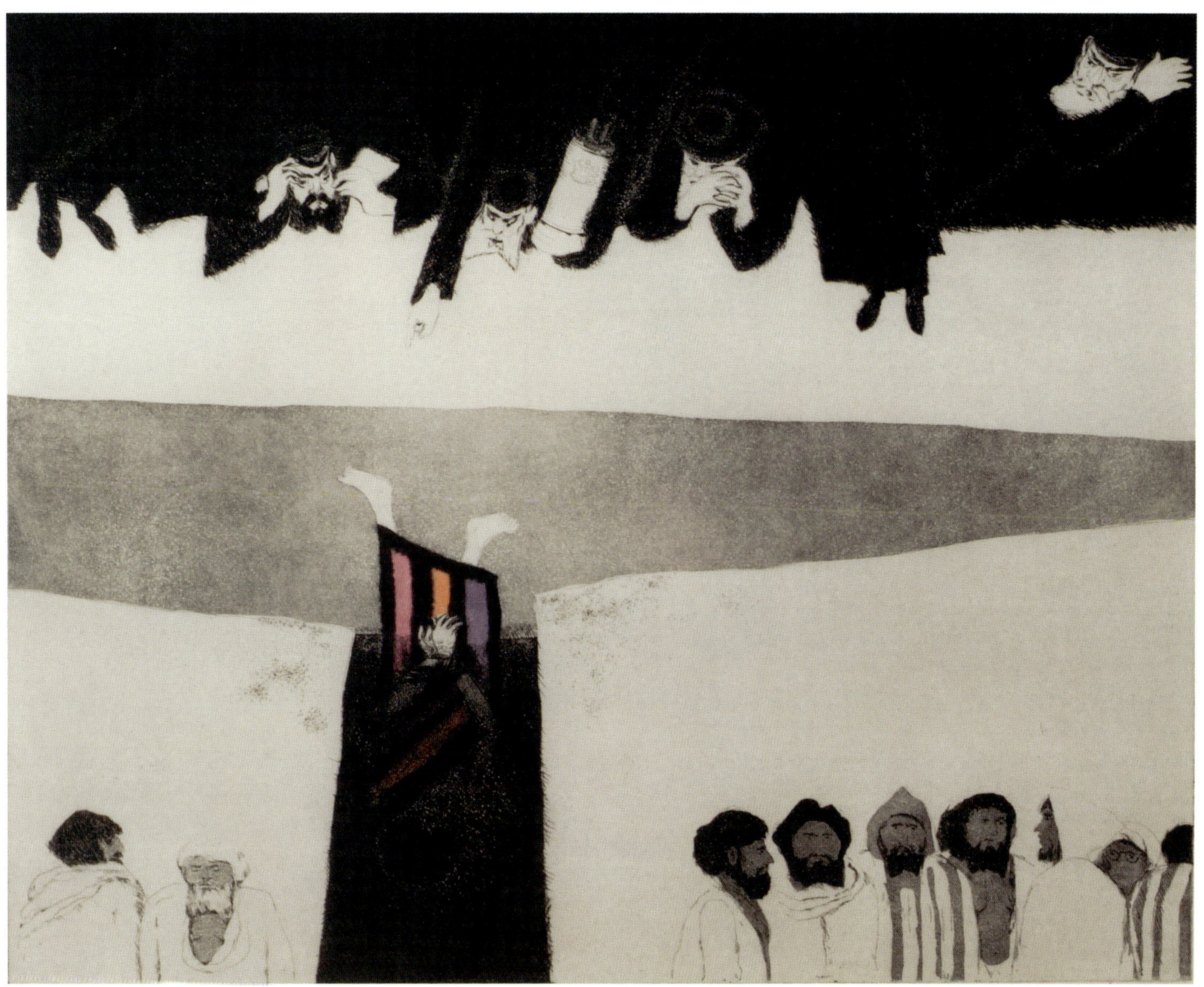

Born in Brooklyn in 1921, Gerson Leiber was interested in a career in art as a young man, so while stationed with the US Army in Hungary during WWII, he took classes at the Royal Academy of Art in Budapest. After the war, he returned to New York and studied printmaking with Will Barnet at the Art Students League and engraving with Gabor Peterdi at the Brooklyn Museum's art school. His prints won many awards and were featured in exhibitions at the Associated American Artists, the Alex Rosenberg Gallery, and the National Academy of Design. Gerson maintains his lifelong commitment to printmaking. He taught etching and engraving at the Printmaking Workshop established by Robert Blackburn, and continues to produce and exhibit his prints.

Joseph and His Brethren,
1966
Gerson Leiber
American, born 1921
Etching
20½ x 24½ in.
Loan from Maxine and Jack Zarrow

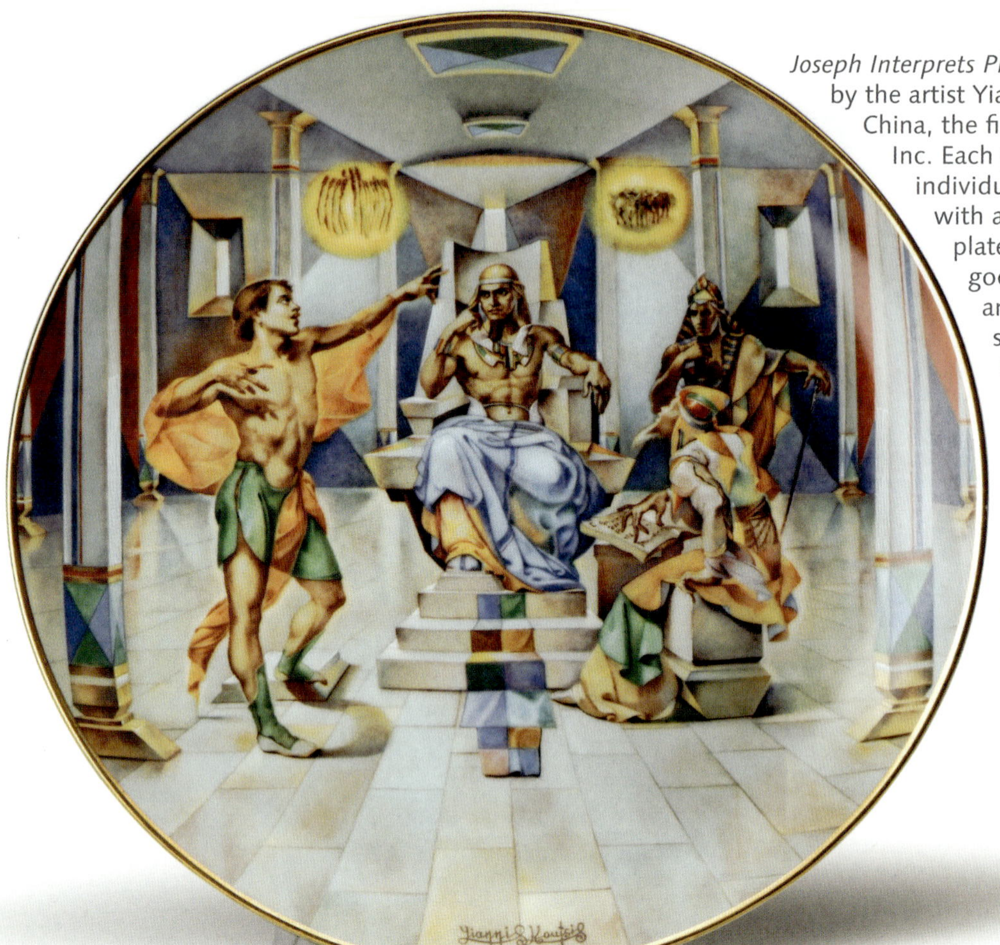

Joseph Interprets Pharaoh's Dream is the twelfth plate in the series *The Creation* by the artist Yiannis Koutsis. The plates are produced on Royal Cornwall China, the finest white porcelain, by the Calhoun Collectors Society Inc. Each plate is 9 inches in diameter with a 24 carat gold rim, individually numbered in a presentation box, and authenticated with a commentary booklet by Jonathan Paradise, Ph.D. This plate shows Joseph and The Pharaoh, who dreamed of seven good ears and seven withered ears; seven fat "kine" (heifers) and seven lean "kine." Joseph's interpretation will come true: seven years of plenty, followed by seven years of famine. With this interpretation, young Joseph becomes Pharaoh's chief advisor. This plate was produced in 1978.

Joseph Interprets Pharaoh's Dream
Yiannis (Giannis) Koutsis
Greek, 20th century
Plate 12 of The Creation Series by Royal Cornwall China
9 in. diameter
Loan from Carolyn and Ron Kriegsman

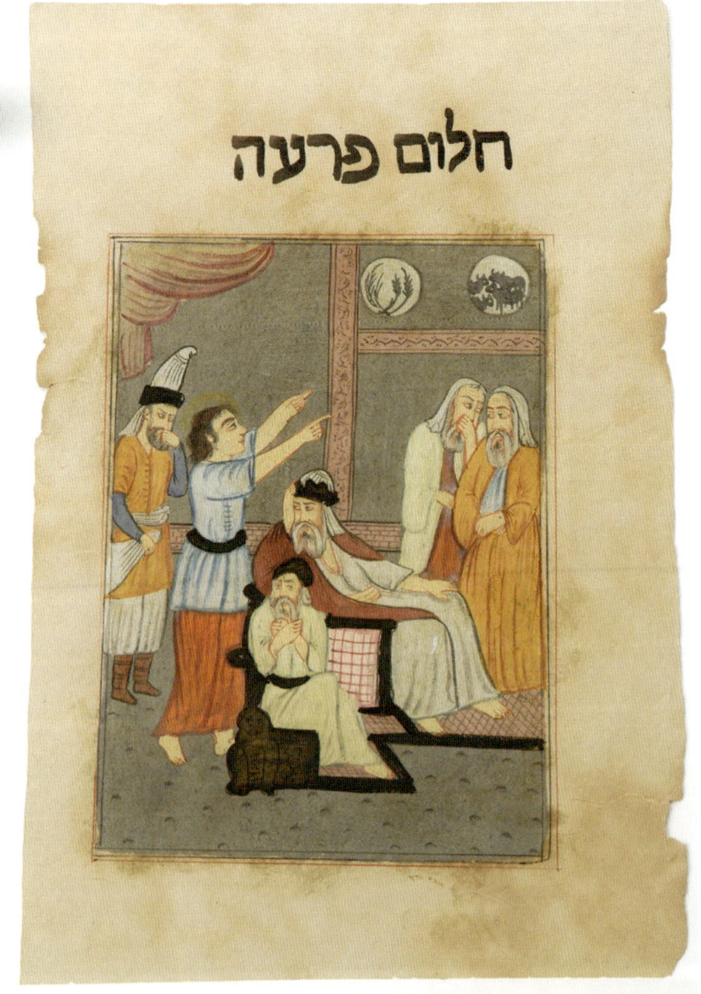

Persian miniature paintings are traditionally created to illustrate great literature, both religious and secular. This painting illustrates Jacob at the meeting when he correctly interprets Pharaoh's dream of famine in Egypt's future.

This illustration, from a Persian Bible study book, shows how Hebrew art follows the traditions of the area in which the object or painting is produced. Jews have resided in Persia since the dawn of the first Persian Empire, and biblical heroes such as Moses and Joseph have long been a part of Persian literature. It is believed that Persian translations of the Bible were achieved in cooperation with Jewish scholars, from the first translations in the sixteenth century.

The style of illuminated Hebrew manuscripts from the late 9th century to the present followed that of the host country in which Jews resided, so that the earliest illustrations from Muslim countries resembled Koran illumination. In the Middle East, manuscript illumination was a high art, and the hand-decorated book was appreciated into modern times.

Pharaoh's Dream
Persia, early 20th century
Pigment on paper
13 x 8½ in.
Gift of Family in honor of Jack Schlanger
73.20

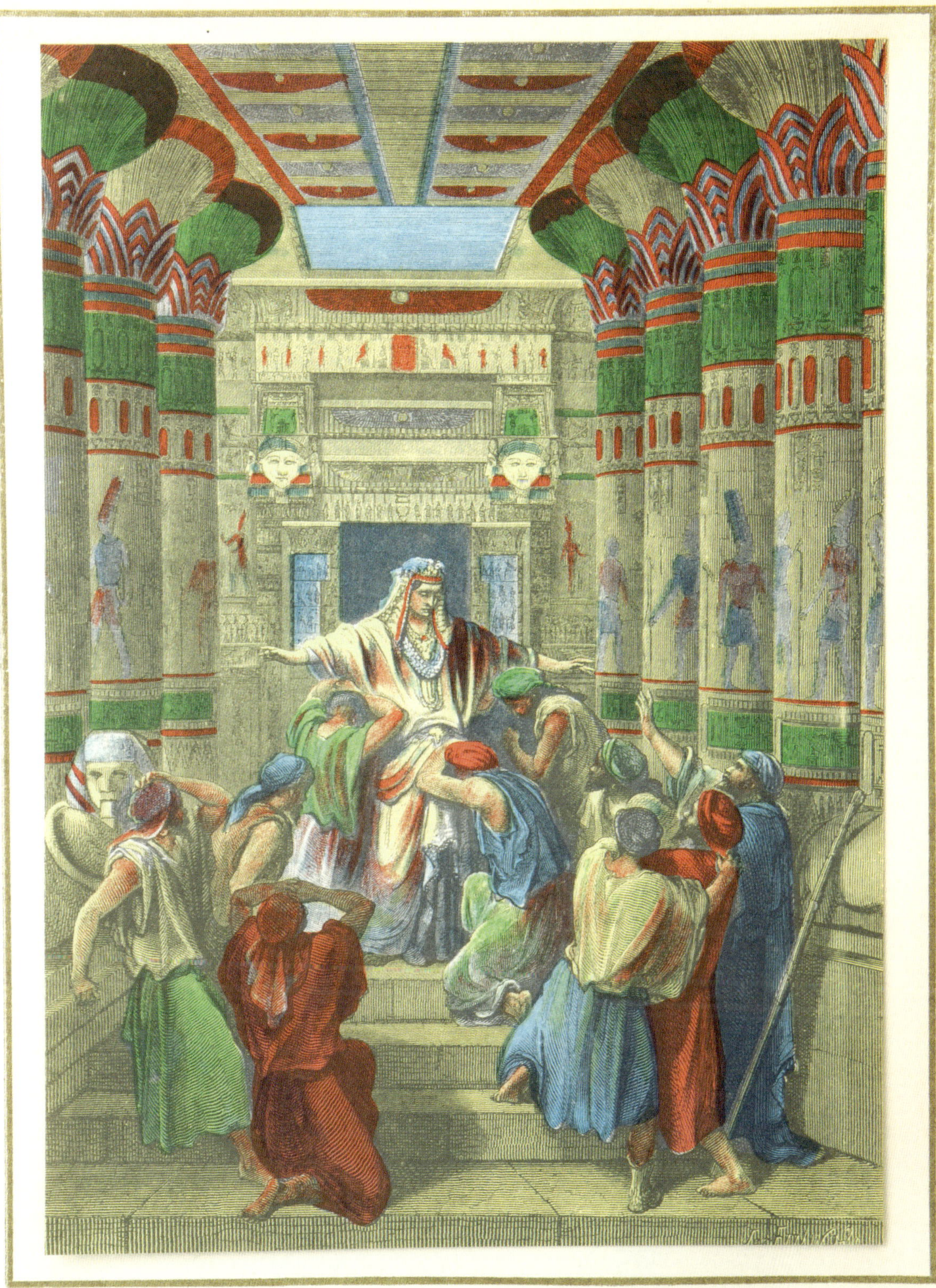

וַיֹּאמֶר יוֹסֵף אֶל אֶחָיו אֲנִי יוֹסֵף

בר׳, מה, ג

This is taken from the larger edition, with a revised English translation and copious explanatory notes by Joseph Loewy and Joseph Guens. It has color illustrations that are tipped in (that is pictures on separate pieces of paper that are glued on pages of the book.) The illustrations are unattributed.

Joseph Revealing Himself to His Brothers
Passover Haggadah
Loewy and Gurens edition,
Tel Aviv, Israel
Chromolithograph
8 x 10 in.
Loan from Phyllis and Howard Raskin

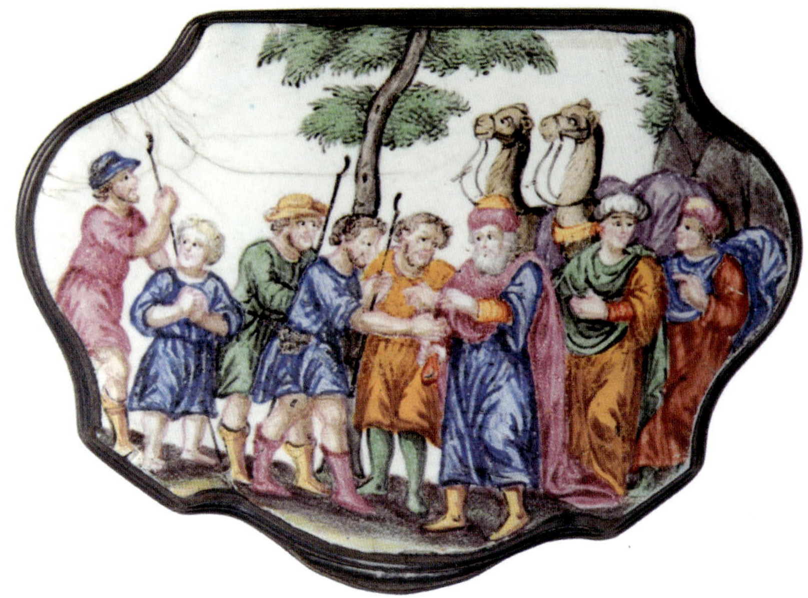

A silver box made in a cartouche form, decorated with painted enamel scenes from the life of Joseph. On the lid is painted the scene of Joseph being sold into slavery by his five brothers, who are making the deal with the caravan traders and taking the money for selling their brother. Inside the box is a whimsical figure of a beetle painted in the bottom of the box.

In the fifteenth century craftsmen in the Limoges area of France first adapted the Venetian skill of painting enamels onto glass by painting enamels onto metals. This technique did not require complex constructions to hold enamels or engraving, and is still used by art enamellers today. Until the eighteenth century most enameling was done on fine art or religious artifacts, but demand for small objects of fine quality by the nobility and upper classes brought about the use of painted enamel on objects for personal use, such as snuff boxes, perfume containers, and dressing table accessories. By the eighteenth century painting on enamel quickly became a new fashion in the courts of Frederick II, the Great of Prussia or the Court at Dresden. Centers of enamel production sprung up in Augsburg and Nuremberg, where the enamel industry produced fine works on watch cases, snuff boxes, and other personal items.

Scenes from the Life of Joseph
Snuff box
Silver and enamel, painted
2 x 3 in.
Germany, ca. 1730
Loan from an anonymous lender

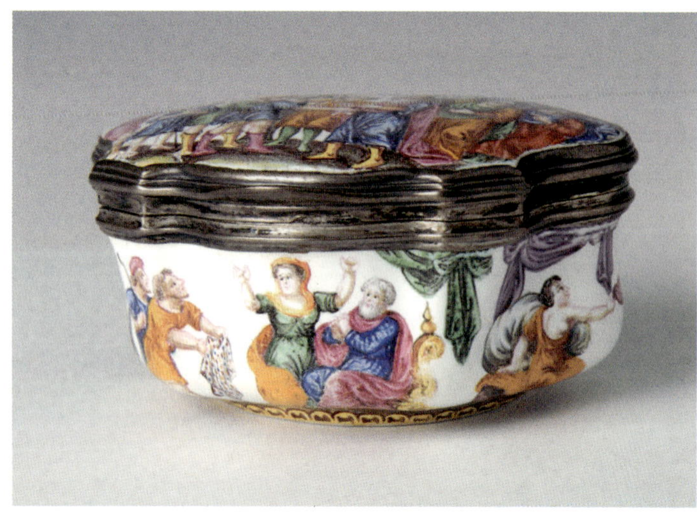

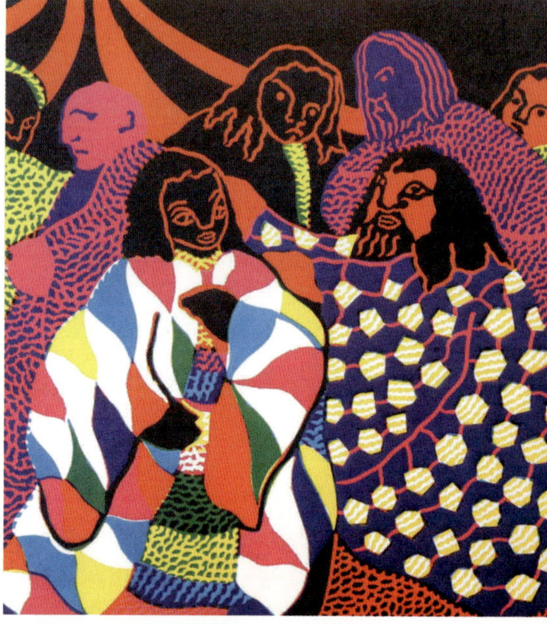

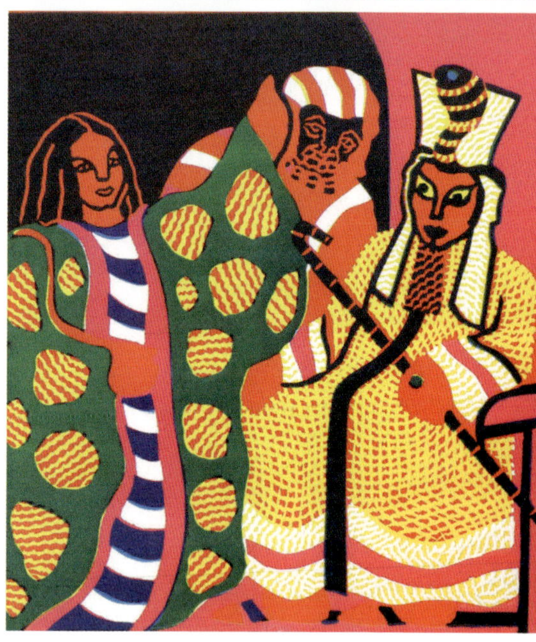

TOP ROW LEFT-RIGHT
Jacob Presents Joseph with the Coat of Many Colors
Joseph is Sold Into Slavery
Joseph and Potiphar's Wife
Joseph in Prison
BOTTOM ROW LEFT-RIGHT
Joseph Interprets Pharaoh's Dream
Joseph's Brothers Seek Grain in Egypt
Joseph and Benjamin
Joseph and Jacob are Reunited

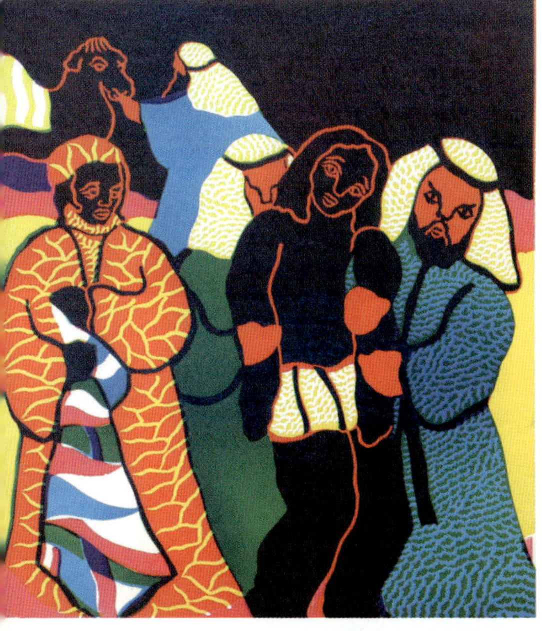
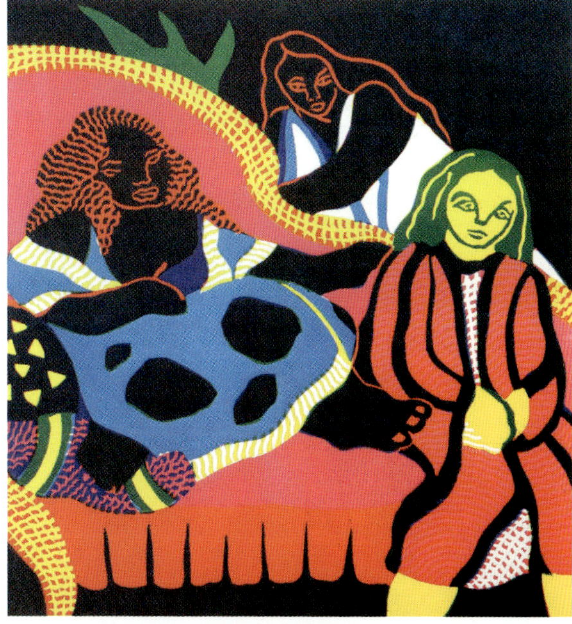
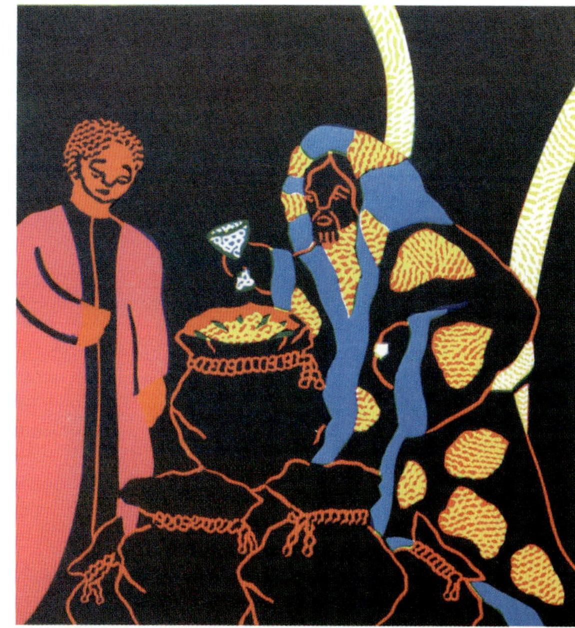
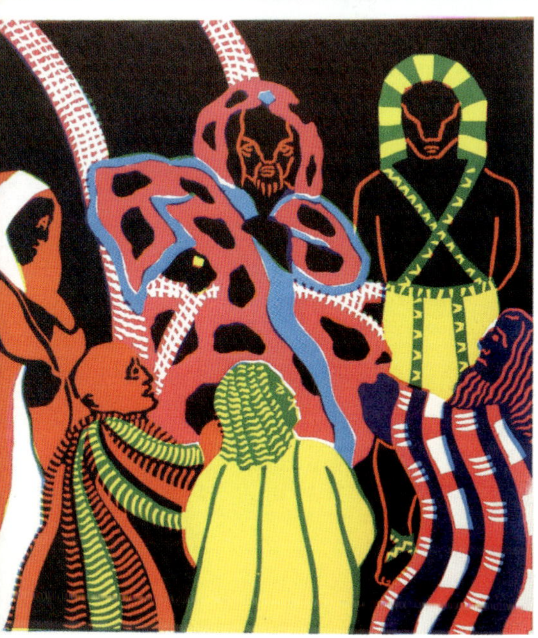
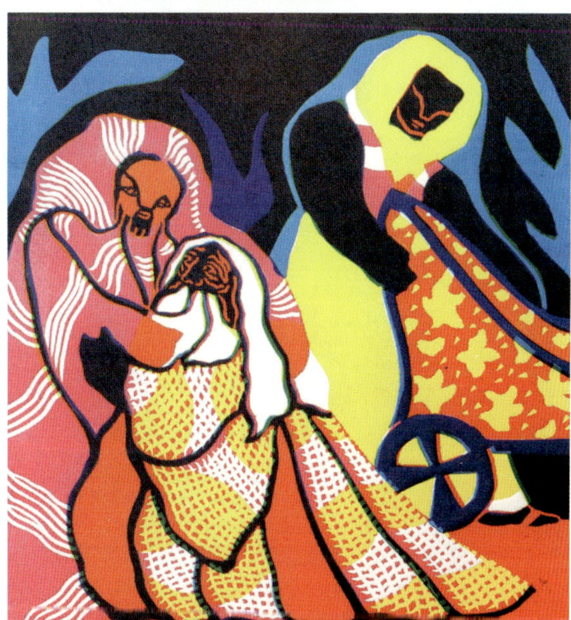
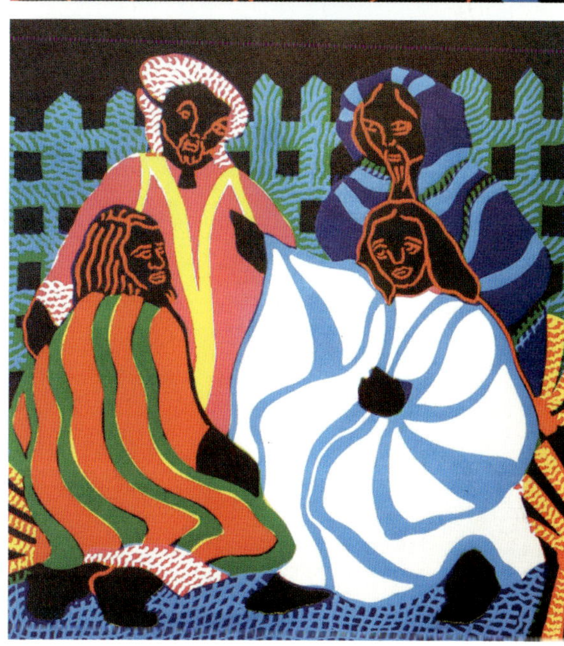

Born in Chicago in 1941, David Bennett studied literature at Harvard University. In 1973, after 10 years as a professional opera singer, he moved to Germany to begin a career in painting, but soon turned to printmaking. Bennett employs the linoleum cutting technique, a technique that enhances his highly decorative style with simplified forms expressed in bright, flat colors. The use of primary colors in his printing allows Bennett to explore ways to achieve greater depth and richness by overprinting and juxtaposing color and form.

"I'm always struck by the fact that Genesis is a fascinating story which runs the entire gamut of human emotions—love, hate, sexual feelings, jealousy, etc.—and does so with the simplicity and succinctness only to be found in the greatest works of art," said Bennett. David Bennett has had solo exhibitions in many cities in Germany and the United States. His works are held in such prestigious collections as the Lenbach Haus Municipal Art Museum, Munich, and the Jewish Museum, New York.

The Joseph Cycle, 1976
David Bennett
American, born 1941
Colored linoleum cuts, Edition Artiste
Edition of 30 with 5 artist's proofs,
17¼ x 16 in.
Loan from Laurel and Arthur M. Feldman

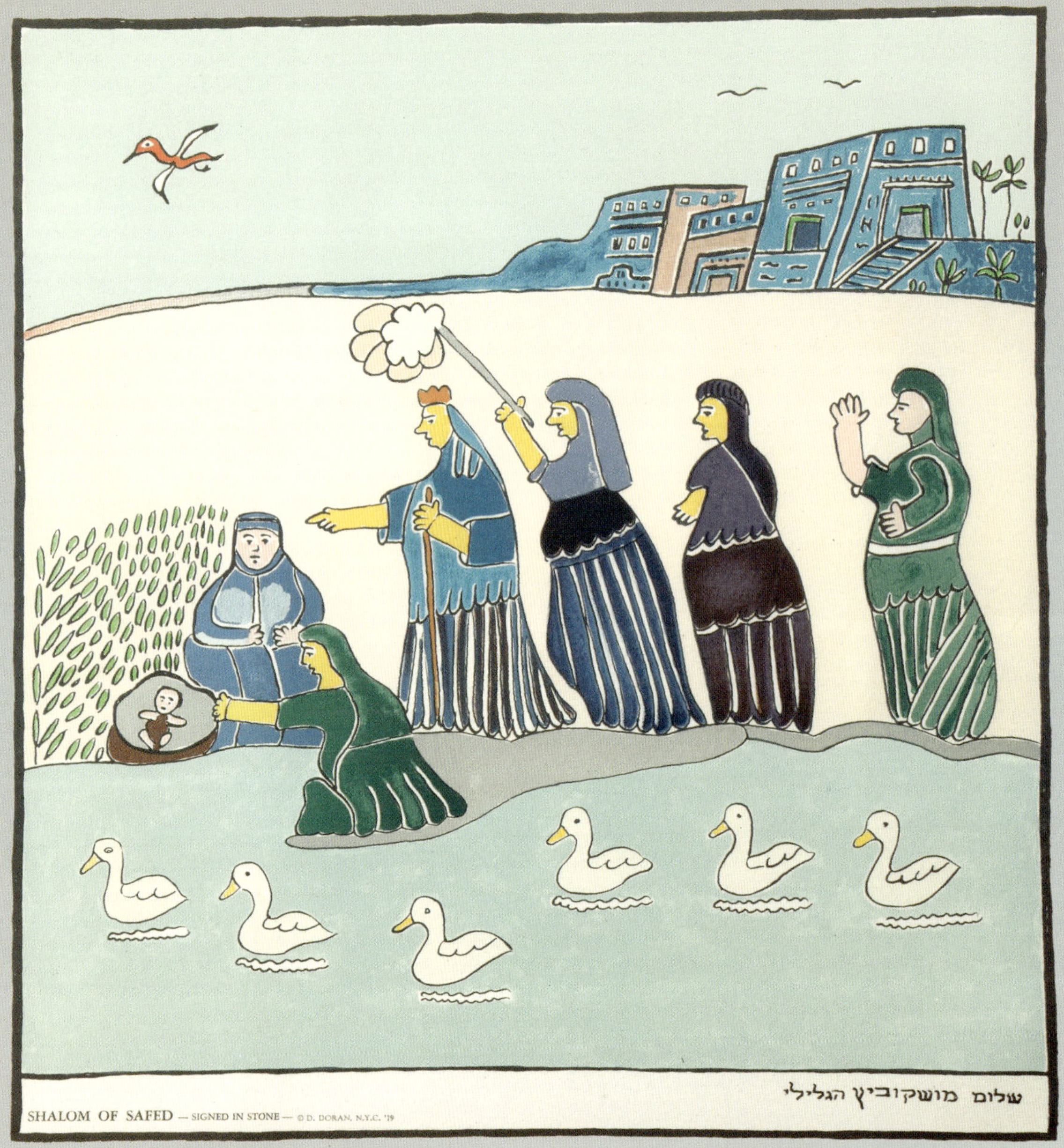

Born in the holy city of Safed in the hills of the Galilee, Shalom of Safed became the sole support of his family after the death of his parents. From his teens on he worked as a watchmaker and silversmith to support his family, then his wife and children. Shalom built colorful wooden toys for his grandchildren, and a friend who loved his work encouraged him to try painting. After much thought, Shalom painted what he knew: stories from the Bible he heard all his life in the holy city. His paintings are pictorial narratives of Bible stories. The form of narrative painting is taken from ancient murals at sites such as the synagogue of Dura-Europos; the action unfolds from right to left, the direction in which Hebrew is read. Shalom of Safed's art, unschooled in academic tradition, is a marriage of his Hassidic literary traditions and the color, light, and landscape of his native Galilee.

In this scene Pharaoh's daughter and her handmaidens find baby Moses tucked in his basket, hidden in the bulrushes. Notice that the story narrative moves from right to left like the Hebrew language, and even the ducks swim from right to left.

Moses Found in the Bulrushes
Shalom of Safed
Israeli, 1895–1980
18¾ x 14¼ in.
Loan from Laurel and Arthur M. Feldman

MOSES

Following the death of Joseph and his brothers in Egypt, the Israelite population, grew into a strong nation. A new Pharaoh, who feared the Israelites were too powerful, set plans in motion to enslave them. Pharaoh issued orders to burden them with hard labor, so they could not raise armies to turn against Egypt. Pharaoh then decreed that every male Hebrew child was to be drowned in the Nile. A daughter of the house of Levi bore a son, and, to save him, placed him in a basket made of bulrushes, and hid it among the reeds on the riverbank. When Pharaoh's daughter came to bathe in the Nile, she discovered the basket. She believed he was a Hebrew child and named him Moses and hired a nurse to care for him until he was old enough to adopt as her son. Moses was raised as a prince in the palace, but he never forgot he was an Israelite. One day as Moses watched the Israelites labor, he saw an overseer beating a slave so cruelly that he overreacted, and killed the Egyptian overseer. Fearing discovery, Moses fled to Midian, where he met Jethro, the high priest, and married one of his seven daughters, Zipporah. Moses was a shepherd in Midian. One day in the field he noticed a bush that was on fire, but not being consumed. And as watched the voice of G-d came from the burning bush, saying, "Moses, I have chosen you to lead my people from their bondage in Egypt." Moses asked how he could convince the Israelites of that, and G-d said, "Throw down your staff." As Moses did, it changed into a serpent! As he picked it up it turned back into a staff. G-d told Moses he would find Aaron, his brother, and Aaron would be spokesman for the Israelites, while Moses worked wonders with his staff.

Moses and Aaron pleaded with Pharaoh to release the Israelites, and to let them worship their own G-d in the wilderness. But Pharaoh wanted to keep the slaves, and made them work harder as punishment for wanting freedom. G-d spoke to Moses and promised that Pharaoh would be punished if he refused to let the Israelites go. Moses followed G-d's instructions as G-d brought nine plagues to punish Pharaoh, each more terrible than the last. Pharaoh still refused freedom for the Israelites. G-d's last blow, the death of all the first-born of the Egyptians, was announced. The Israelites were commanded to protect their homes by marking their doorways with the blood of a lamb. The first-born of all the Egyptians died, and Pharaoh released the Israelites to leave the country, after 430 years.

The Story of Moses is from the Bible, THE BOOK OF EXODUS.

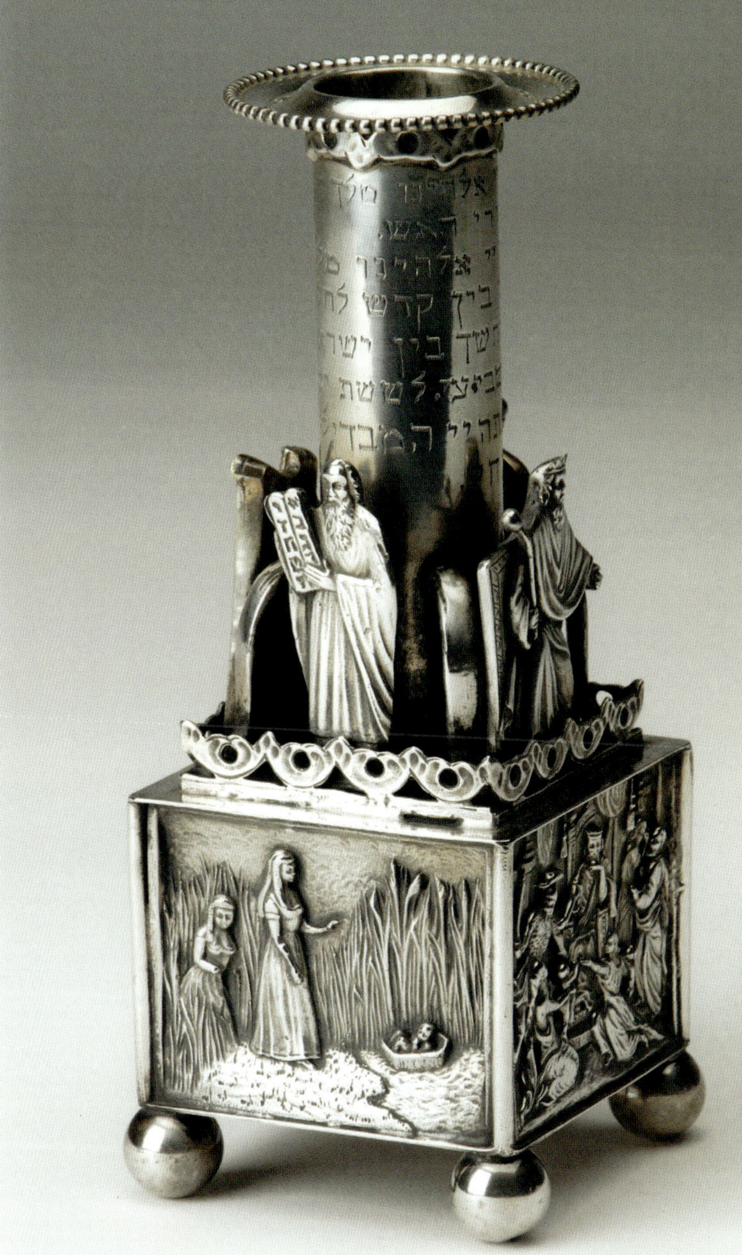

This combination spice box and candlestick serves two functions during the weekly Shabbat rituals at table, and features biblical scenes on each panel of the four-sided spice holder. On one panel is *Moses in the Bulrushes*, next is *The Decision of Solomon*, then the *High Priest Aaron*, and finally *Scenes from the Life of King David*. Above each scene the figure featured in each panel stands, holding an object that symbolizes his story: Moses with the tablets or David with the harp.

COMBINATION BESAMIM CONTAINER AND HAVDALAH CANDLE HOLDER
Germany, 19th century
Silver, 7 in. high
Presented by Mr. and Mrs. Ira E. Sanditen
in memory of Herman Sanditen 1968.1

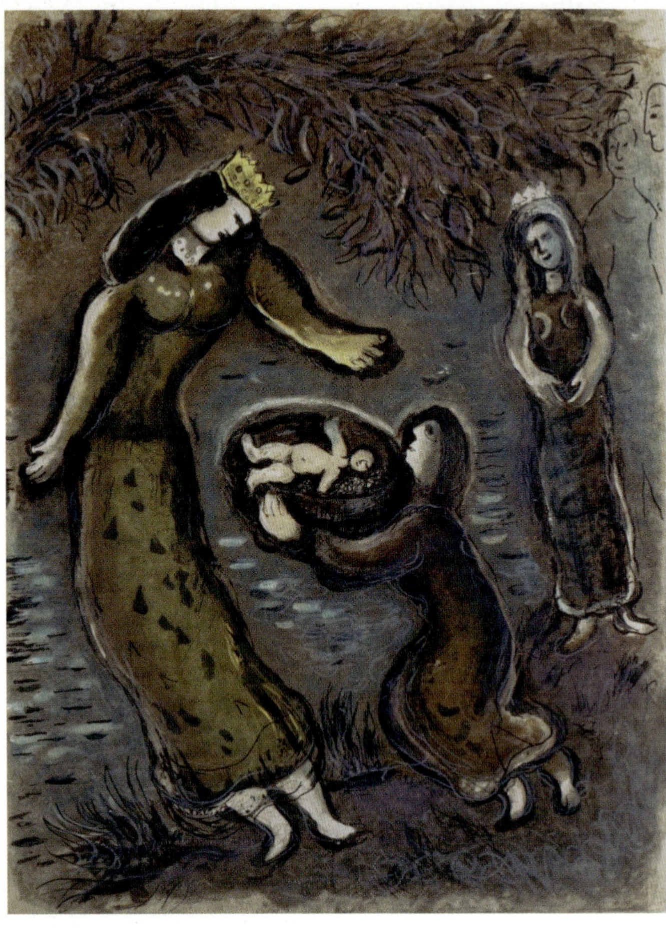

In this Chagall version of the same story, the handmaid has found Moses in the basket, picked him up, and is offering Moses to Pharaoh's daughter.

Marc Chagall, a Russian painter, printmaker, and stained-glass artist, was born in the ghetto of the village of Vitebsk, Russia, and grew up in the Jewish shtetl that would later provide imagery for many of his paintings. He persuaded his parents to let him study art, which eventually led him to St. Petersburg and Paris. Joining other expatriate artists of The School of Paris, Chagall developed his personal vision, influenced by the shtetl and modernized by Cubism. In the 1930s Chagall traveled in the Near East, visiting the Holy Land, Syria, and Jerusalem researching themes and local color.

In 1966, Leon Amiel published Chagall's portfolio of lithographs titled *The Story of the Exodus*, This edition was made up of twenty-four large color lithographs, and 285 signed portfolios were produced.

Pharaoh's Daughter and Moses, 1966
Marc Chagall
Russian, 1887 - 1985
Original color lithograph, 19 x 14 in.
Loan from Sue and Rick Arlan

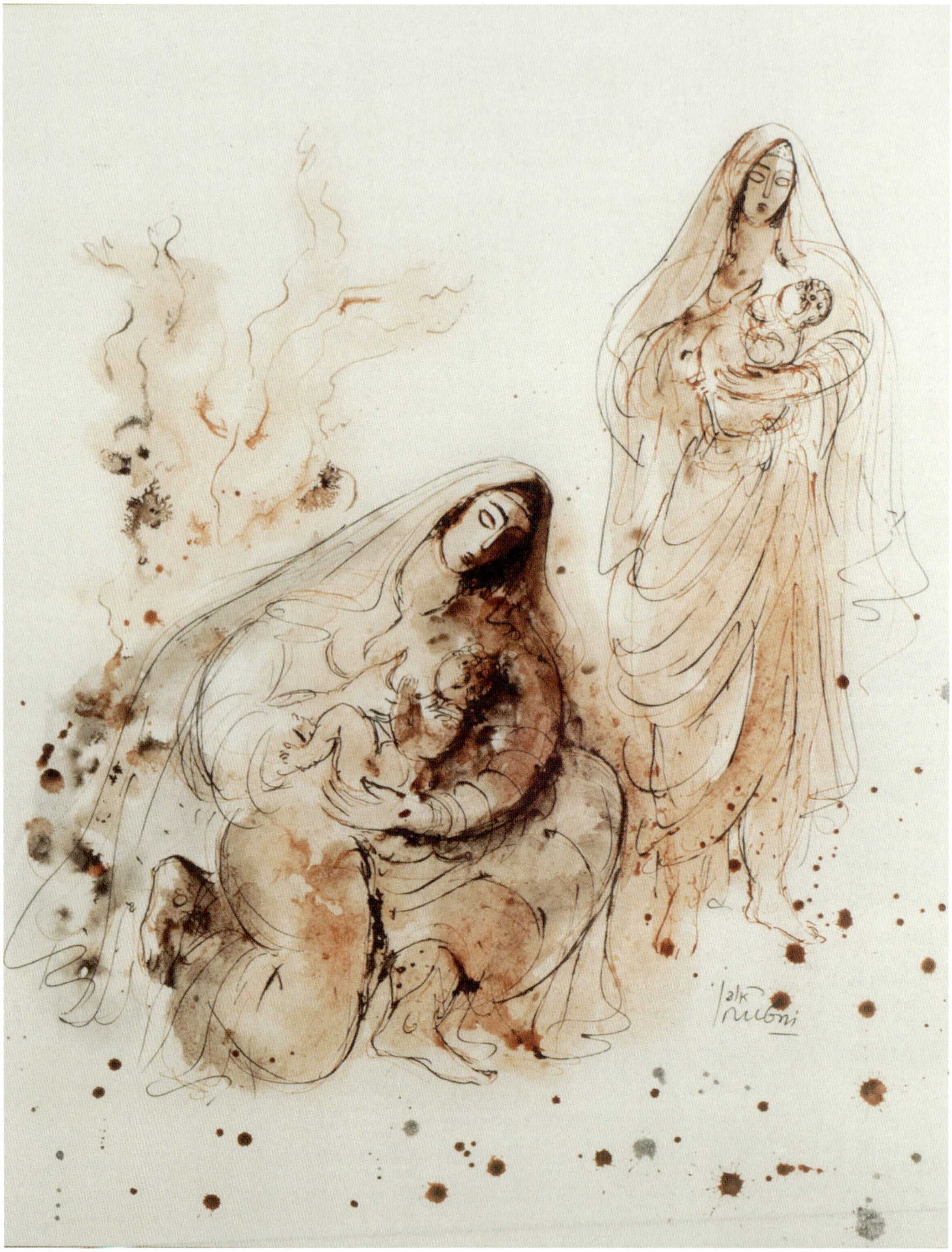

Small differences are found in every artist's rendition of a scene from the Bible. Here are two women at the river's edge holding a child, as if the sequence of the story is being illustrated. The colors of the Holy Land are seen in this lithograph, an example of Rubin's work that focused on biblical images and themes. From Abraham to Moses, Rubin illustrated the stories of the Bible in paintings and lithographs. He first exhibited his work in New York, and since then, has exhibited many times in New York, Paris, Los Angeles, London, Venice, Geneva, Tel Aviv, and Jerusalem. Recognized as one of the most significant artists in the history of Israeli art, Rubin was a significant contributor to Israeli artistic culture.

Moses and Pharaoh's Daughter, 1972
Reuven Rubin
Israeli, 1893 – 1974
Lithograph
30½ x 24½ in.
Loan from Cynthia and Yohanan Zomer

THE EXODUS

Pharaoh, with chariots and horsemen, pursued the Israelites, who reached the shores of the Red Sea, divinely guided by day by a pillar of cloud, and by night by a pillar of fire. The Israelites passed safely between the waters, which parted before them while engulfing Pharaoh and his entire army. Moses, Miriam, and his people sang a song of praise to G-d. After three months the Israelites arrived in the desert of Sinai and made camp at the mountain. G-d announced to them through Moses that He would make them His people, a kingdom of priests and a holy nation. The Israelites accepted this covenant, and after they prepared themselves, G-d, through Moses' mediation, and with thunder and lightning, clouds of smoke and noise of trumpets, revealed Himself to them on Mount Sinai and pronounced the Ten Commandments.

Moses then went again to the mountain to receive the two tablets containing the Ten Commandments and the entire Torah. Moses went up the mountain and stayed there forty days and forty nights, without food or sleep. Finally, G-d gave Moses the two stone Tables of Testimony, containing the Ten Commandments, written by G-d Himself.

Moses had promised the children of Israel that he would return after forty days. When he did not return on time, the people asked Aaron to make a golden idol to replace Moses as their intermediary to G-d. Aaron tried to delay them, but the people managed to melt their gold and form an idol in the shape of a calf. As they began to celebrate, Moses returned to camp. He was so shocked he threw the tablets to the ground and shattered them. Then he took the idol and ground it into dust. After the people repented, Moses went back to Mount Sinai and received another set of tablets. After Moses returned again from Mt. Sinai, he said G-d had ordered them to build a Tabernacle, a place of G-d's presence in the midst of Israel. G-d asked them to contribute gold, silver, copper, precious stones, wool, and linen for its construction, and everyone brought rich gifts to build G-d's sanctuary.

The Story of the Exodus is from the Bible,
EXODUS 1 - 32.

America's oldest existing art porcelain studio, Cybis is recognized as one of the world's foremost creators of fine porcelain art. Boleslaw Cybis, founder of the Cybis Studio, came from Wilno, Lithuania with his wife in 1939. Cybis, who studied at the St. Petersburg Academy of Fine Arts and the Academy of Fine Arts in Warsaw, was selected to paint murals for the Polish Pavilion at the 1939 New York World's Fair. He finished his commission, enjoyed the fair, and then he and his wife headed for home. After they sailed for Poland word came that Germany had invaded their homeland. The ship immediately returned to the United States, and the couple was stranded. They formed a small company, Cybis Art Productions, and sold their porcelain figures to stores in New York City. A larger studio was established in Trenton, New Jersey—still in business today—where, for more than 55 years the Cybis studio has produced outstanding art porcelain figurines. Examples of those figures can be found in many museums and private collections throughout the United States.

THE EXODUS
Cybis Porcelain, Closed Limited Edition, 20th century
Porcelain, 19¼ x 16 x 5¾ in.
SMMJA Collection

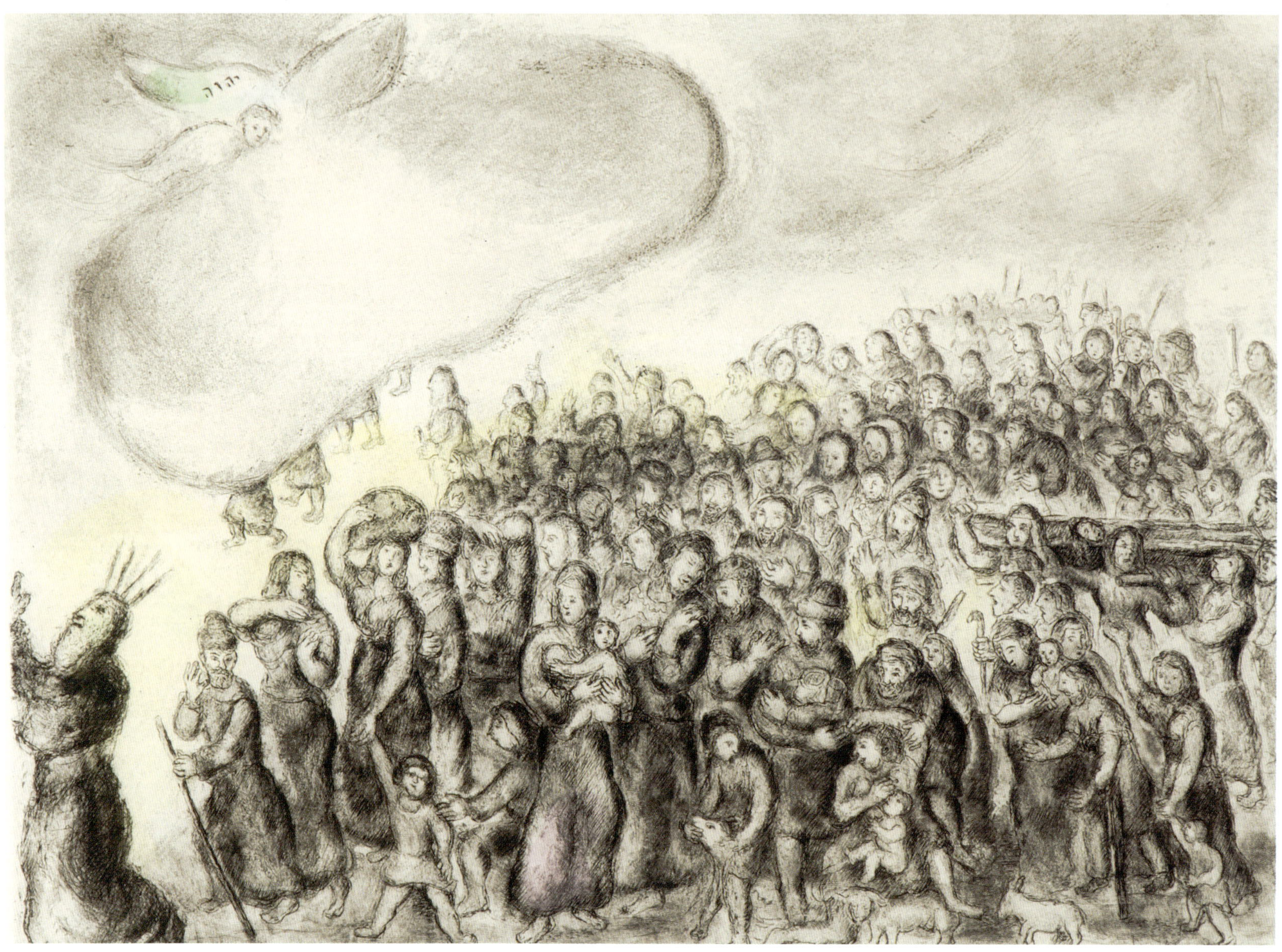

Illustrating the Bible with 105 etchings was one of the most involved printmaking projects Marc Chagall ever attempted. It is the largest number Chagall ever did on a single subject, and he meticulously reworked each plate until he was satisfied. Covering the major events of the Old Testament, Chagall begins with the Creation, continues through the cycle of Abraham and continues with Exodus, the Kings, the prophets, and favorites such as Queen Esther. Although the series begins with simple figures the compositions evolve in seriousness and complexity, concluding with the large, agitated figures of the prophets.

Marc Chagall, a Russian painter, printmaker, and stained-glass artist, was born in the ghetto of the village of Vitebsk, Russia, and grew up in the Jewish shtetl that would later provide imagery for many of his paintings. He persuaded his parents to let him study art, which eventually led him to study in St. Petersburg and Paris. Joining other expatriate artists of The School of Paris, Chagall developed his personal vision, influenced by the shtetl and modernized by Cubism. In the 1930s Chagall traveled in the Near East, visiting the Holy Land, Syria, and Jerusalem. He was researching themes and local color for his *Drawings for the Bible*, a commission from long-time supporter and art dealer Ambroise Vollard. Chagall's illustrated Bible was finally published in 1956, 17 years after Vollard's death.

In 1966, Leon Amiel published Chagall's portfolio of lithographs titled *The Story of the Exodus*, This edition was made up of twenty-four large color lithographs, and 285 signed portfolios were produced.

Exodus from Egypt, 1966
Marc Chagall
Russian, 1887–1985
Hand-colored etching from *The Story of the Exodus*, 21 x 23 in.
Loan from Sanford (Sandy) Cardin

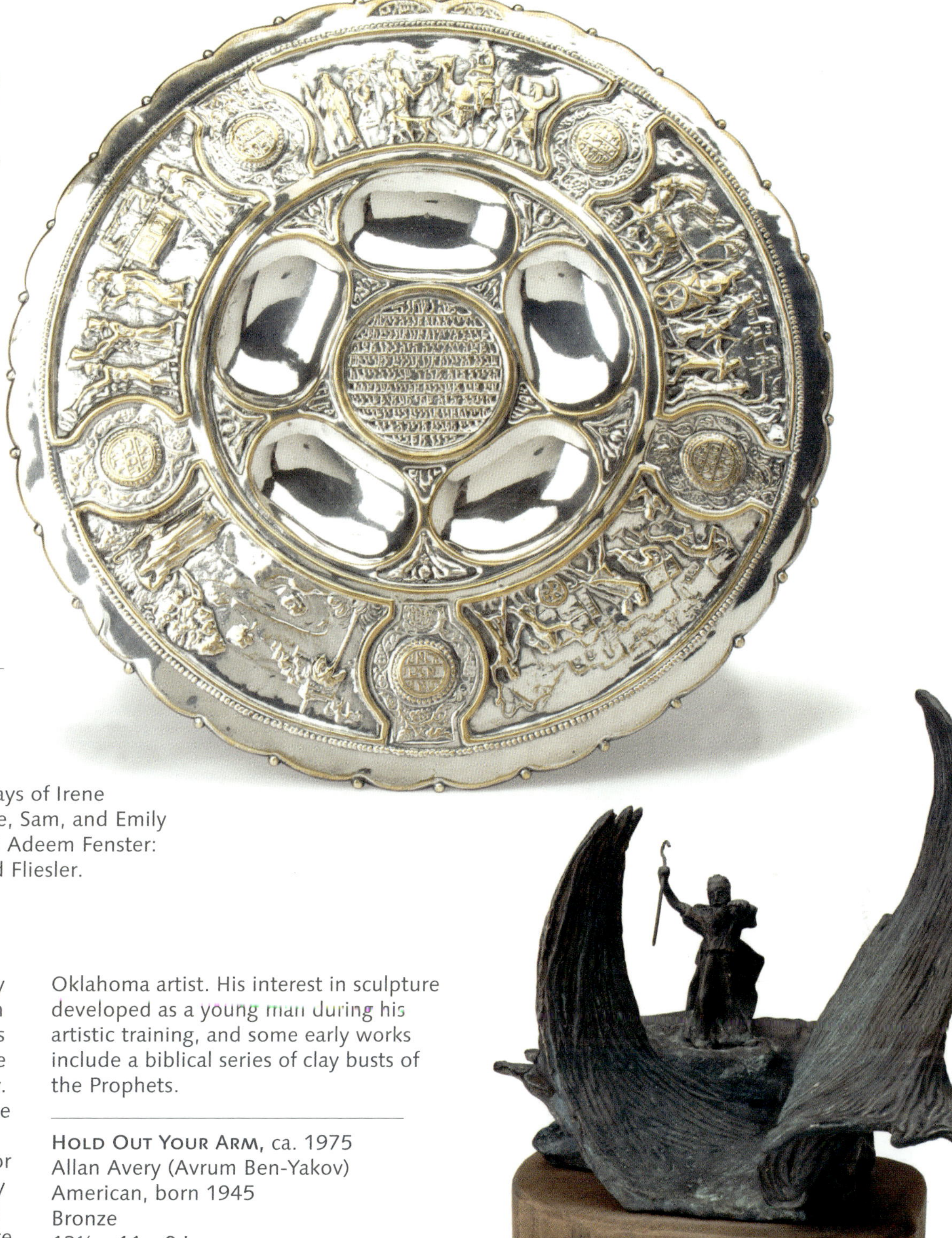

This classic Seder plate is considered a masterpiece of Jerusalem's Bezalel School of Arts and Crafts (today Bezalel Academy of Art and Design), the first modern design school for Jewish ritual objects. Its outer border is composed of five vignettes relating to the story of Passover that alternate with Hebrew inscriptions engraved on roundels. The center section features five condiment sections around a central inscription. Bezalel artists such as Ze'ev Raban worked to create a contemporary Hebrew style that reflected the belief that the artistic traditions of the local Palestinian communities were closest to the forms and styles of art of the ancient Hebrews.

Bezalel Passover Plate
Palestine, ca. 1920
Silver-plated brass
13 in. diameter
Dedicated to honor the 80th birthdays of Irene and Irving Fenster by George, Marcie, Sam, and Emily Fenster: David, Sheela, Amman, and Adeem Fenster: Paula and Sam Brust, Ellen and Jared Fliesler.
SMMJA Collection

This small original bronze sculpture, by Tulsa Jewish community member Allan Avery, depicts Moses raising his arm as G-d split the Red Sea down the middle for the Israelites to pass through safely. This sculpture is one of a series of three biblical sculptures, all included in the *Sons of Adam* exhibition. Avery, Curator of the Arkansas River Historical Society and The Tulsa Port of Catoosa, studied art growing up in Tulsa. He took private art instruction with Maggie Gough, studied at the Philbrook Museum School of Art, and studied with Inez Henson, an Oklahoma artist. His interest in sculpture developed as a young man during his artistic training, and some early works include a biblical series of clay busts of the Prophets.

Hold Out Your Arm, ca. 1975
Allan Avery (Avrum Ben-Yakov)
American, born 1945
Bronze
12½ x 11 x 9 in.
Gift of the artist
03.2

Illustrating the Bible with 105 etchings was one of the most involved printmaking projects Marc Chagall ever attempted. It is the largest number Chagall ever did on a single subject, and he meticulously reworked each plate until he was satisfied. Covering the major events of the Old Testament, Chagall begins with the Creation, continues through the cycle of Abraham, Exodus, the Kings, the Prophets, and favorites such as Queen Esther. Although the series begins with simple figures the compositions evolve in seriousness and complexity, concluding with the large, agitated figures of the prophets. In this plate, *Crossing of the Red Sea*, Moses raises his arm at the signal from the angel, G-d's messenger, and the Israelite nation crosses between the walls of water. At one end Pharaoh's army in chariots is beginning to overtake the Israelites and any moment will be crushed by the returning waters. In 1966, Leon Amiel published Chagall's portfolio of lithographs titled *The Story of the Exodus*, This edition was made up of twenty-four large color lithographs, and 285 signed portfolios were produced.

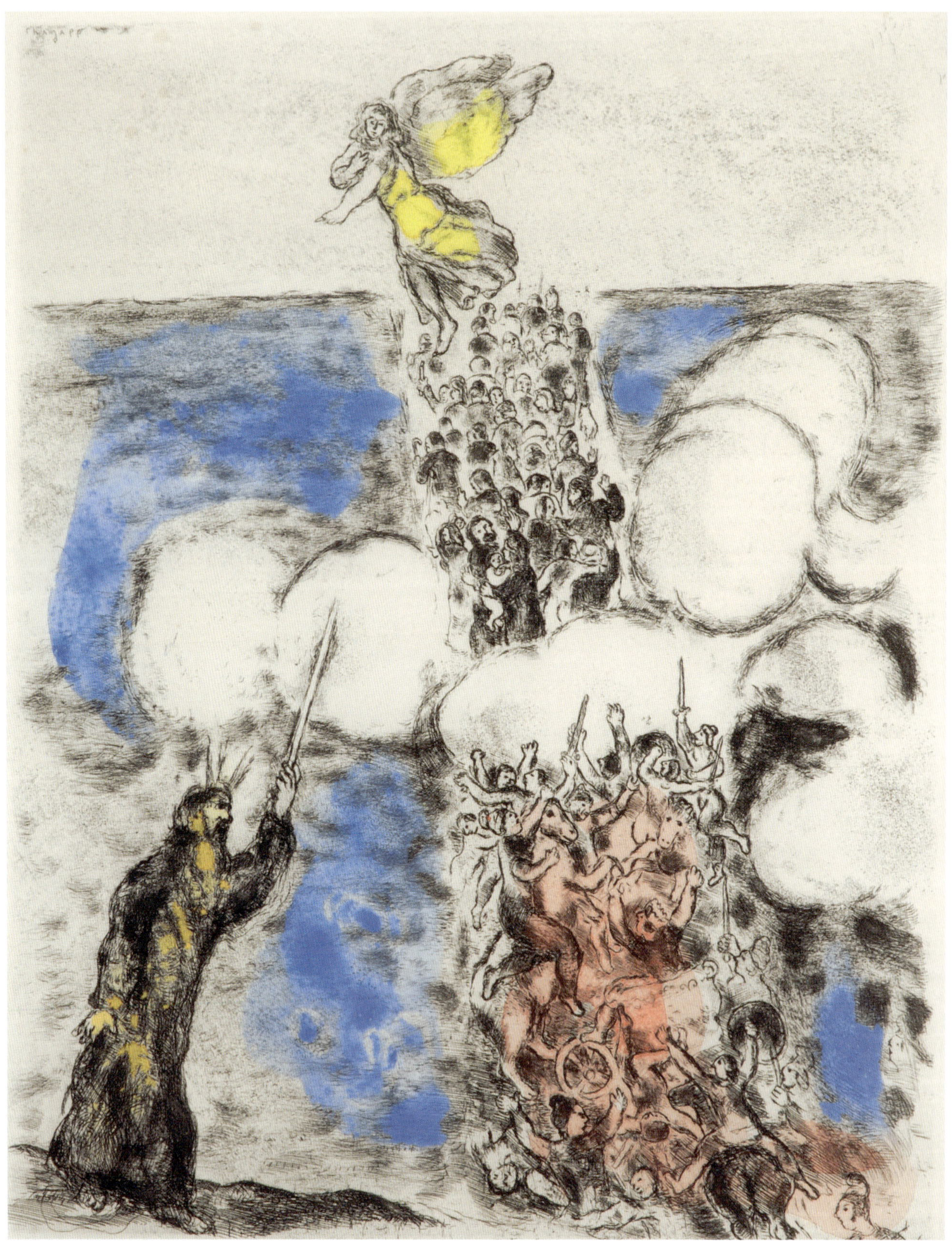

Crossing of the Red Sea, *1966*
Marc Chagall
Russian, 1887 – 1985
Hand-colored etching from *The Story of the Exodus*
12 x 9 in.
Loan from Sanford (Sandy) Cardin

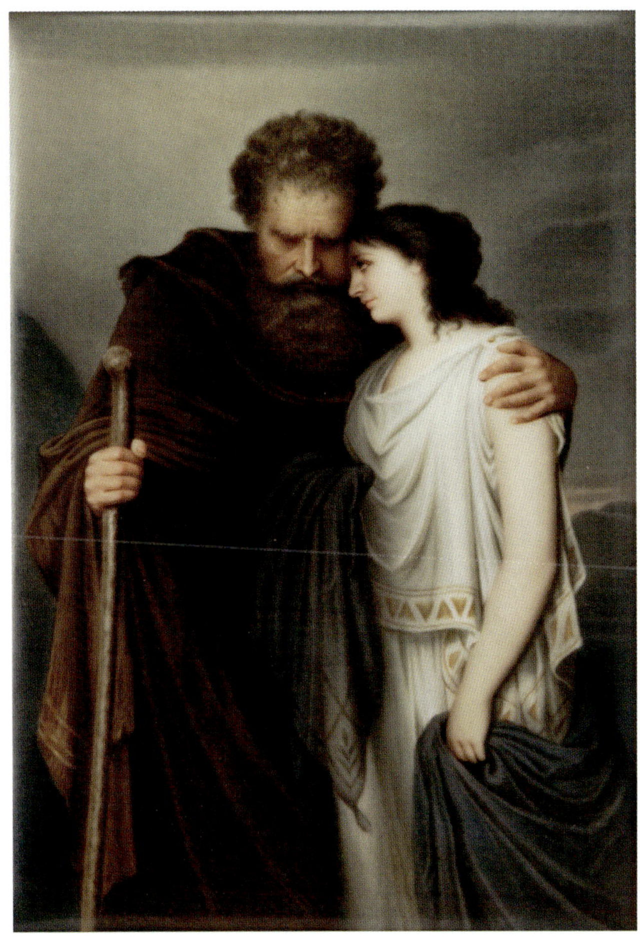

Paintings on porcelain plaques were first produced in Europe during the 19th century, and were often copies of popular paintings. KPM, Berlin's royal factory, produced plaques of the highest quality, which are marked with the KPM insignia. The initials KPM stand for, in German, *Konigliche Porzellan Manufaktur*, and in English, King's Porcelain Manufactory. The king mentioned in the company name is Frederick the Great (Frederick II, King of Prussia), who is said to have run this factory personally to produce work that satisfied his own tastes. Over the years, KPM (or Berlin) made high-quality paintings on porcelain featuring subjects that ranged from portraits to Old Testament figures to reproductions of popular paintings.

Untitled (Moses and Miriam)
KPM Porcelain plaque, ca. 1860-1880
Berlin, Germany
Loan from Joe Degen

Miriam's Song of Thanksgiving is the fifth plate in the series *The Promised Land* by the artist Yiannis Koutsis. The plates are produced on Royal Cornwall China, the finest white porcelain, by the Calhoun Collectors Society Inc. Each plate is 8½ inches in diameter with a 24 carat gold rim, individually numbered in a presentation box, and authenticated with a commentary booklet by Jonathan Paradise, Ph.D. This plate shows "Miriam the prophetess ... took the tambourine in her hand; and all the women followed her with tambourines and dances." Exodus 15:20–21

Miriam's Song of Thanksgiving, 1980
Yiannis (Giannis) Koutsis
Greek
Plate five of *The Promised Land* Series by Royal Cornwall China
8½ in. diameter
Loan from Carolyn and Ron Kriegsman

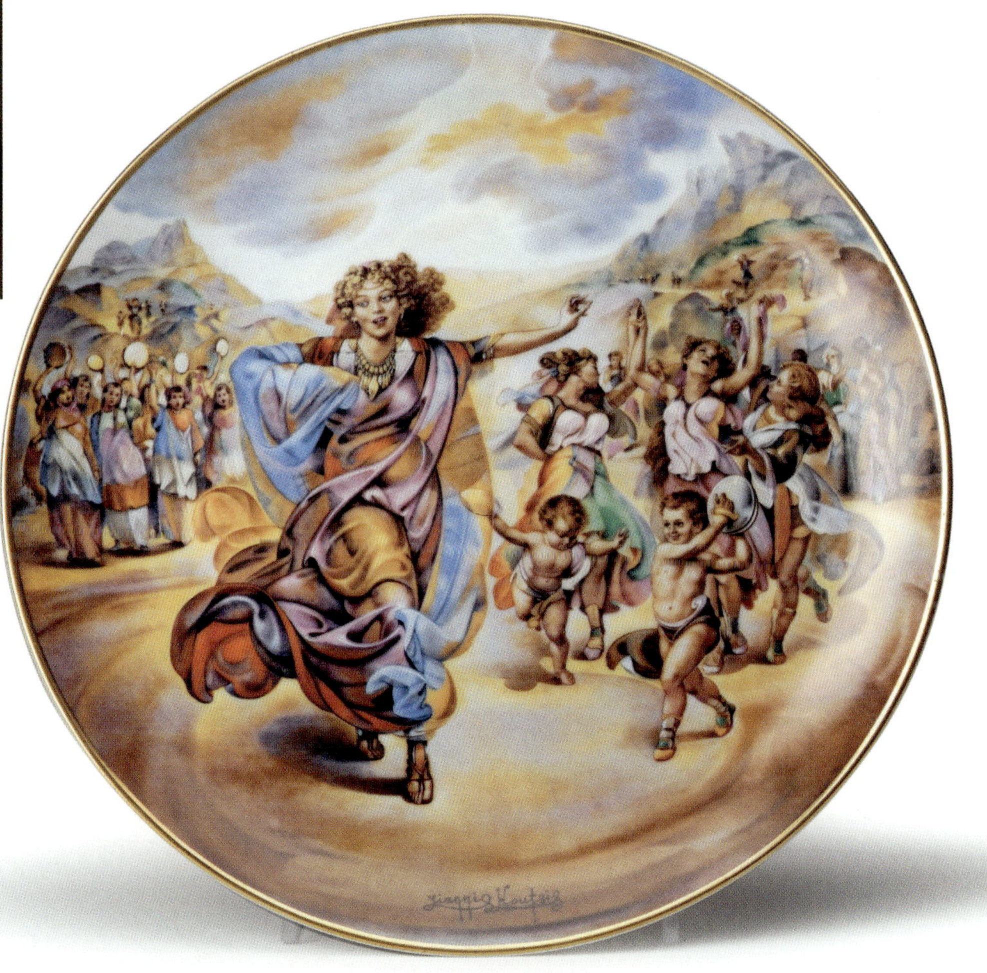

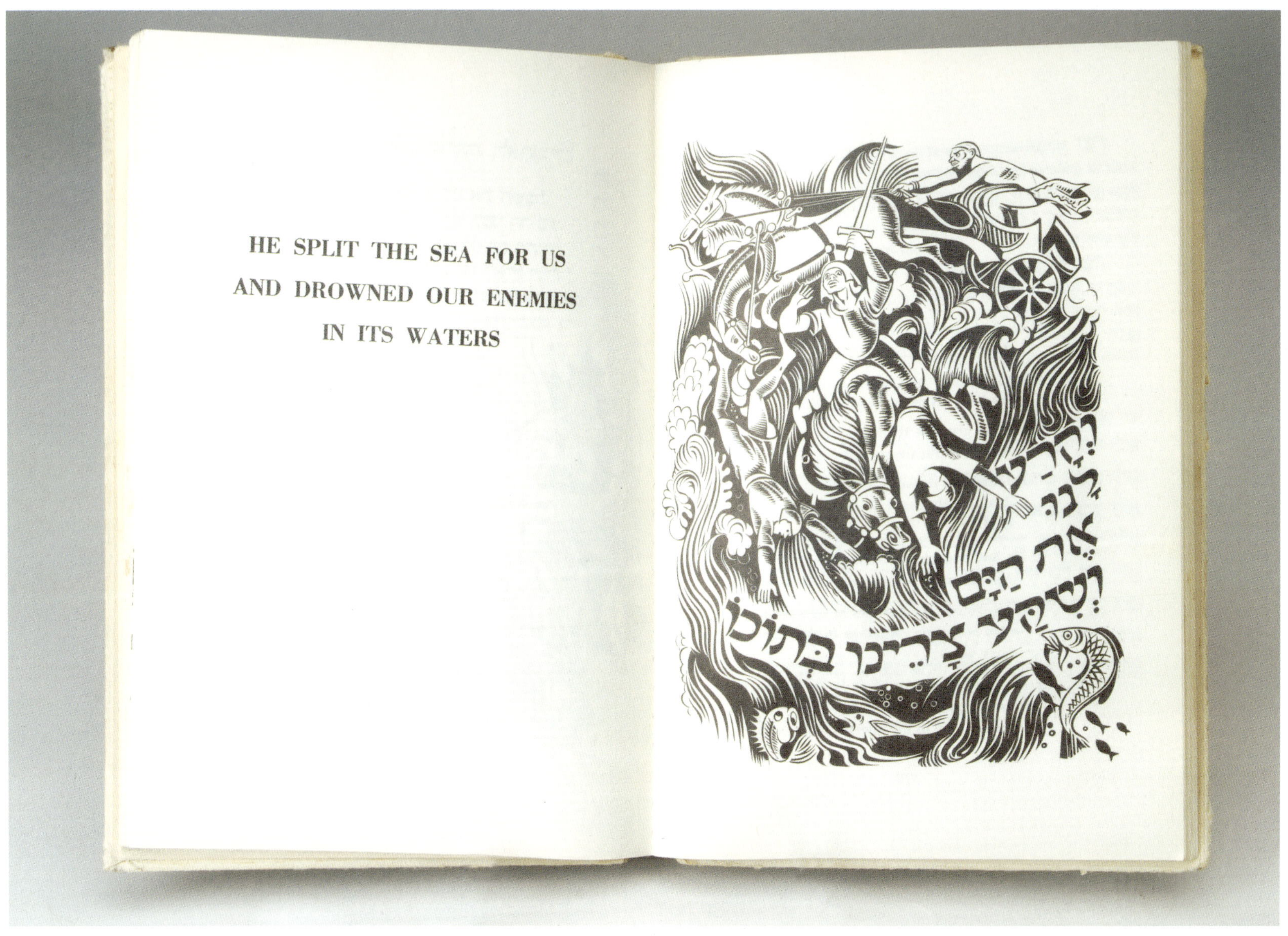

Illustrated for children, this active representation of the parting of the Red Sea shows the sea crushing and tumbling Pharaoh's soldiers in the rushing waters. Siegmund Forst, originally from Vienna, created graphics and illustrations for Hebrew textbooks and Haggadot that revolutionized the look of American Jewish publications. His vision of modernity brought the classic text of Jewish ritual into the 20th century and had a major impact on Jewish popular culture and the way in which Biblical heroes, Zionist pioneers, and Americans celebrating Jewish holidays were portrayed.

The Children's Passover Haggadah
Translated by Ben-Ami Scharfstein
Illustrated by Siegmund Forst
Shilo Publishing House, USA, 1945
6 x 9¼ in.
99.19.8mmmm

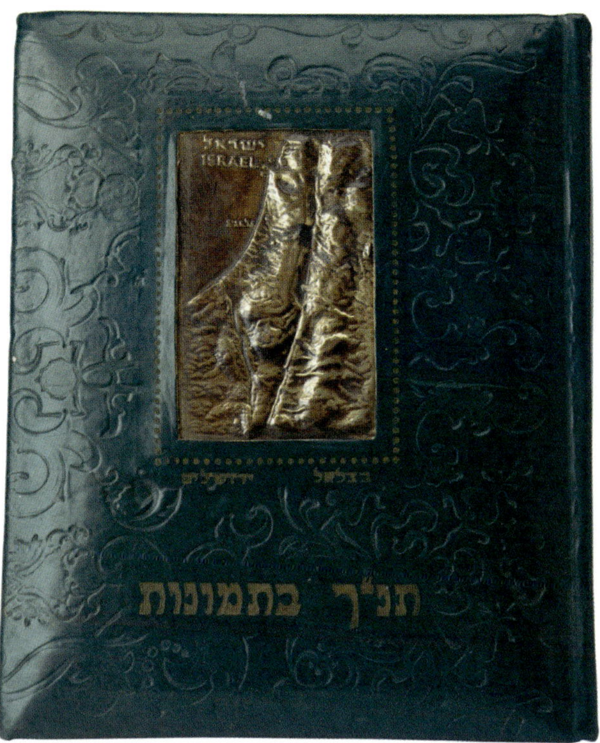

This 20th century printing of Gustav Doré Bible illustrations is bound in a Bezalel tooled leather cover with an embossed copper rectangular insert (2 x 3 inches) showing a map of Israel on the front cover. The book contains full-page Doré engravings of the Five Books of Moses. Doré, a successful artist in the mid-nineteenth century, illustrated the works of Poe, Milton, Balzac, Byron, and Dante. He produced hundreds of illustrations for the Bible during his lifetime, and they continue to be published in Bibles today.

Illustrations to the Bible
Paul Gustav Doré
French, 1832–1883
Hefetz, Printed in Jerusalem
Loan from Eva Unterman

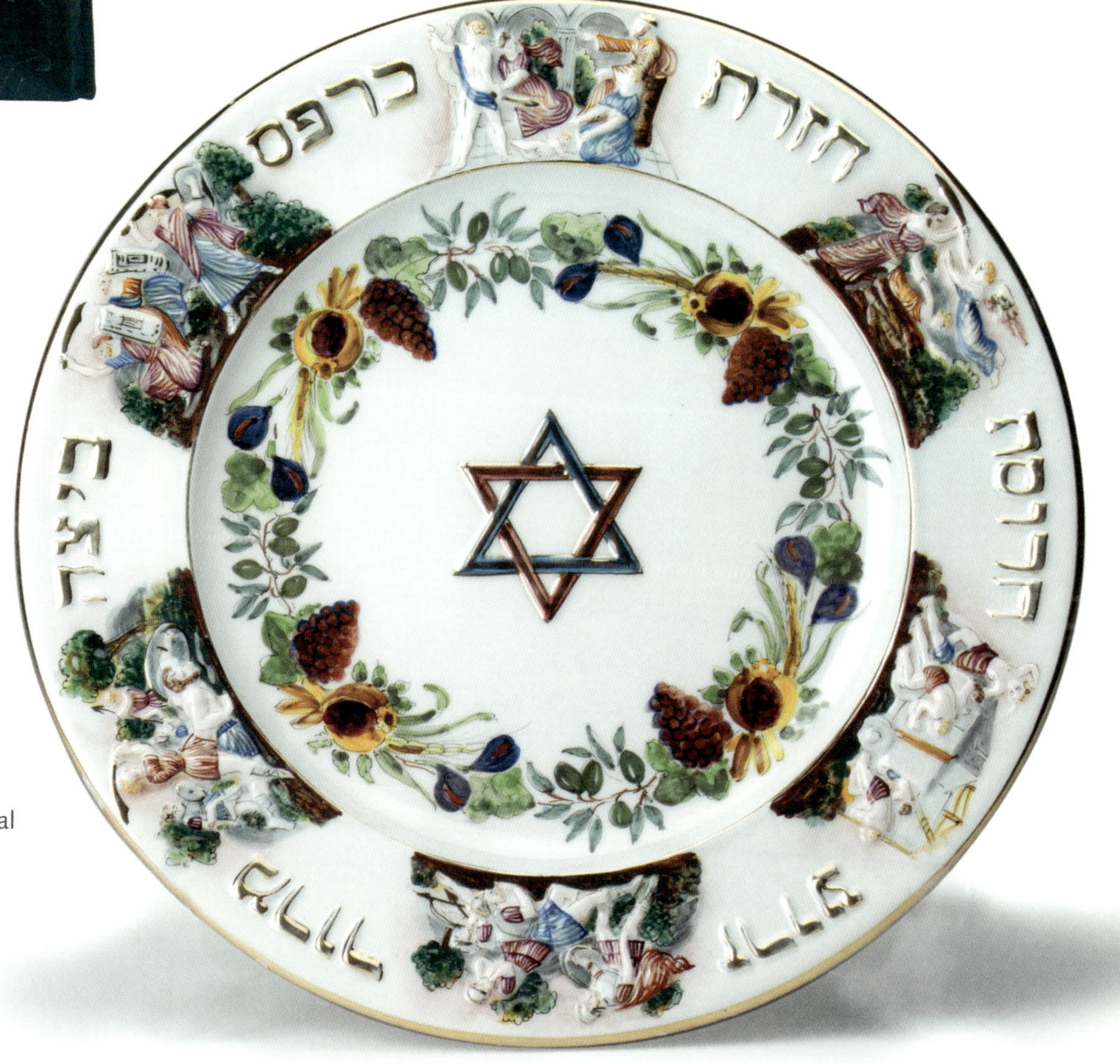

This large Capodimonte porcelain Seder plate, made in Italy, is decorated around the rim with scenes relating to Passover and Hebrew inscriptions. A central Star of David is surrounded by a hand painted floral wreath design.

Seder Plate
Italy, 20th century
Porcelain
14 in. diameter
Loan from Temple Israel

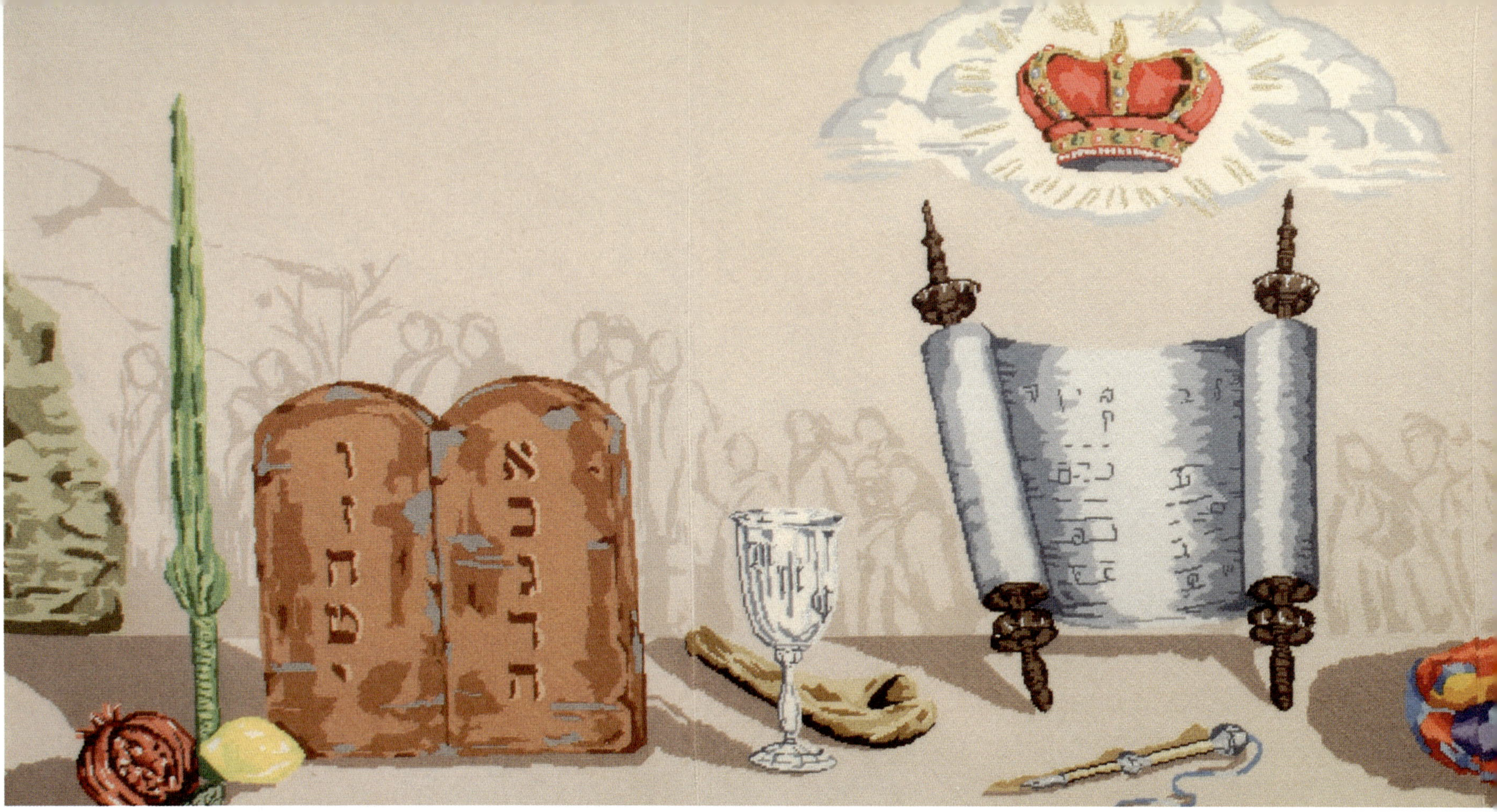

This panel of joined needlework was created by Dr. and Mrs. Cash, and designed by Su Hall of Tulsa, Oklahoma. Mrs. Cash confided that this was the first piece of needlework the couple had attempted, and they had no idea that it was such a monumental project. Worked in wool, the panel tells the story of Exodus by illustrating Moses, the Tablets of the Law, the Torah and Pointer, the components of the Passover Seder, and the shadowy line of Israelites making their way to the Promised Land.

THE EXODUS
Needlepoint panel
Wool
87¾ x 36½ in.
Loan from Goldie Cash

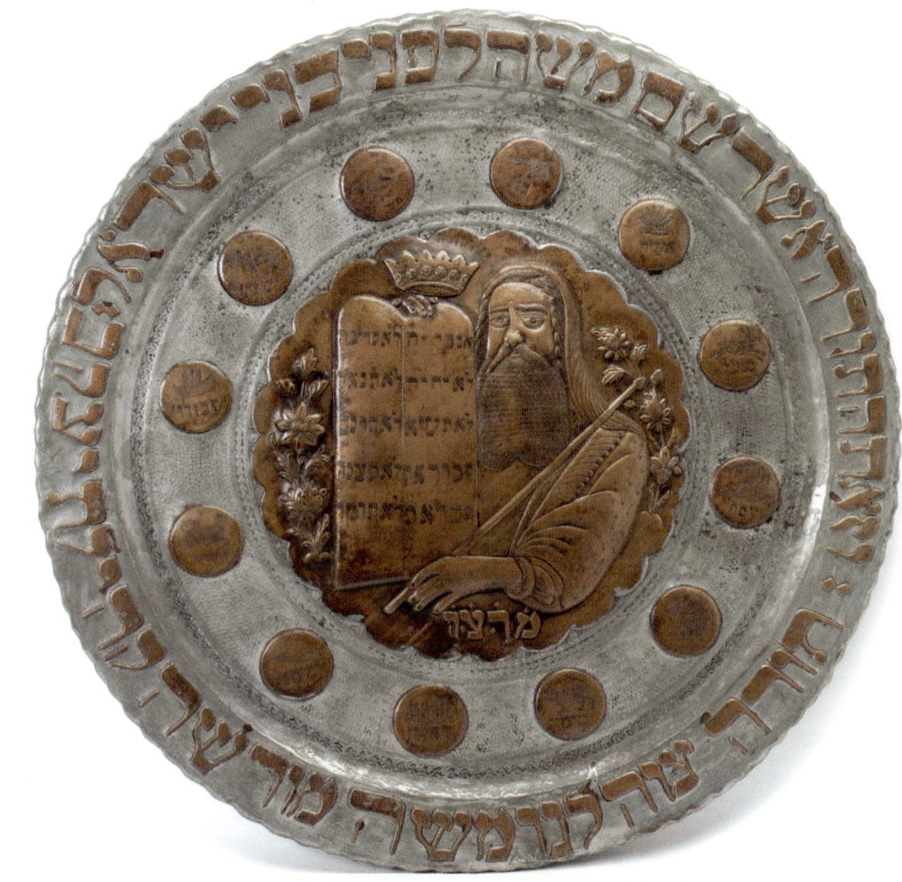

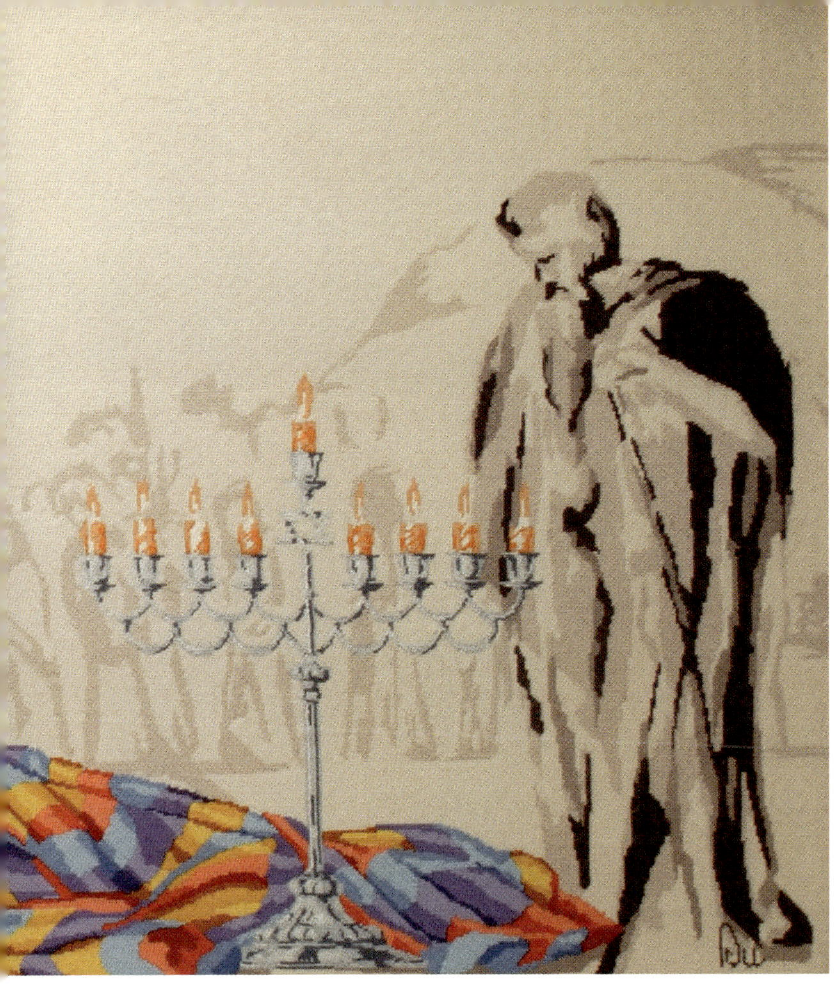

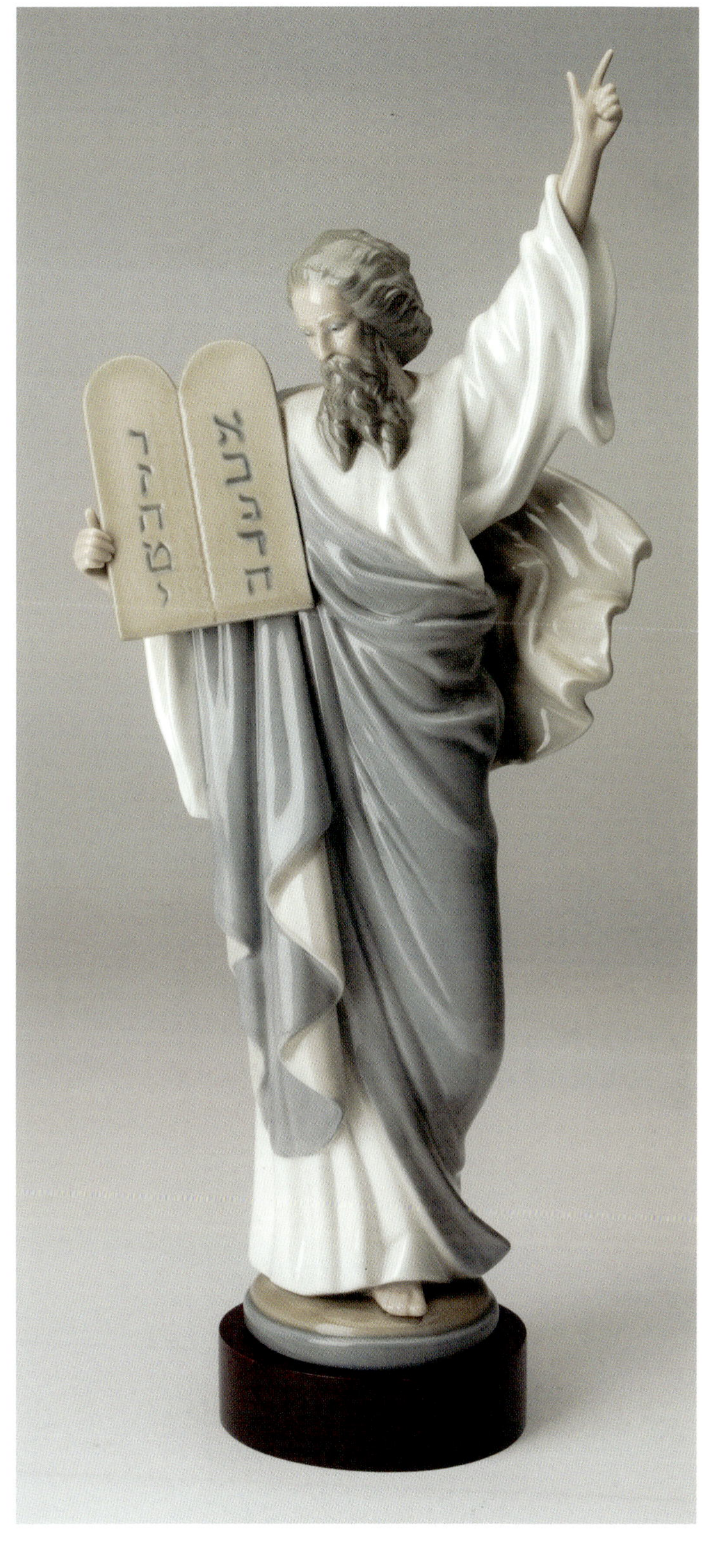

LEFT: Elaborate engraving of Moses with representations of the Ten Commandments, and the Twelve Tribes of Israel. Hebrew phrases surround the outer border, which translate as "This is the Torah that Moses brought before the children of Israel." Oftentimes Persian Jewish families are seen serving fruit on a tray such as this, other times it is used as a wall hanging.

Moses and the Tablets of the Law
Persian tray, 20th century
Tinned copper
23 in. diameter
Loan from Congregation B'nai Emunah

This porcelain Moses, sculpted by Francisco Catalá, was created in 1982 and retired in 2001. Lladró was founded in 1953 when Juan, José, and Vicente, three artistic brothers, formed a small family company in Almácera, Spain. They began sculpting figures in clay, drawing on their personal experiences. The small workshop became a large company, and the three founding brothers are still present in the day-to-day activities of the company, supporting the creation of new and innovative design.

Moses, 1982
Lladró figure
Porcelain, 17¾ x 7½ x 4½
Loan from Shirley and Robert Dormont

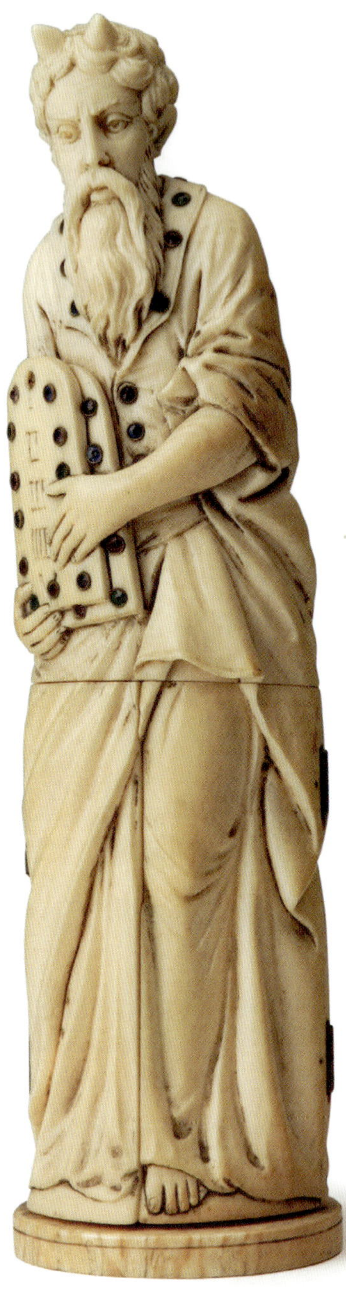

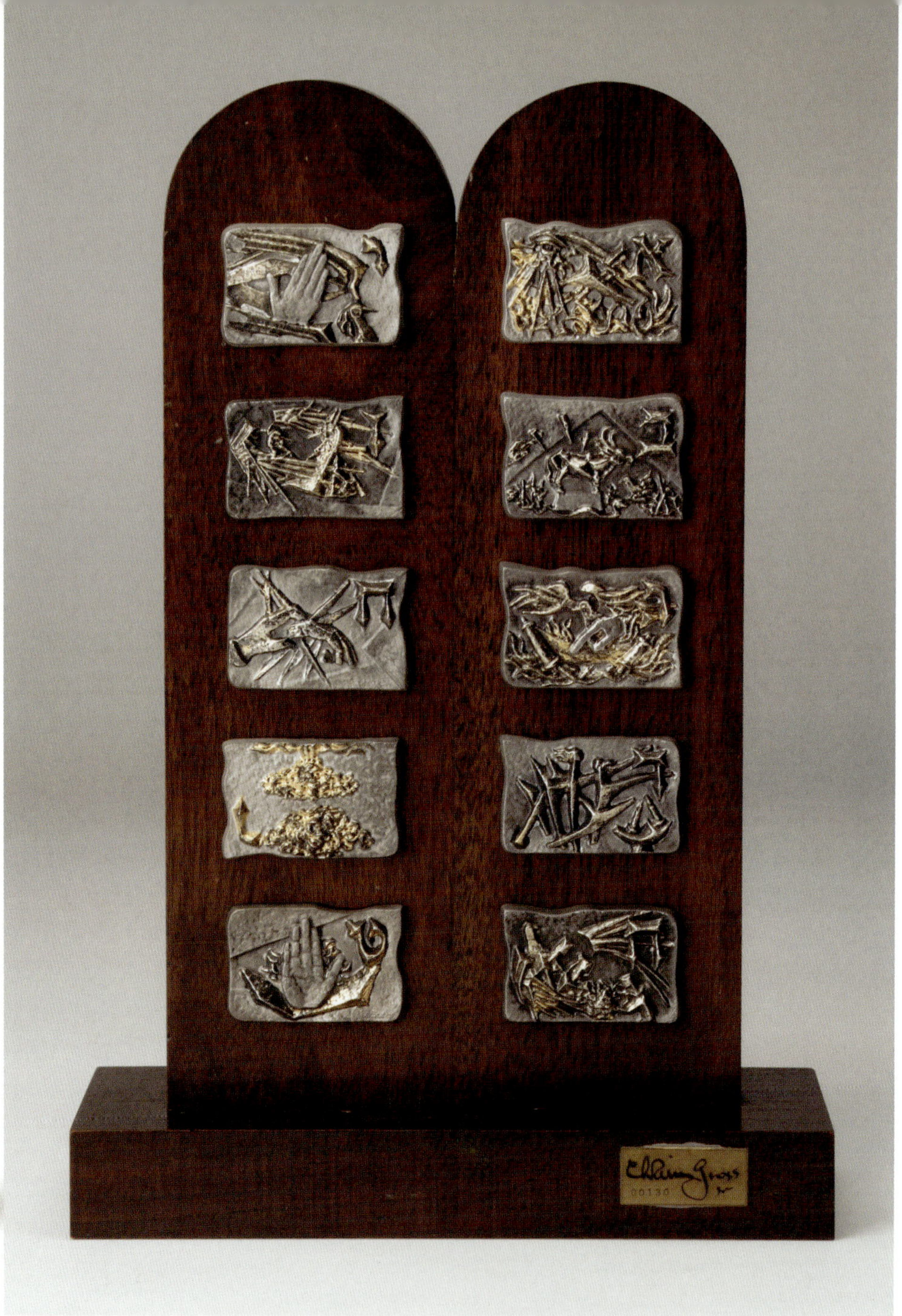

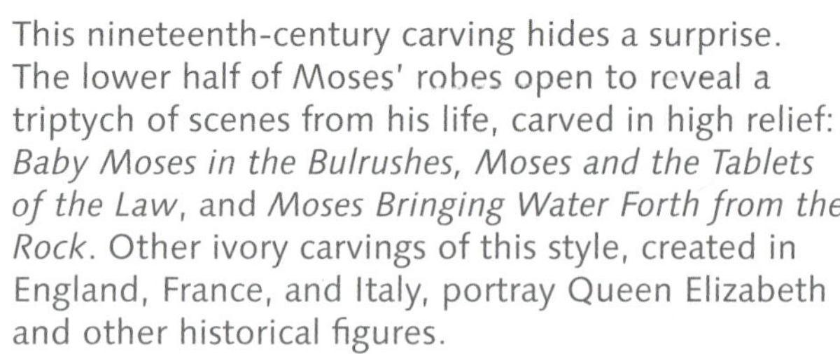

This nineteenth-century carving hides a surprise. The lower half of Moses' robes open to reveal a triptych of scenes from his life, carved in high relief: *Baby Moses in the Bulrushes*, *Moses and the Tablets of the Law*, and *Moses Bringing Water Forth from the Rock*. Other ivory carvings of this style, created in England, France, and Italy, portray Queen Elizabeth and other historical figures.

Moses Triptych
Italy, 19th century
Ivory, garnet
8¼ x 2½ in.
Gift of Mr. and Mrs. Herman Kaiser, 1965.47

This miniature replica of the Chaim Gross sculpture, *The Ten Commandments* was created as a limited edition series. The original sculpture, commissioned by the New York Board of Rabbis, is installed in the International Synagogue at New York's JFK Airport.

Chaim Gross, an Austrian born American sculptor, immigrated to the United States in 1921. He studied in Vienna and New York, and created sculpture primarily by carving directly in wood. His works are included in major museums and private collections throughout the United States.

The Ten Commandments
Chaim Gross
American, 1904–1991
Silver, rhodium, gold, wood
7½ x 12 x 3 in.
Limited edition, numbered 130
Gift of Alan Livingston, on behalf of his mother, Mrs. Gertrude Livingston
2004.13.2

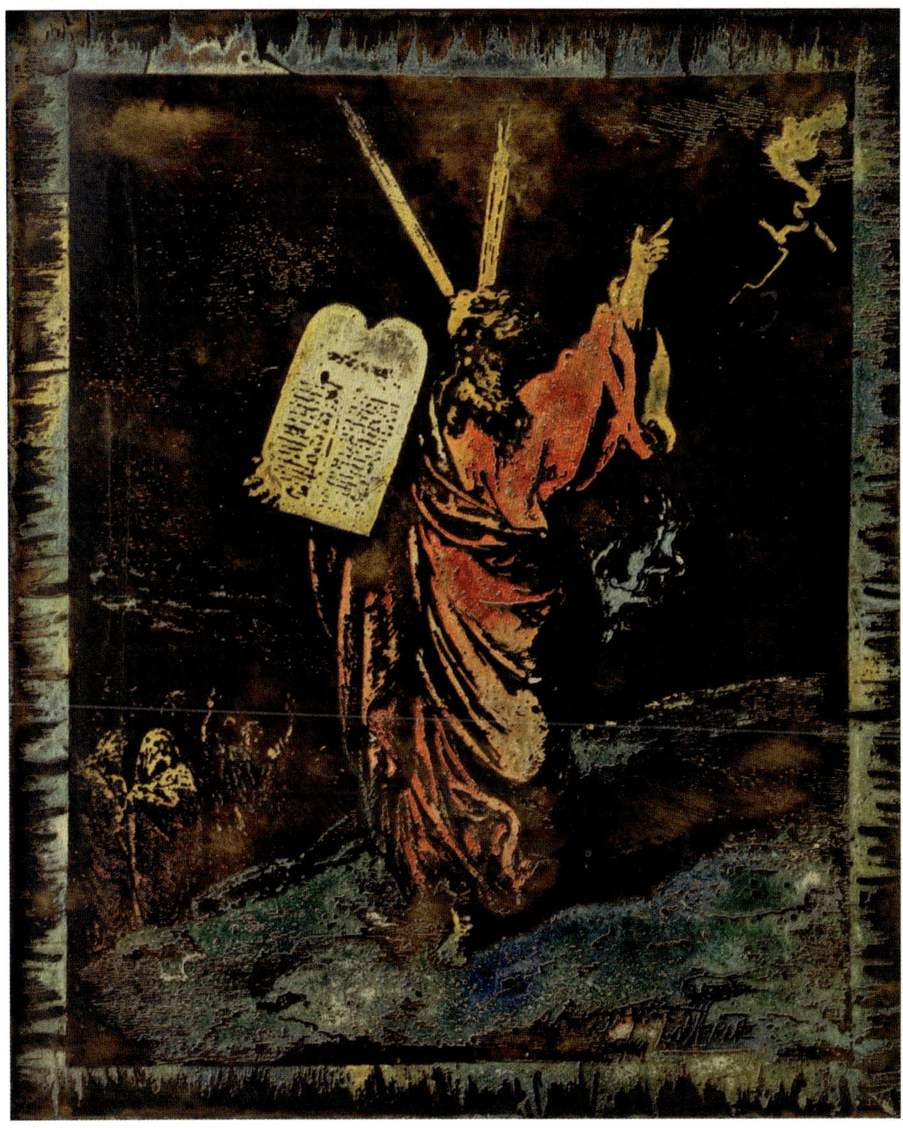

This bronze acid-etched panel with a portrait of Moses was signed by Philip and Kelvin Laverne. The LaVernes are American modernist furniture designers and artists whose preferred medium is acid-etched bronze. Formed into plaques, coffee tables, or occasional tables, the works are etched and patinated with a series of colors to enhance the subject matter.

Moses
Philip and Kelvin LaVerne
American, 20th century
Bronze panel
12 x 15 in.
Loan from Isabel Sanditen

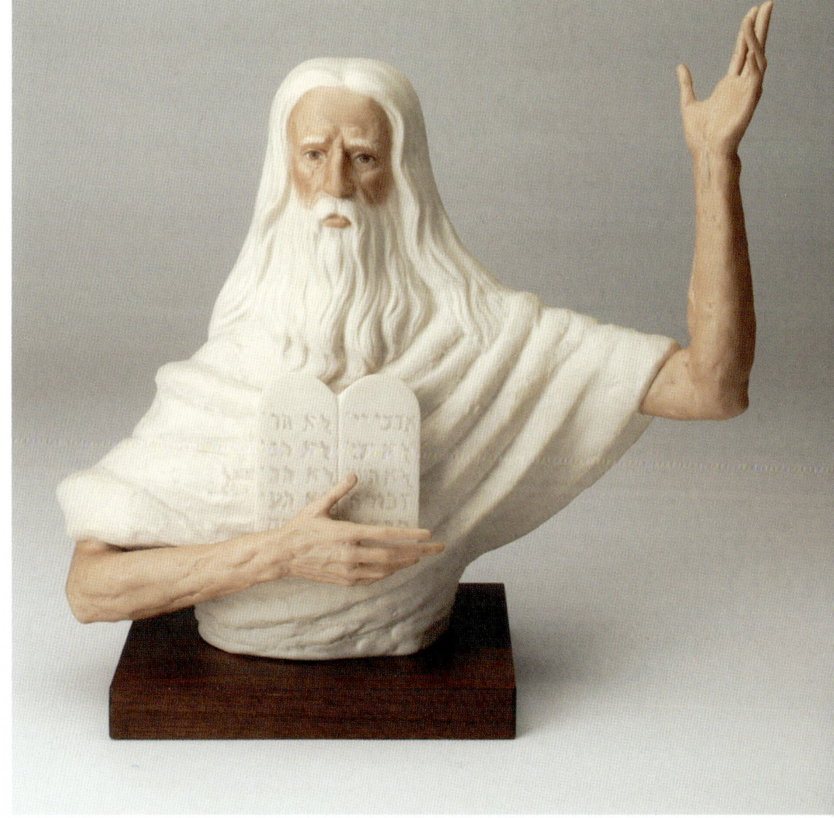

Born in Budapest in 1919, Laszlo Ispanky found his artistic talents as a boy. He studied at Hungarian Fine Art Academy, but found life as an artist difficult under Communist rule, and made his way to America in 1956. Ispanky began his American career as a designer for Cybis Porcelains. In 1966, he established his own studio in Pennington, New Jersey and since 1976, has worked for Goebel of North America. He works in stone, wood, or metal, as well as porcelain. Mr. Ispanky's work also can be seen at the Smithsonian Institution in Washington, D.C., The Cincinnati Children's Zoo, The Basketball Hall of Fame in Springfield, Massachusetts, as well as a piece on exhibit at the New Jersey State Museum in Trenton.

Moses, ca. 1980
Laszlo Ispanky
Hungarian, born 1919
Porcelain, 19 x 12 x 6¾ in
Loan from Isabel Sanditen.

Seymour Rosenthal, born in the Bronx in 1921, began drawing at the age of five and is still drawing today. As a young man he worked delivering clothing, and then became a lithographer in Manhattan, joining the Local One-L Amalgamated Lithographers of America. Rosenthal loved working as a lithographer, but his dream was fulfilled when he became a full-time artist. The Museum of Modern Art has many Rosenthal lithographs in the permanent collection, as does the Indianapolis Museum of Art and other important museums, temples and universities throughout the country.

Moses and the Broken Tablets
Seymour J. Rosenthal
American, born 1921
Etching, pencil-signed by the artist
14 x 11 in.
SMMJA Collection

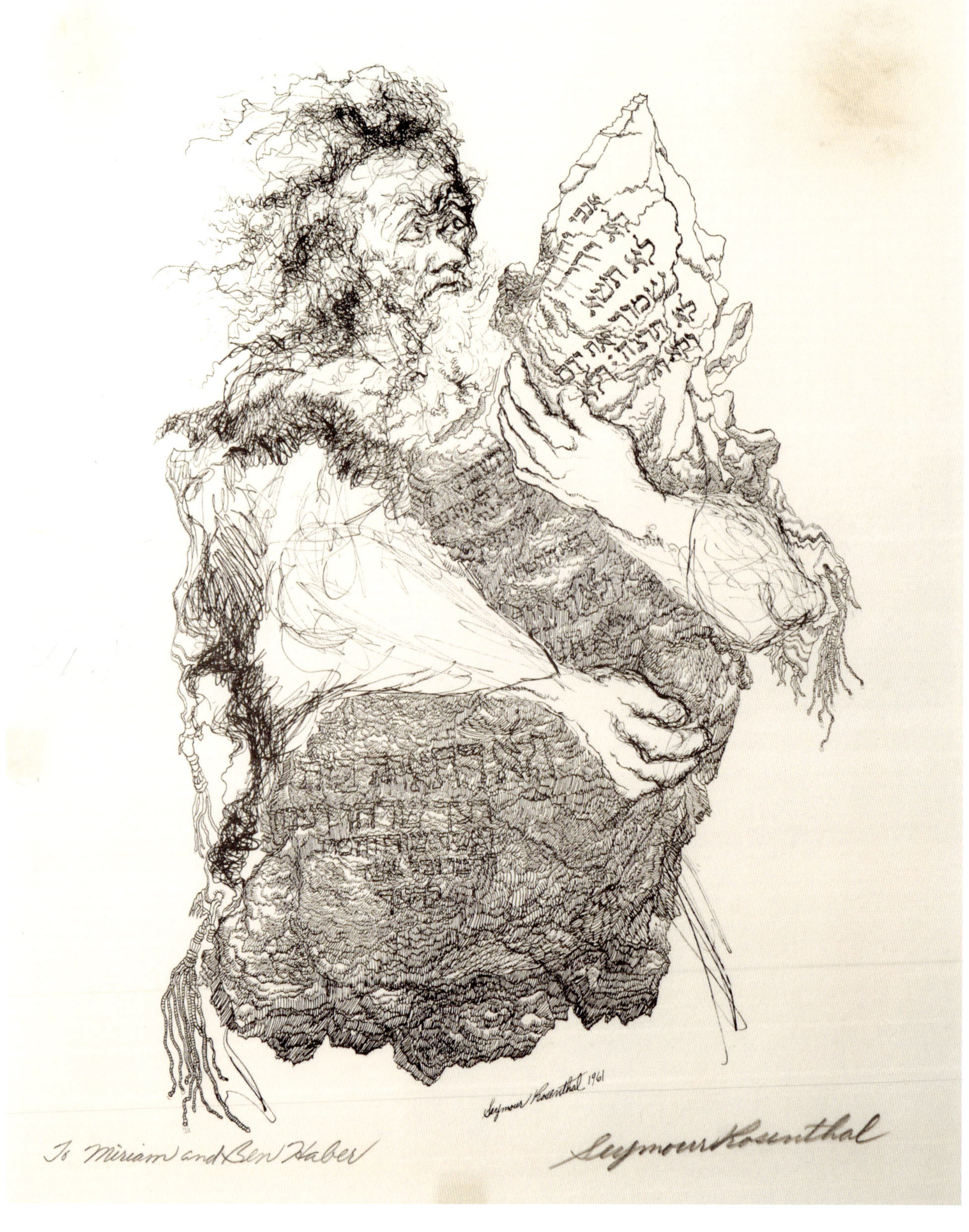

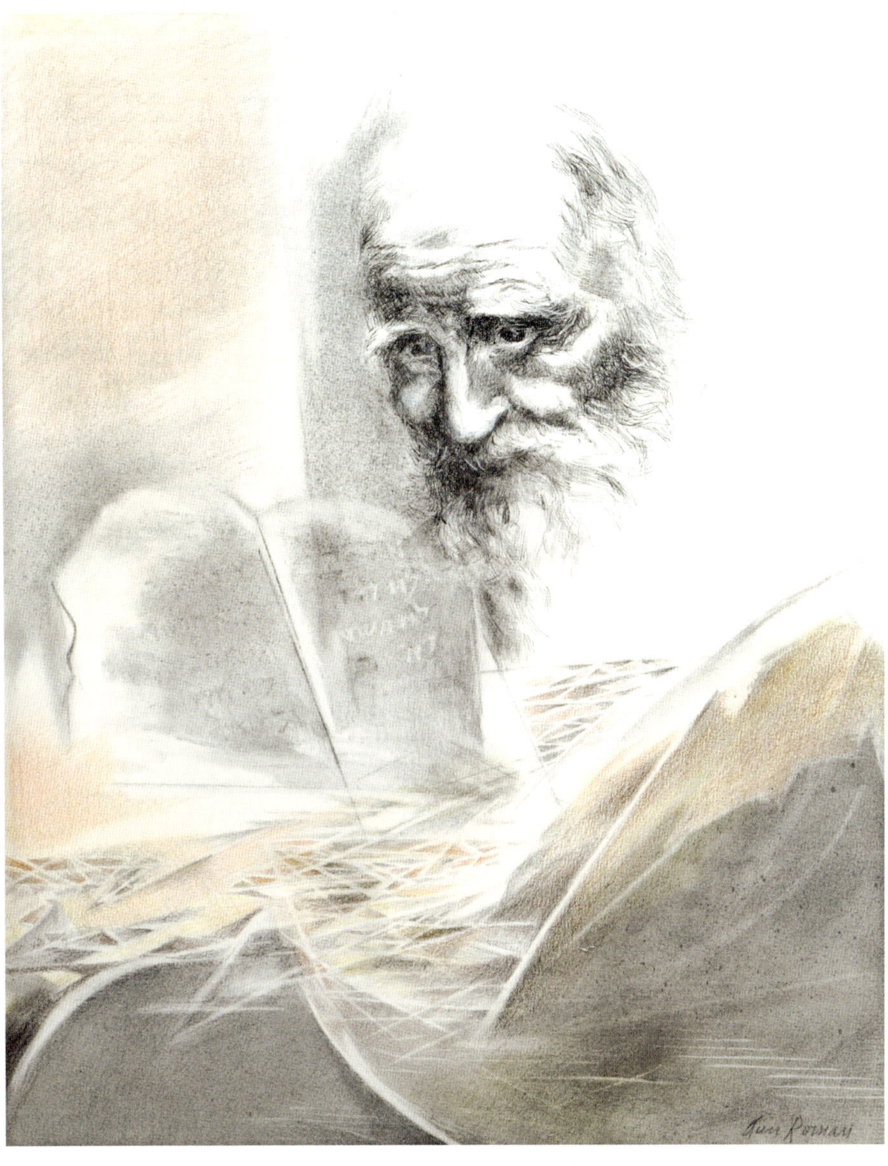

Born and raised in Chicago, Ann Roman studied at the Art Institute and participated in the Chicago art community for the span of her lifetime. She taught art at her private studio for decades and participated in the Musarts Club of Chicago, the Ballet Art Group, and the American-Jewish Arts Club. Roman exhibited not only with those organizations, but was also honored with one-woman shows at the Mandel Brothers Gallery, the Hyde Park Art Center, the South Shore Gallery, the Palmer House and the Art Institute.

This ink drawing was loaned by her cousin and lifelong friend, Rita Moskowitz.

The Decalogue, 20th century
Ann Roman
American
Ink on paper, 29 x 33 in.
Loan from Rita Moskowitz

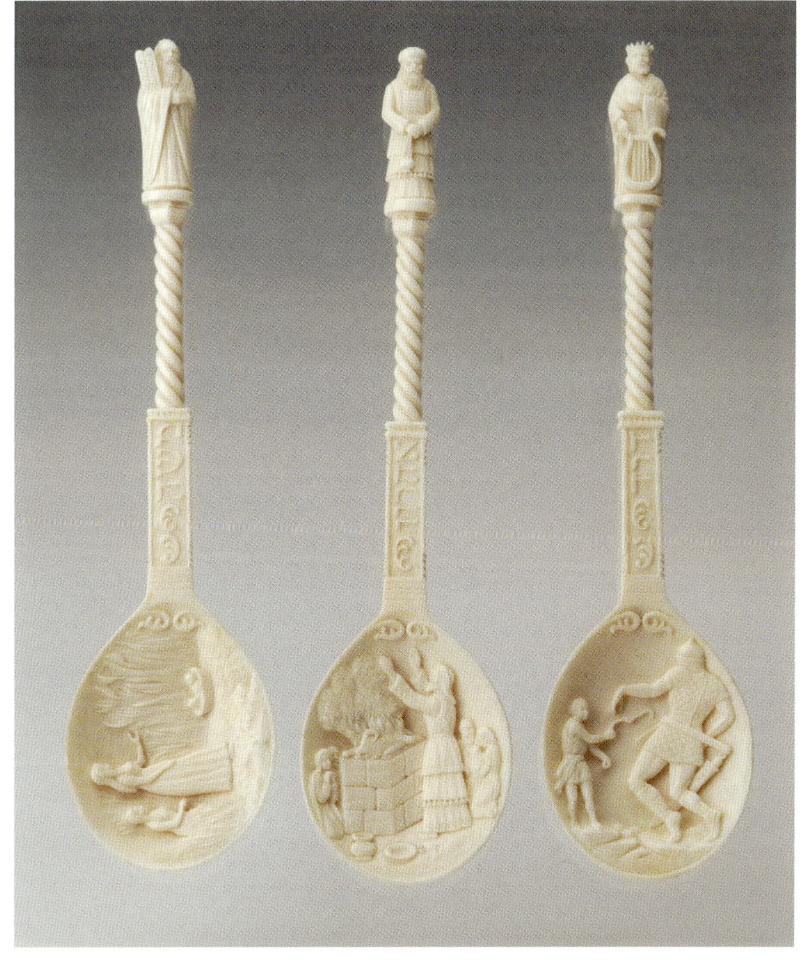

Three spectacular ivory spoons, each carved with a Bible story and character, are a mystery in origin. One features David and Goliath, one illustrates the High Priest Aaron at the altar, and the last is Pharaoh's Daughter finding Moses in the bulrushes. The set of spoons are presented in a turn-of-the-century hinged case, obviously made for presentation. The workmanship could be European or Near Eastern in origin, but the purpose of the set, other than as a decorative gift, is not apparent.

Ivory Spoons
European, early 20th century
8 x 2 in.
Gift of Mr. and Mrs. Maurice Gimp, 67.43

This vibrantly colored painting portrays the brothers Moses and Aaron in their roles as leaders of the nation of Israel. Moses cradles the tablets as precious objects while Aaron, dressed in his priestly garments, raises his hand in a gesture of blessing.

Isaac Frenel, born in Odessa, Russia, was a great grandson of the famed Rabbi Levi Yitzhak of Berdichev. After beginning his study of painting in Odessa, he immigrated to Israel in 1919 as part of the first settlers of the third Aliya. In 1920, Frenel traveled to Paris to study at the École des Beaux-Arts and at the studio of the painter Matisse. Returning to Israel in 1925, Frenel opened the studio of painting arts of the Histradut in Tel Aviv. Frenel's paintings were more influenced by contemporary art in Paris than orientalist trends of the Bezalel School in Jerusalem.

Frenel made Safed his home in 1934, where a museum of his works was opened at his house in 1973.

Moses and Aaron
Isaac Frenel
Israeli, born Russia 1889–1981
Oil on canvas, 54 x 41 in.
Loan from Kip and Gail Richards in care of the Tulsa Jewish Retirement Center

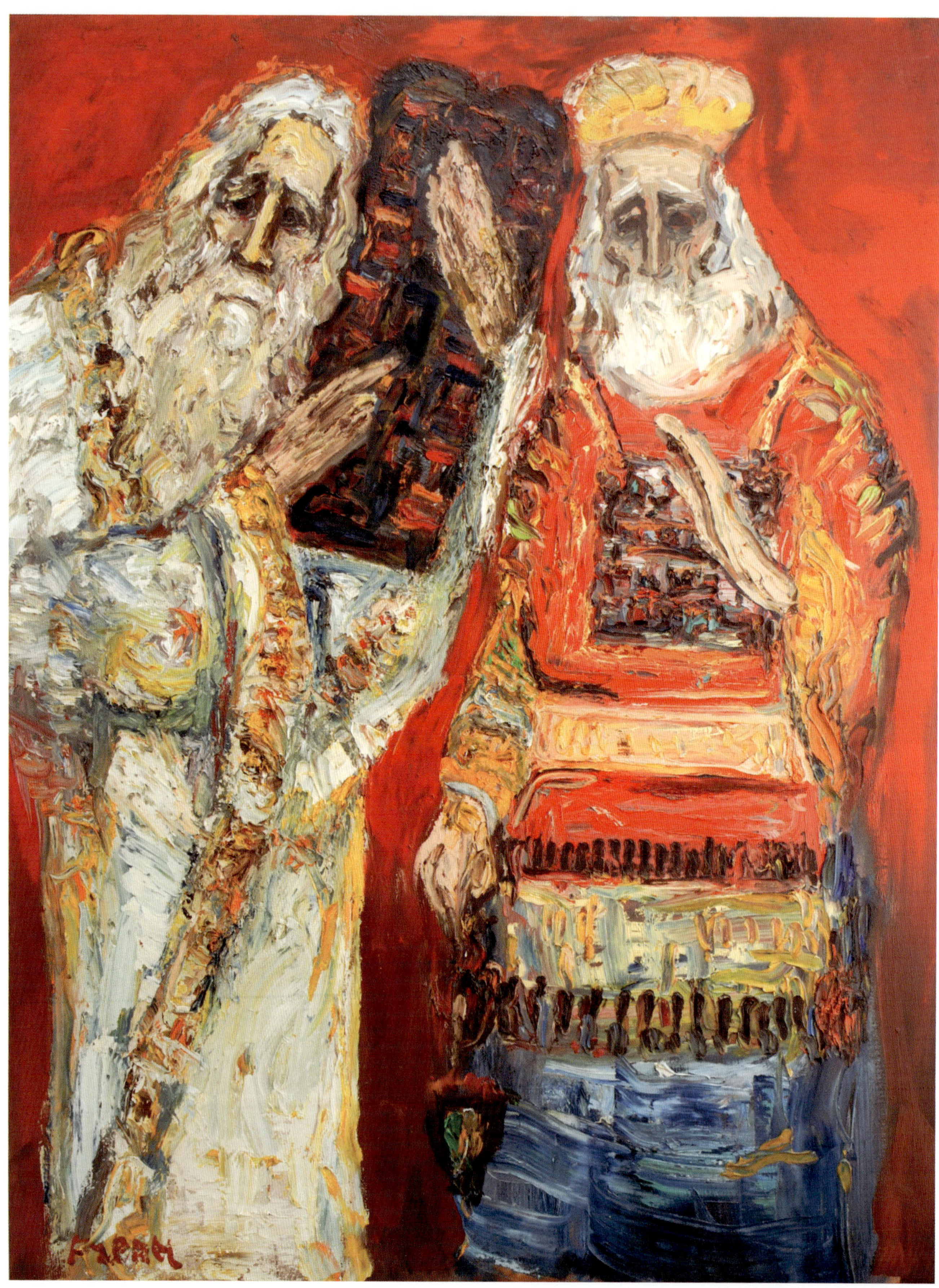

AARON

G-d selected Aaron as priest to serve in the Tabernacle. The vestments of the High Priest consisted of a white linen tunic, trousers, girdle, and a white turban. Other ornaments proclaimed his high office; the *Ephod,* a tunic with two onyx-stones on the shoulder-piece, on which were engraved the names of the tribes of Israel; the breastplate set with four equal rows of precious stones, each engraved with names of the Twelve Tribes of Israel; the *Me'il,* a sleeveless purple robe fringed with small golden bells and pomegranate tassels; and a turban which bore a gold plate with the inscription *Holy unto G-d.* Aaron and his sons had to take care of the offerings to G-d and to bless the children of Israel.

THE TABERNACLE

Two men, Bezalel and Oholiav, gifted with divine wisdom and artistic knowledge, were in charge of the Tabernacle construction. They designed and made the holy Tabernacle and its furnishings, according to the plan G-d revealed to Moses.

The Tabernacle was a tent that could be moved from place to place. A woven curtain separated the tent into two chambers: the front chamber was called the Holy Place, and the inner chamber was called the Holy of Holies. The roof and walls were covered with carpets. The tent of the Tabernacle stood in a wide court, enclosed by curtains. The two Tablets which Moses had brought back from Mount Sinai were kept in the Ark, which stood in the Holy of Holies.

The Holy Tabernacle was always covered by a pillar of clouds during the day, and by a pillar of fire during the night. As long as the pillar of clouds rested over the Tabernacle, the children of Israel remained in the same place. When the clouds rose up, it was a sign for them to continue their journey. Thus they camped and traveled according to G-d's command.

The Story of Aaron is from the Bible, EXODUS 1 – 40.

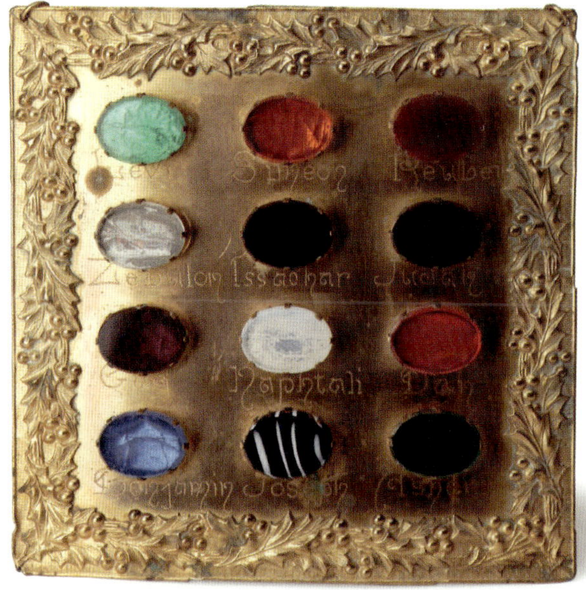

This elaborate replica of the breastplate of the High Priest is made from engraved brass, and decorated with patterned binding and Bohemian glass stones representing the Twelve Tribes of Israel. No marks identify the maker of this work, but its stamped holly border may indicate its origin is English.

BREASTPLATE OF THE HIGH PRIEST
Brass, Bohemian glass
7½ x 7½ in.
Gift of Steven Whysel
2006.5

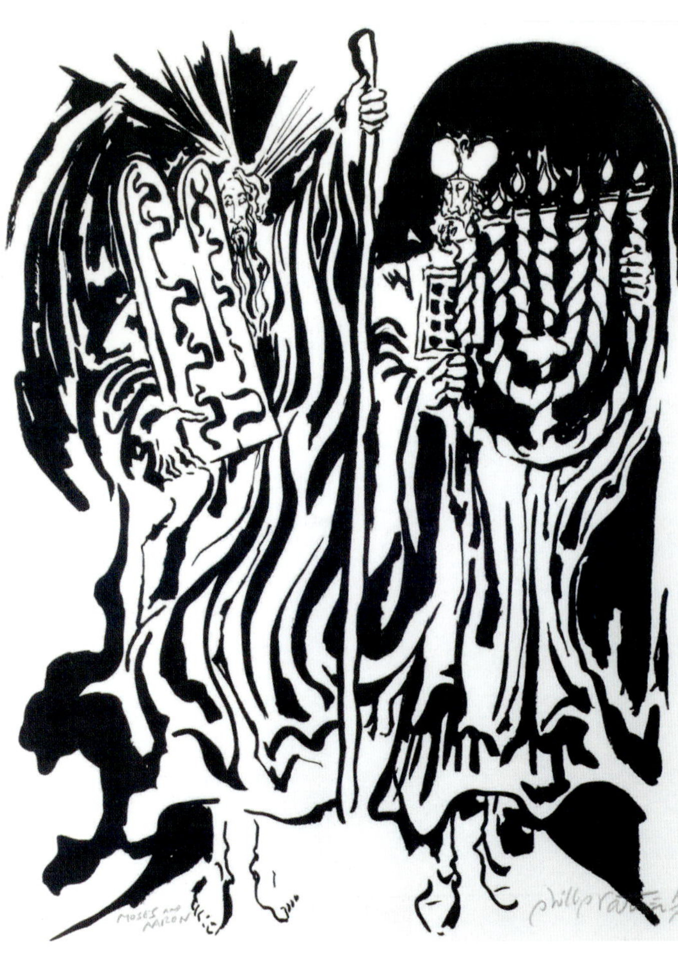

A multi-media artist and native of Washington, D.C., Phillip Ratner has spent many years working in sculpture, painting, etched glass, tapestry, drawing and the graphic arts. In 1984, he opened The Israel Bible Museum in Safad, Israel. Ratner also spent time in Israel using sculpture, painting and graphics to design more than 250 works of art relating to the Hebrew Bible. Ratner has degrees from Pratt Institute and American University, and for 23 years taught in Washington, D.C. area public schools. He continually builds his reputation as an international artist. His work is included in the permanent collections of the Smithsonian, the United States Supreme Court, the Library of Congress, the White House, The Statue of Liberty and Ellis Island.

Moses and Aaron, 20th century
Phillip Ratner
American, born 1938
Lithograph
Loan from Estelle Finer

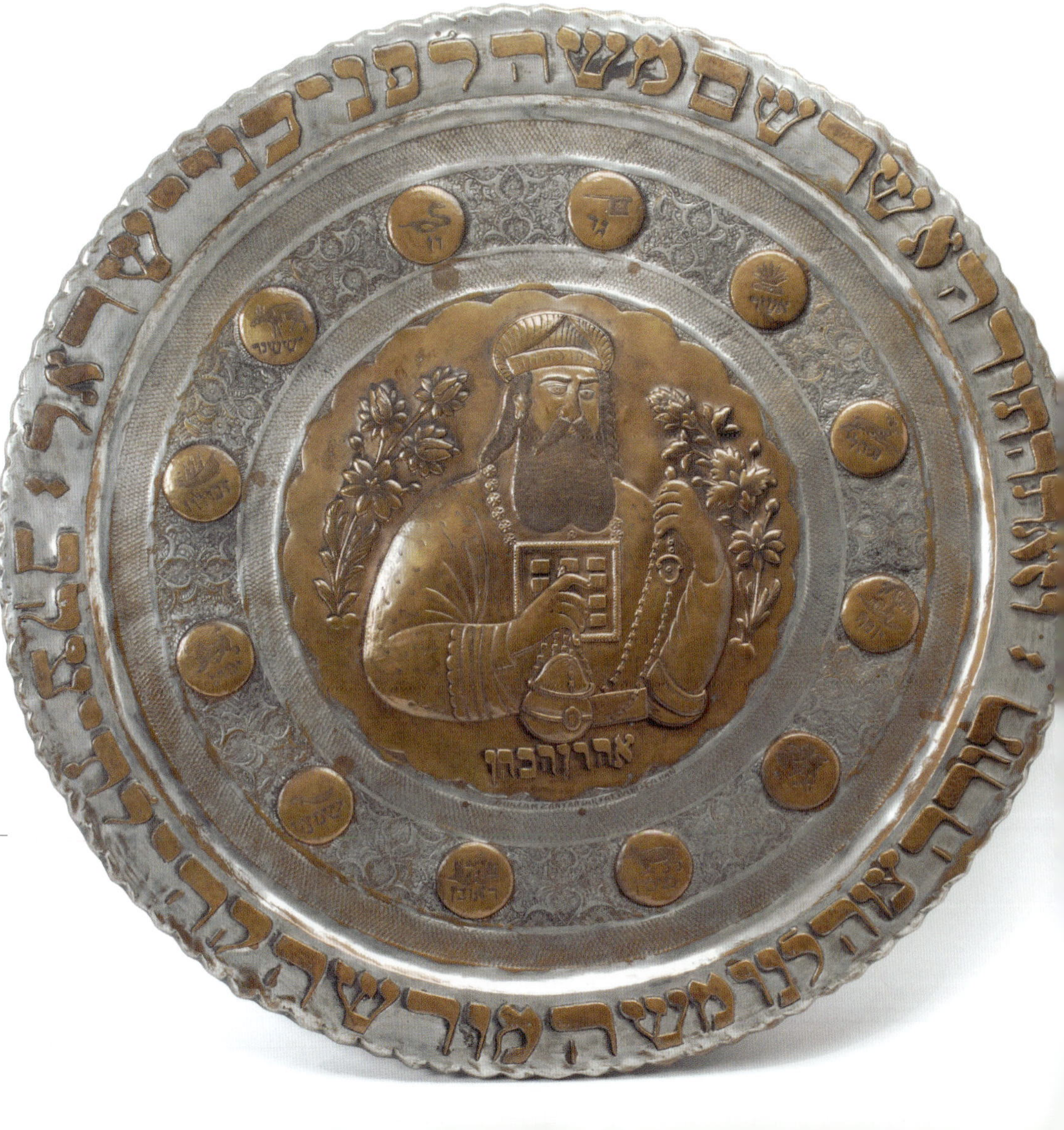

Elaborate engraving of Aaron with representations of the *Urim Thumim* and the Twelve Tribes of Israel. Hebrew phrases that surround the outer border translate as "This is the Torah that Moses brought before the children of Israel."Interestingly, the phrase is the same on both similar trays (see *Moses and the Tablets of the Law*), even though this tray depicts Aaron the High Priest and is labeled as such below the figure. Oftentimes Persian Jewish families are seen serving fruit on a tray such as this, other times it is used as a wall hanging.

Aaron, High Priest
Persian Tray, 20th century
Tinned copper
23 in. diameter
Loan from Zella Borg

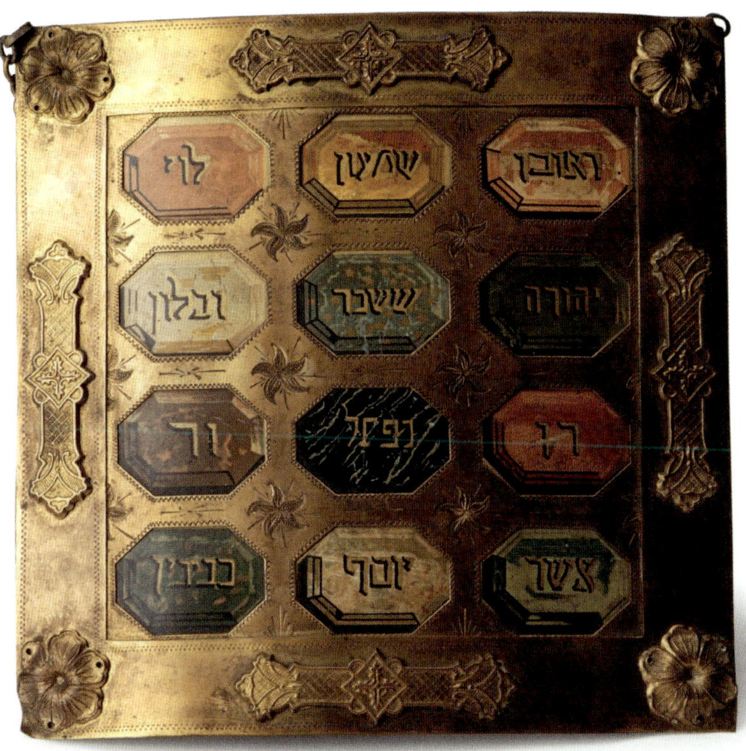

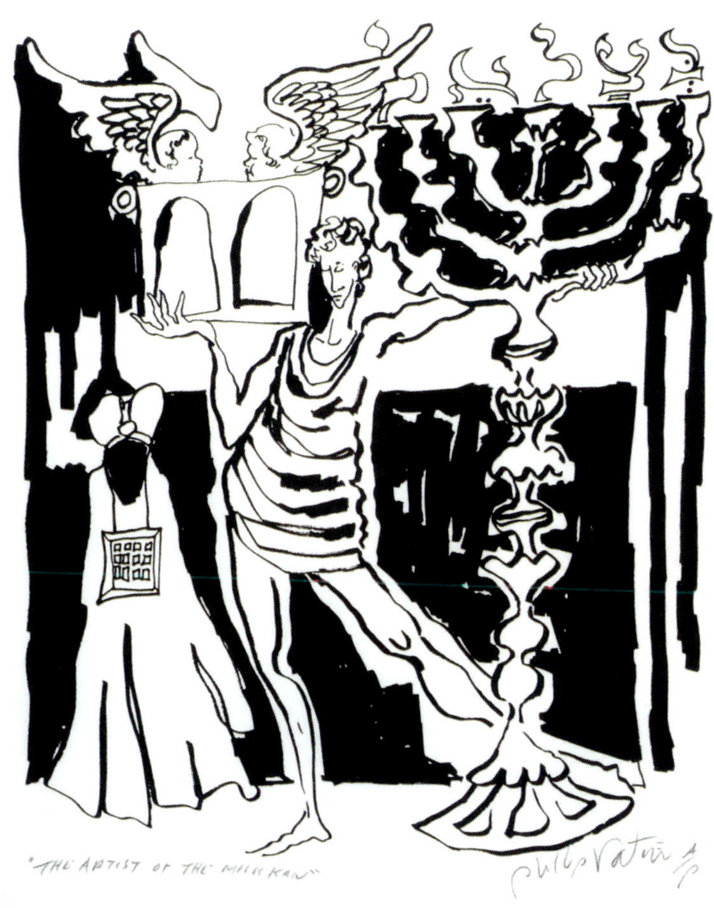

This version of an ancient priestly breastplate was found during demolition of a 19th century Odd Fellows Hall in Pennsylvania. As it was not created for Judaic use, it was not a Torah Shield, but may have been used in a ritual of the Odd Fellows organization.

Breastplate of the High Priest
Brass with lithography decorations
8 x 8 in.
Gift of Stanton Klein
83.20

Bezalel, Artist of the Mishkan, 20th century
Phillip Ratner
American, born 1938
Lithograph
Loan from Estelle Finer

In the 1930s Chagall traveled in the Near East, visiting the Holy Land, Syria, and Jerusalem. He was researching themes and local color for his *Drawings for the Bible*, a commission from long-time supporter and art dealer Ambroise Vollard. Chagall's illustrated Bible was finally published in 1956, 17 years after Vollard's death.

In 1966, Leon Amiel published Chagall's portfolio of lithographs titled *The Story of the Exodus*, This edition was made up of twenty-four large color lithographs, and 285 signed portfolios were produced.

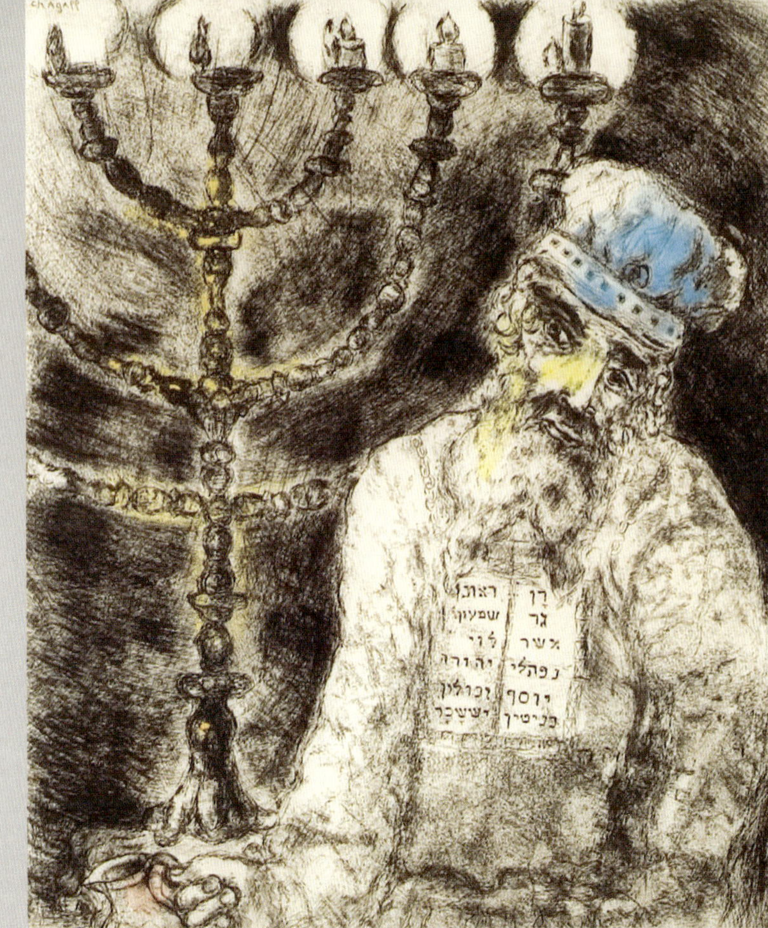

Aaron and the Lamp, 1966
Marc Chagall
Russian, 1887–1985
Hand-colored etching from *The Story of the Exodus*
12 x 9 in.
Loan from Marge Singer and Kenneth Renberg

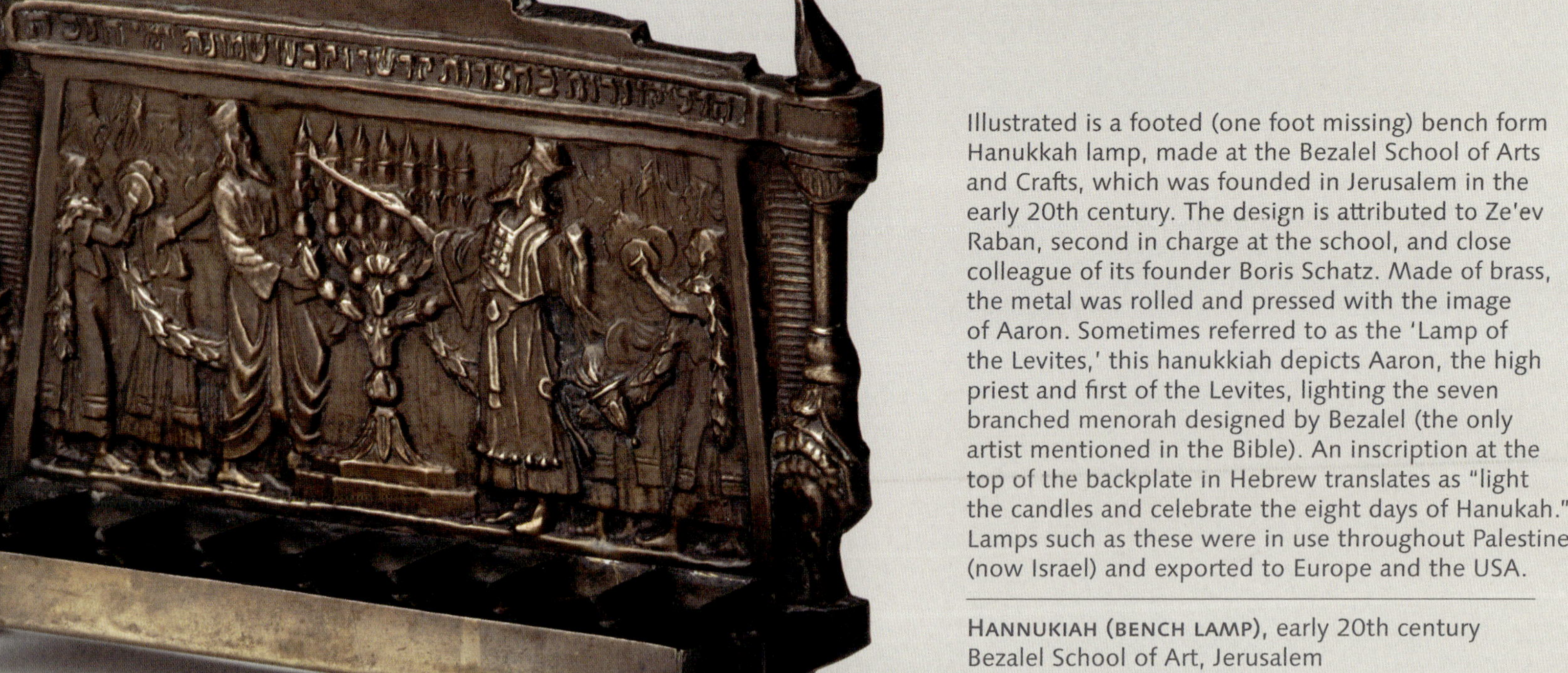

Illustrated is a footed (one foot missing) bench form Hanukkah lamp, made at the Bezalel School of Arts and Crafts, which was founded in Jerusalem in the early 20th century. The design is attributed to Ze'ev Raban, second in charge at the school, and close colleague of its founder Boris Schatz. Made of brass, the metal was rolled and pressed with the image of Aaron. Sometimes referred to as the 'Lamp of the Levites,' this hanukkiah depicts Aaron, the high priest and first of the Levites, lighting the seven branched menorah designed by Bezalel (the only artist mentioned in the Bible). An inscription at the top of the backplate in Hebrew translates as "light the candles and celebrate the eight days of Hanukah." Lamps such as these were in use throughout Palestine (now Israel) and exported to Europe and the USA.

Hannukiah (bench lamp), early 20th century
Bezalel School of Art, Jerusalem
Brass, pressed and rolled
5 x 6 ½ x 2 in.
Loan from Rosalee Minsky

For the 1962 publication of a deluxe book on the making of the Jerusalem Windows, Charles Sorlier, Chagall's Master Printer at the Mourlot workshop, made twelve 20-color stone lithographs after Chagall's final models for the windows under Chagall's supervision. The work was published by Andre Sauret in an edition of unknown size.

The Tribe of Levi, 1962
Marc Chagall
Russian, 1887 - 1985
Lithograph, hand signed by Marc Chagall in pencil
9½ x 12¾ in.
Loan from Irvin Frank

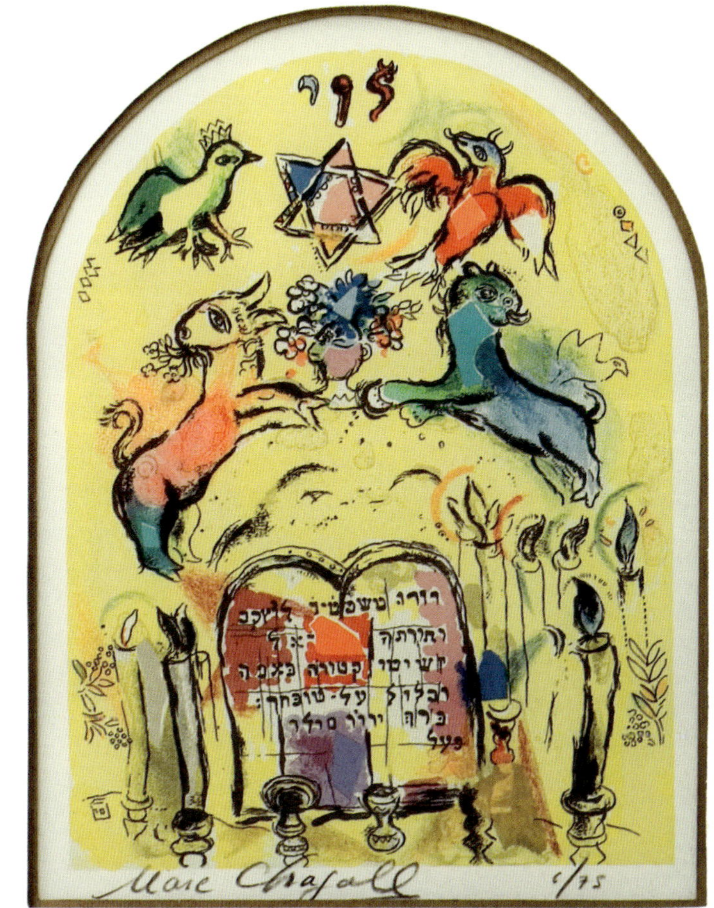

THE TWELVE TRIBES OF ISRAEL

The Tribes of Israel are historically the descendants of the twelve sons of Jacob, who was named Israel. Each of Jacob's twelve sons was the father of the Tribe bearing his name. The Twelve Tribes are: Asher, Benjamin, Dan, Gad, Issachar, Joseph, Judah, Levi, Naphtali, Reuben, Simeon, and Zebulun. When the Hebrews left Egypt, they left as Tribes. When they camped at Mt. Sinai, they camped as Tribes. When they entered and settled the Land of Israel, they settled as Tribes.

Each Tribe had its allotted portion of the Land and for many generations there was little "intermarriage" among them. Each Tribe had its flag, its colors, its particular tasks, and even its unique personality traits. The symbols of the Twelve Tribes match the twelve months of the year and the twelve signs of the Zodiac.

Made for the burgeoning tourist trade in Israel, this brass plate/wall hanging is stamped around the outer rim with the twelve symbols of the Twelve Tribes of Israel, which correspond to the twelve signs of the zodiac. The characteristic green patina was used on brass goods made in Israel by such companies as Pal-Bell and Oppenheim from the 1940s to the 1960s.

Decorative Passover Plate
Israel, ca. 1945 –1960
Brass, 10" diameter;
99.27

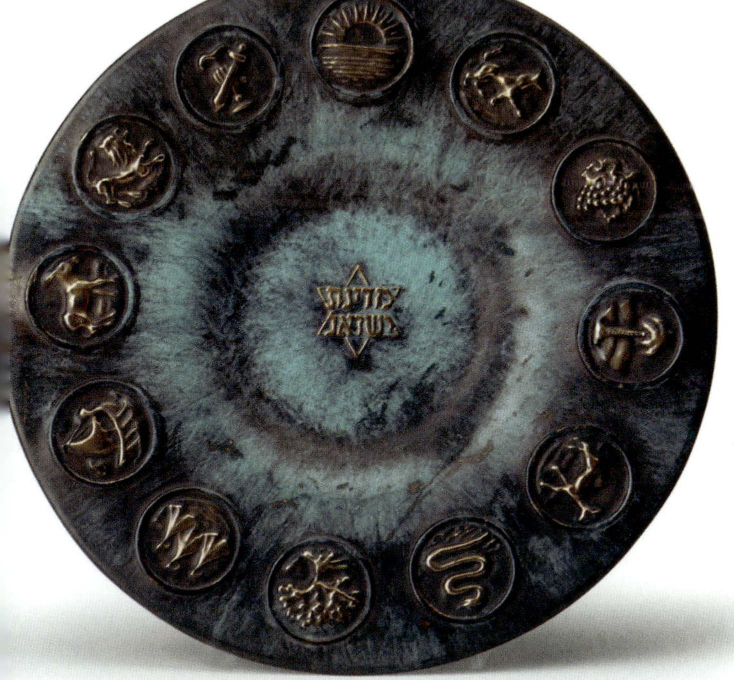

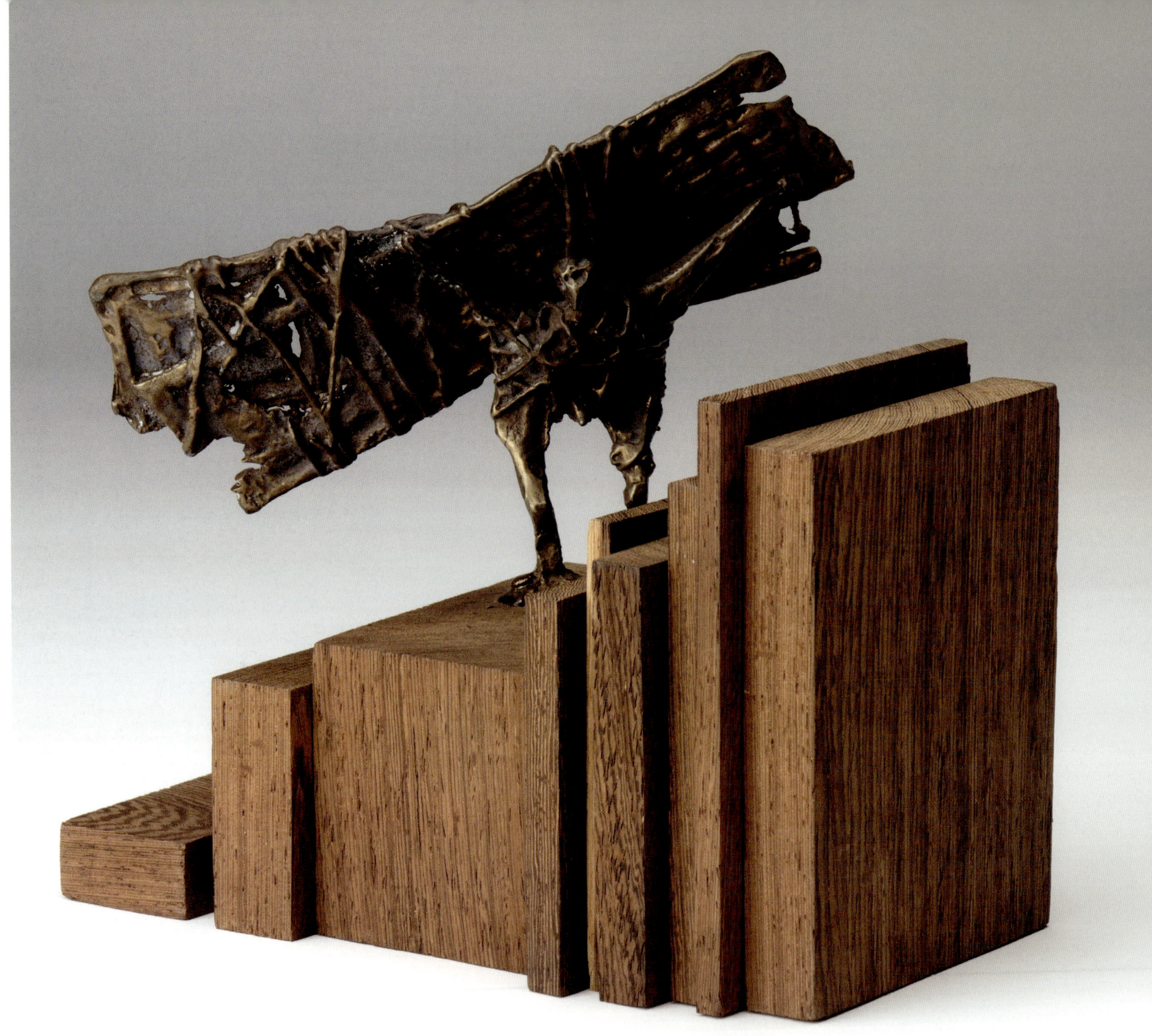

Samson and the Gates of Gaza,
ca. 1960–1970
Aharon Bezalel
Israeli, born Afghanistan 1926
Bronze, 7 x 8 x 4 in.
Loan from Isabel Sanditen

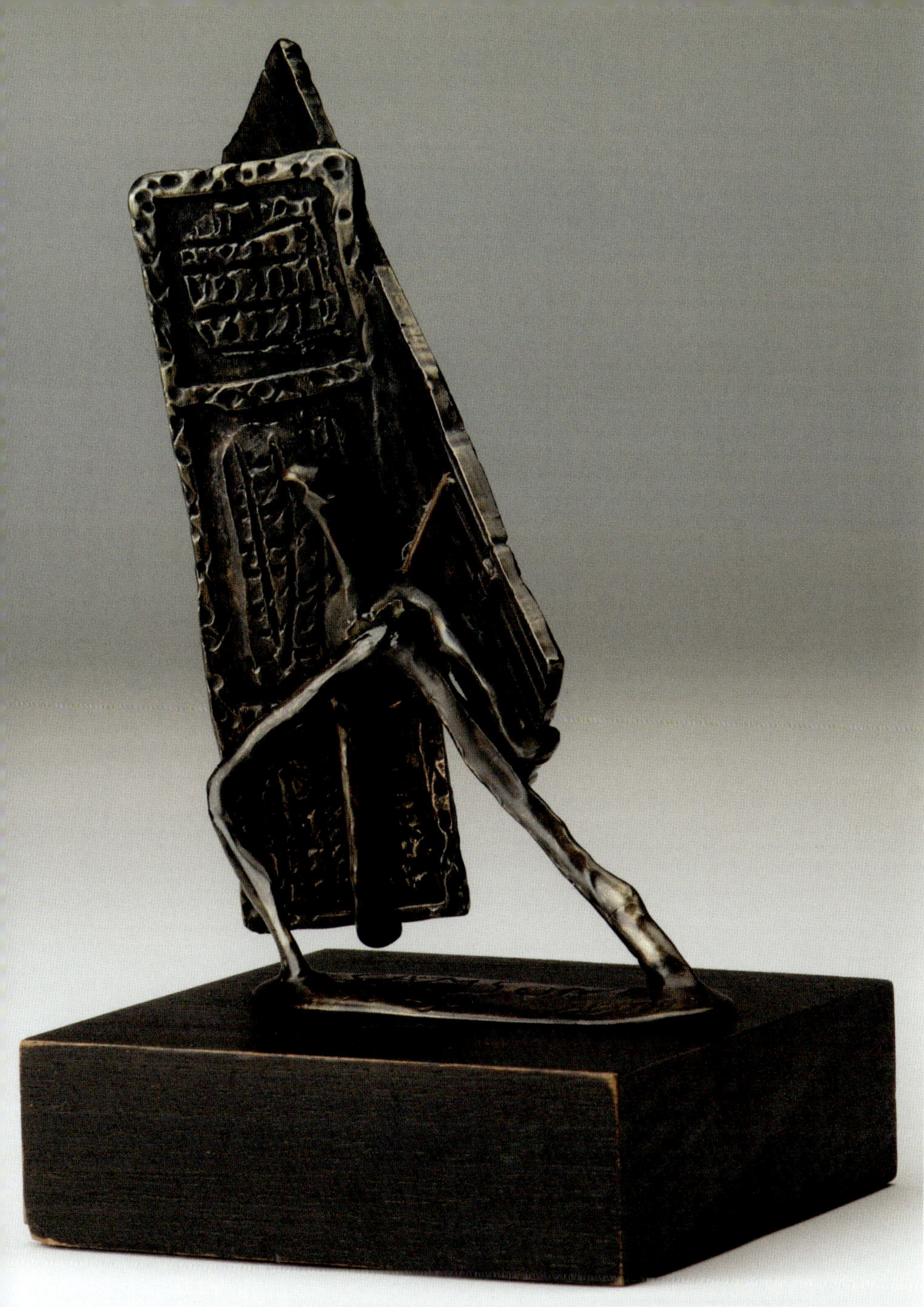

SAMSON

At the time of Samson's birth, a strong and cruel nation, the Philistines, began to trouble Israel. They lived by the seacoast, and for years they controlled the tribes of Israel whose land adjoined their country. They worshiped a god called Da'-gon, whose idol they set up in the temple of their chief city, Gaza. An angel told Samson's parents he would grow up and deliver their country from Philistine rule, that Samson should be dedicated to do special work for G-d as a Nazarite, and that he should never cut his hair or drink wine.

Samson and his parents followed the angel's guidance, and Samson grew to be a man of immense physical strength. On one occasion, he went into battle against the Philistines, who were Israel's feared enemies, and killed a thousand warriors with the jawbone of an ass. Another time, Samson visited the city of Gaza, and the Philistines decided to take him prisoner. When Samson learned of their plot, he walked to the city walls at midnight and removed the two huge doors that guarded the entrance into the city, put them on his shoulders, and carried them away. The next morning the Philistines discovered he had escaped, taking the gates of the city with him.

The story of Samson is from the Bible, JUDGES 13 – 16

Born in Afghanistan as a son of a Kabbalist rabbi, Aharon Bezalel grew up on Bible stories. During the 1950s, in the form of small wood sculptures, he began to tell the stories he knew so well. At the time, modern Israeli artists were exploring Israel's connection to its biblical roots, and Bezalel's small sculptures touched the heart of that effort, helping Bezalel find his place in Israeli art. Although the semi-abstract influences of Giacometti and Henry Moore are evident in Bezalel's early wood and bronze figures, the underlying biblical narrative is told without representing each character as metaphor.

Aharon Bezalel has lived, worked, and taught art in Jerusalem for many years. He works primarily in bronze and wood, and has shown all over the world. His works are included in museums and galleries world-wide.

SAMSON AND THE GATES OF GAZA,
ca. 1960–1970
Aharon Bezalel
Israeli, born Afghanistan 1926
Bronze, 7 x 8 x 4 in.
Loan from Isabel Sanditen

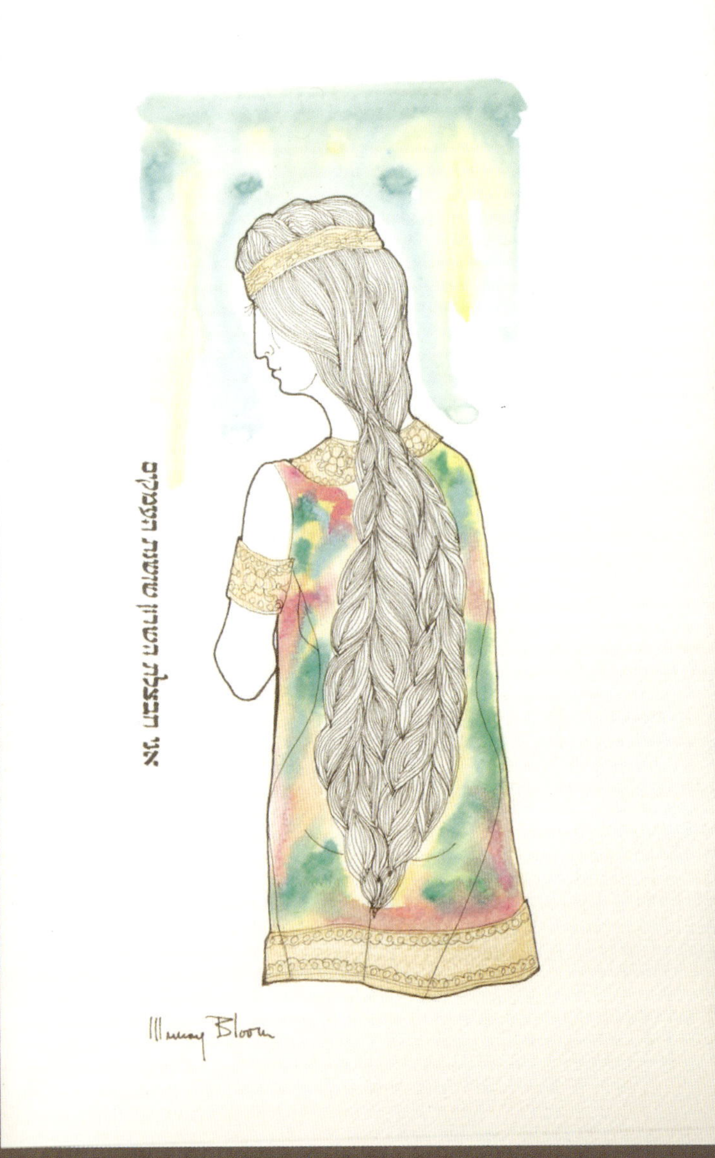

RUTH

Ruth, a young Moabite girl who married into the Israelite nation, lost her husband after just a few years of marriage. She lived with her mother-in-law, Naomi, who sent her one day to follow after the reapers and gather grain which they let fall, for she had no food in her house. The landowner, Boaz, one of Naomi's kinsmen, saw her at her work, and asked who this beautiful woman might be. He learned she was Naomi's daughter-in-law, and said to her kindly, "Come every day and gather all that you wish and then stay for lunch with my workers." Privately he ordered the reapers to let fall more than usual of the ears, so that she could gather plenty.

Ruth went home and told Naomi about Boaz, and Naomi told her, at the end of the harvest, to dress up and go find Boaz where he slept on the threshing floor, and lie at his feet. Naomi knew that according to Hebrew custom the nearest of kin may marry a widow; she also knew that Ruth had pleased Boaz and she wished them both happiness. When Boaz awoke, he saw Ruth, and said, "Blessed are you, Ruth, for you are kind and did not go after the young men. I am a near kinsman and I will marry you." So Ruth and Boaz were married, and she bore him a son, who became the father of Jesse, who was the father of David.

The story of Ruth is from the Bible, RUTH 1 – 4

A small ink and watercolor drawing portrays Biblical matriarch Ruth was one of a series of paintings of Biblical Women conceived by artist Murray Bloom, but never completed. Inscribed on the work is the passage "Whither thou goest" from the Book of Ruth.

Bloom, born in New York City in 1937, began his career in the arts in high school, dividing his interest between painting and photography. He studied at NYU, Columbia, HUC, and The Art Students League before moving to Israel in 1972. He spent six years there as a photographer for the *Jerusalem Post* and an art teacher at the Bezalel Academy of Art and Design, returning to America in 1978. His career grew in scope as he exhibited and taught in Los Angeles and New York, and in his retirement he is pursuing his great love, photography.

RUTH, ca. 1990
Murray Bloom
American, born 1937
Ink and watercolor on paper
12 x 18 in.
Gift of Abe Brand and Dorothy Gimp-Brand in memory of Moe Gimp
1993.37

ESTHER

Ahasuerus, King of Persia, put aside his queen, Vashti, for disobedience, and began looking for a new queen. He invited all the eligible young women to his court for a beauty contest. Esther, a Jewish girl, was chosen from the participants to become queen. Her Uncle Mordechai told Esther not tell Ahasuerus she was Jewish. One day Mordechai discovered a plot to assassinate the king and reported it to the palace. He was never rewarded, but the report was recorded.

The king then chose Haman, an enemy of the Jews, to be his chief advisor. Haman was an arrogant man who expected everyone to bow down to him. When Mordechai refused to bow to him, Haman convinced the king to destroy the Jewish population of Persia. Haman then cast lots to determine the day of the Jews' annihilation

When Mordechai heard the news, he went to Esther and recounted the details of the evil decree, asking her to intercede on the Jews behalf. Esther agreed to try, and dressed in royal garb, went before the king. She put herself in danger knowing that to appear before the king without a summons was death. But the king welcomed her and agreed to appear at a banquet with Esther and Haman. That night, the King discovered that Mordechai had never been rewarded for saving him from the assassination plot of two servants. When Haman appeared, the King decided that Haman should decide Mordechai's reward. Haman, intending to obtain the King's permission to hang Mordechai, unwittingly answered the King's questions. The King asked Haman, "What should be done for the man the King wishes to reward?" Haman, believing that Ahasuerus intended to reward him, replied that the honoree should be dressed in royal clothing, ride upon a royal horse. And be led through the city streets by an official proclaiming "This is what is done to the man the King wishes to honor." Ahasuerus agreed and instructed Haman to carry it out for Mordechai, Crestfallen, Haman followed the King's orders. At Esther's second banquet Haman's downfall continued. Esther revealed Haman's villainous plot and the fact that she was Jewish. She asked the King to "grant me my soul and my people." Ahasuerus ordered that Haman be hanged on the gallows intended for Mordechai. The King elevated Mordechai to a position of great influence and allowed him to issue edicts permitting the Jews to fight their enemies. On the thirteenth and fourteenth of *Adar* the Jews won tremendous victories and were saved from the threat of total annihilation.

The story of Esther is from the Bible, ESTHER 1 – 10

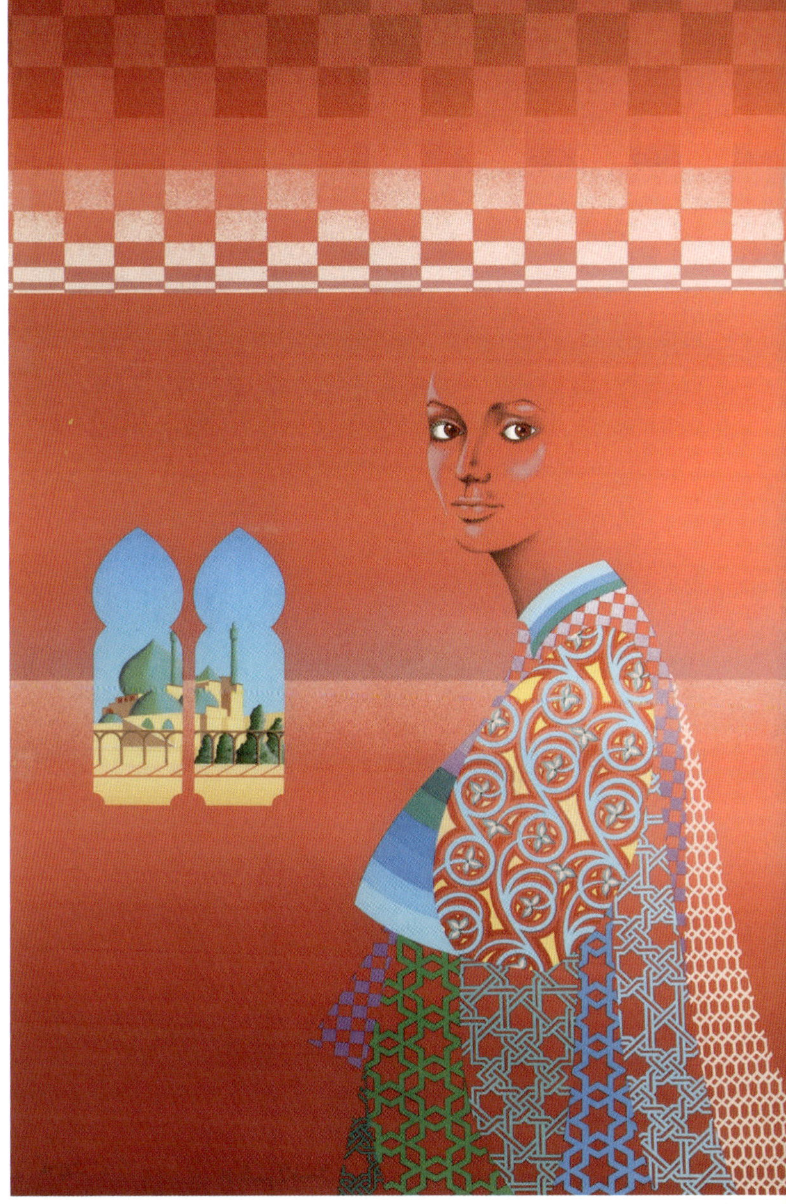

This colorful lithograph of *Queen Esther* is adapted from a series of paintings commissioned by Yeshiva University Museum titled *The Book of Esther*. In this work Esther is portrayed in royal costume, surrounded by a Persian landscape.

QUEEN ESTHER, 1981
Murray Bloom
American, born 1937
Lithograph; 44/200
41 1/8 x 29 1/4 in.
Gift of friends in honor of Flora Solow's 80th birthday.
1982.2

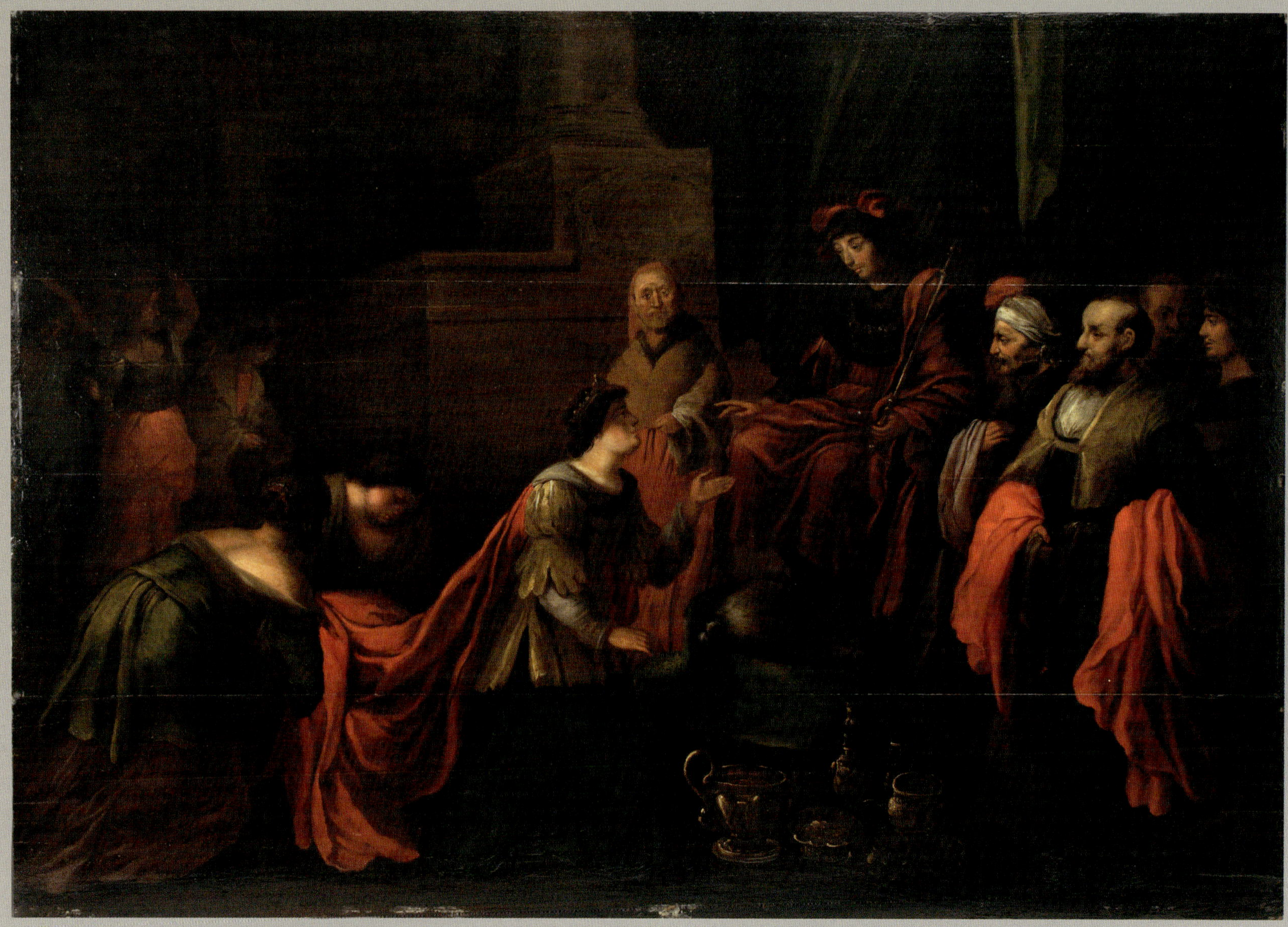

A fine Netherlandish panel painting, this work presents Queen Esther imploring King Ahasuerus to spare her people from destruction. Rembrandt Harmensz van Rijn, master of the Dutch school, lived from 1606 to 1669. Born in Leiden, he moved to Amsterdam in 1624 to study painting in the school of Pieter Lastman. Rembrandt's reputation as a painter grew after he settled in Amsterdam, and when his reputation and commissions were at their height, Rembrandt opened an atelier or school in his home. Between 1628 and 1661 he worked with more than forty students, each of whom studied with him for a few years, then left to establish their own careers.

Most paintings were produced in studios during the seventeenth century. The atelier functioned like a factory. Often the master would lay out the painting, his students would fill in large areas, and he would sign it. In the atelier specialists were trained to only paint heads, hands, or backgrounds. Rembrandt attracted many students, a fact that increases the potential for this painting, *Esther and Ahasver*, to be a correct attribution to the Rembrandt Atelier.

ESTHER AND AHASVER, ca. 1606–1669
Rembrandt Atelier
Dutch School, 17th century
Oil on panel
48 x 60 in.
Gift of Mr. and Mrs. Cedric Marks
1971.1

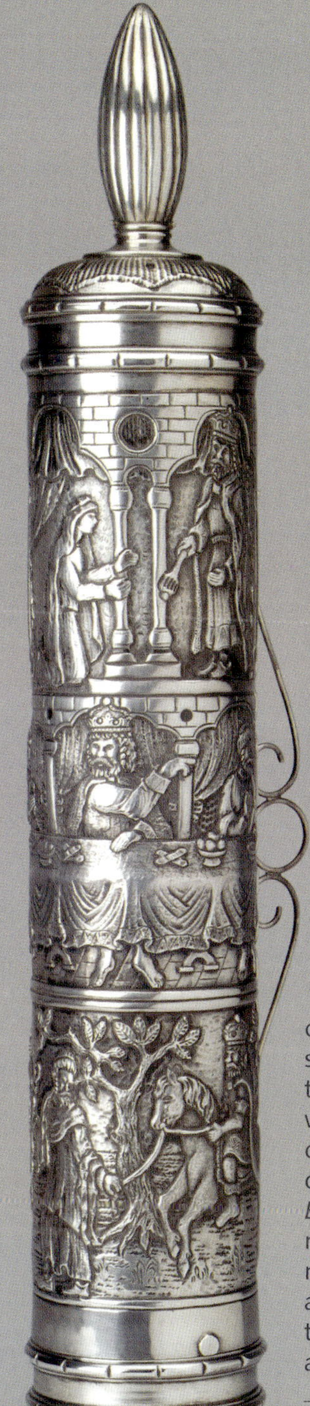

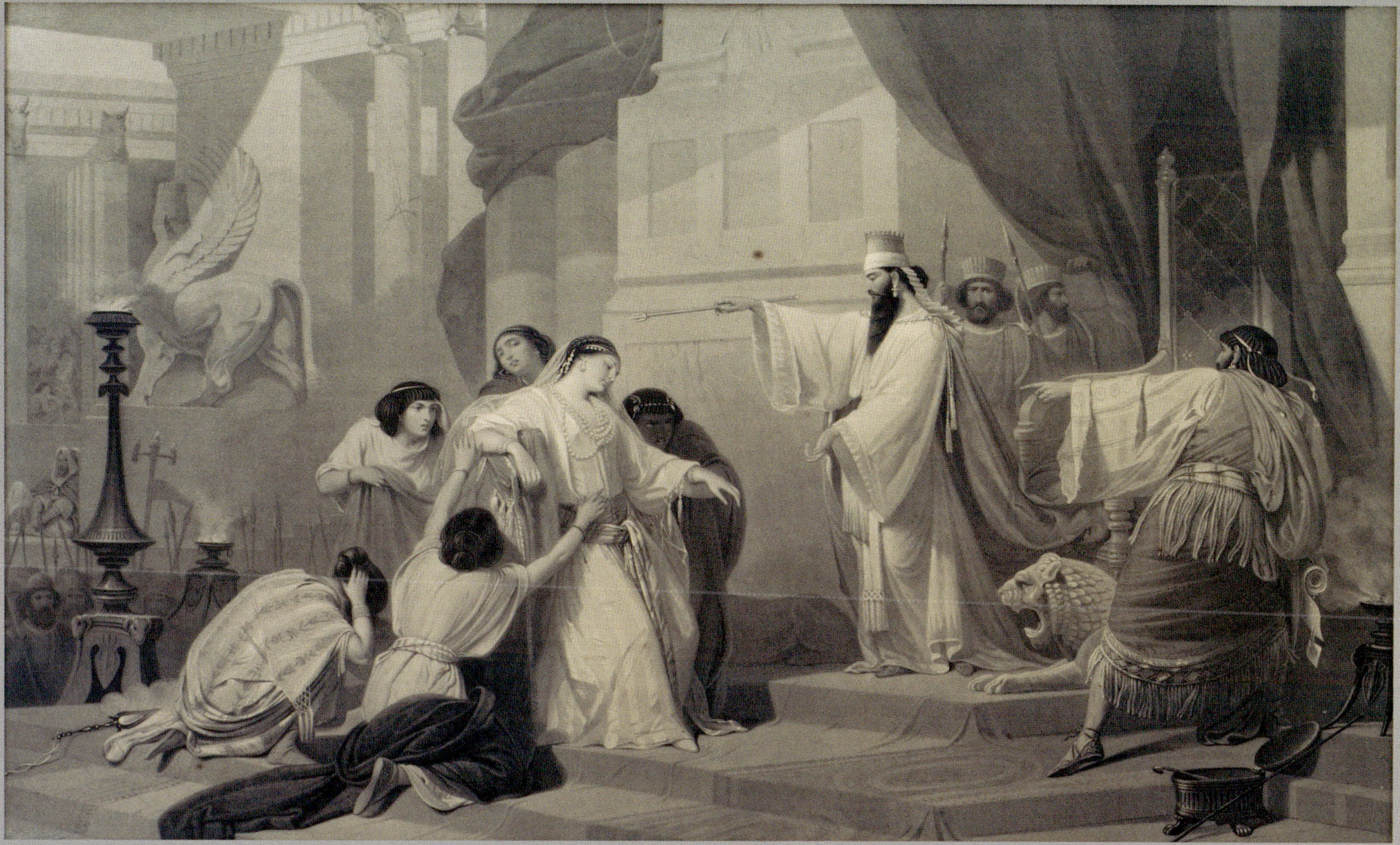

The *Megillat Esther* exemplifies the traditional combination of two objects: the scroll and the ornamental case. The silver case, embossed from top to bottom with scenes from the Purim story, is made to house a parchment scroll, on which is written the *megillah*. The *Megillah* contains ten chapters of text from the Book of Esther. Scrolls of varying quality are available, from plain to illustrated. The *Megillat Esther* is read twice on *Purim*, the 14th day of the Jewish month of *Adar*, once in the evening of *Purim* and once the next morning. The evening ceremony is at the synagogue, and the reading is accompanied by boos and noises from the audience when the names of the characters in the story are read aloud.

Megillat Esther and Case, 20th century
Dutch
Silver, ink on parchment scroll
25¾ x 7½ x 7½ in.
Gift of Temple Emanuel, Ponca City, Oklahoma
88.12.1

A nineteenth century steel engraving, this work was most likely engraved after a popular painting of the time. These engravings were often sold in folios or by subscription to middle-class households, increasing the availability of fine art to the Victorian populace.

Esther Imploring the Assyrian,
ca. 1870–1880
Henry Chopin, 1804–1880
Steel engraving, 28 x 42 in.
Loan from Congregation B'nai Emunah

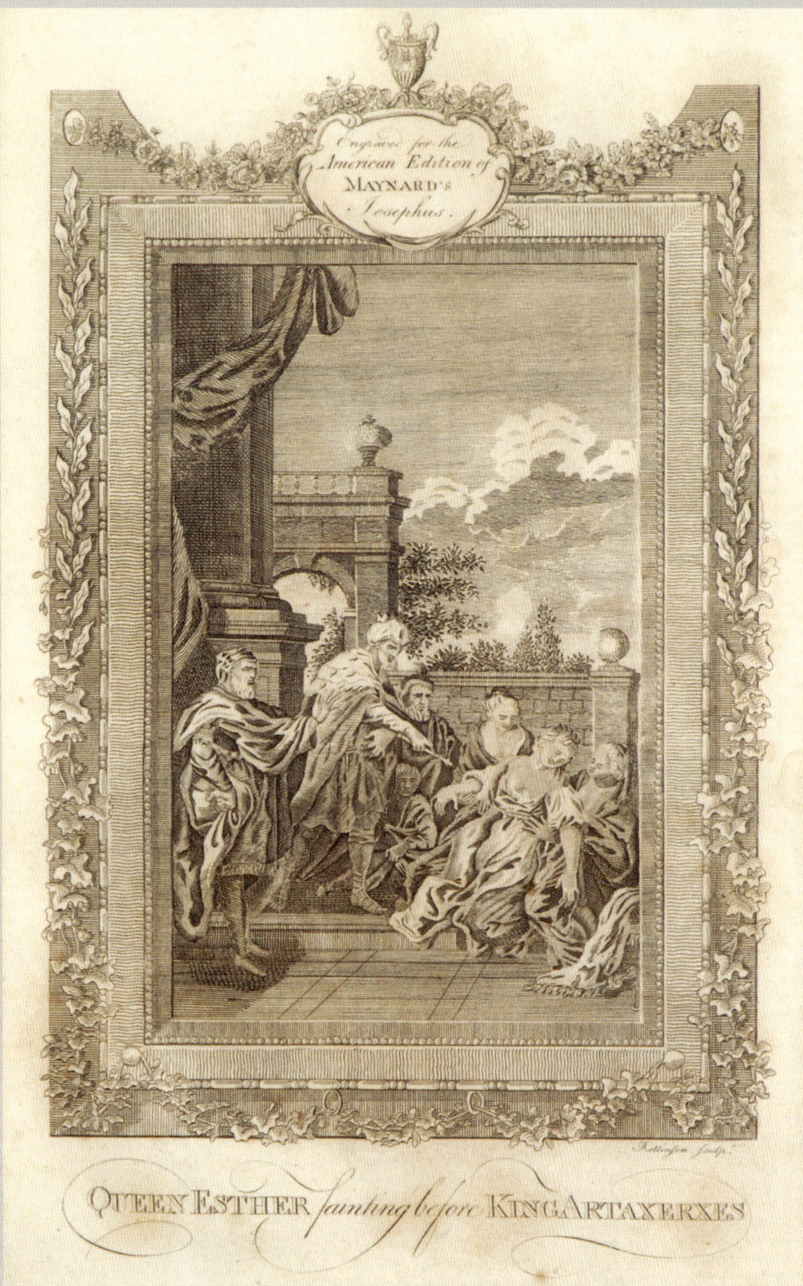

This work was engraved to illustrate the 1791 edition of *The Whole Genuine and Complete Works of Flavius Josephus, The Learned and Authentic Jewish Historian, Celebrated Warrior*, translated from the original in the Greek language and edited by George Henry Maynard and the Rev. Edward Kimpton. New York: William Durrell, 1792. It is embellished with 60 engraved plates, including two maps and a folding plan of Jerusalem.

This is one of the great illustrated books printed in the new United States of America during the 18th century. Almost by necessity, the roster of "American artists" responsible for these large engravings forms a Who's Who of early American craftsmen. Seven of these plates were executed by Alexander Andersen, who is generally considered America's first professional book illustrator. There are fourteen plates each by Amos Doolittle and Cornelius Thiebout. William Rollinson made six, J. Allen five, and two are the work of Benjamin Tanner.

Queen Esther, 1792
Copperplate engraving
Gift of Gerald and Charlotte Richards in honor of their granddaughter Lisa Benjaminov
1972.9

Wedding chests originated in France and Italy around the fifteenth century. The purpose of such a chest was to convey the bride's dowry goods to her new home and store them for her use. The invention of the chest form, the *cassone*, is attributed to the late Italian renaissance, and became a low chest with carved panels that illustrated scenes from Gothic and Biblical literature.

This bridal chest may have been a gift for a bride named Esther and a groom named Solomon, as the front panels depict, on the left, Queen Esther before King Ahasuerus; and on the right, Solomon's decision.

Bridal Chest, 17th century
European, Southern Germany
Carved oak
Gift of Dorothy Gimp in memory of Maurice E. Gimp
42 x 20¾ x 38 in.
1975.31

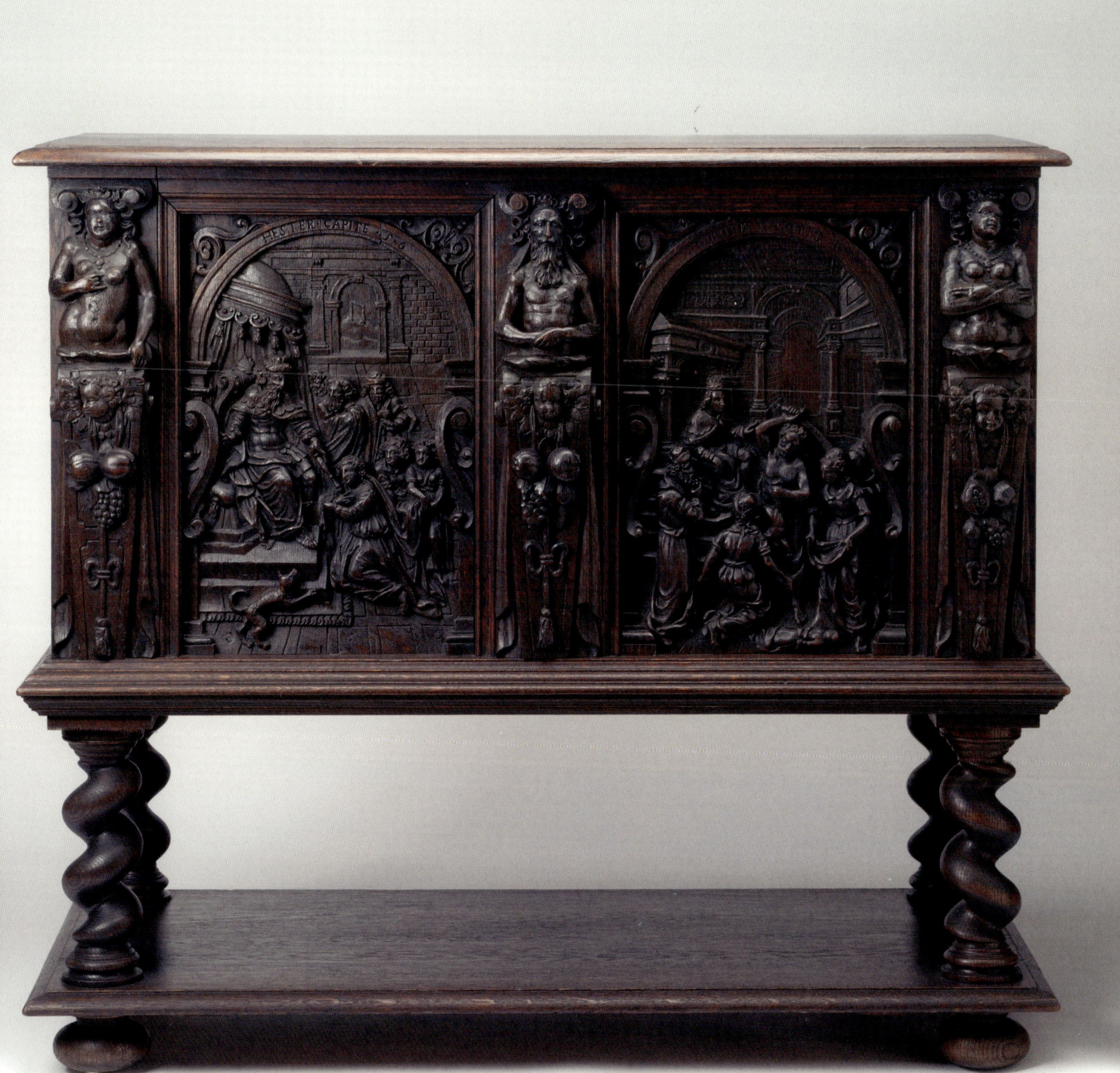
HESTER CAPITE 5 6

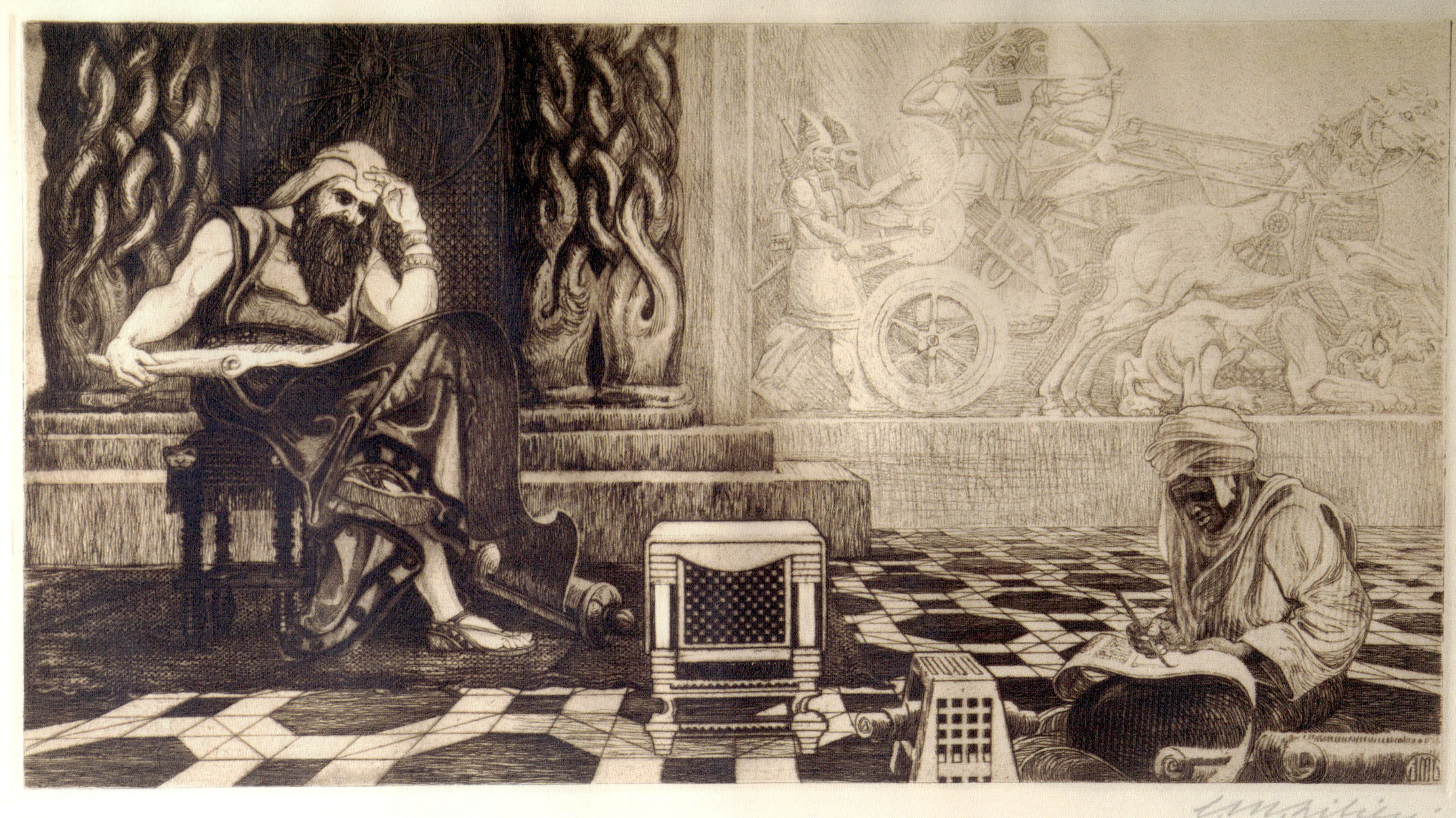

Ephraim Moses Lilien grew up in Galicia and moved to Germany in 1899, where he became involved in the movement to restore Jewish statehood. Lilien began his career as an illustrator in the *Jugendstil* (German Art Nouveau) movement. He worked in India ink until 1908, when he learned the etching process, which he continued to use for most of his career. Interested in Zionism and the search for a national art, Lilien traveled through Palestine taking photographs of the land and its people. He returned to Germany and began to create a series of etchings. He used his photographs to create Biblical scenes of the Holy Land, which were distributed in several formats: prints, etchings, posters, postcards, and illustrated books of the Bible. This etching, *Ahasuerus and Scribe*, may be taken from volume seven (Ruth, Jonah, Esther and Daniel) of *Die Bucher Der Bibel* (The Books of the Bible) which Lilien illustrated for publication in 1912. His signature is engraved in the plate in the lower right corner of the plate, but no date is included.

Ahasuerus and Scribe, 1921
Ephraim Moses Lilien
German, 1874–1925
Etching
19 x 27¾ in.
Loan from an anonymous lender

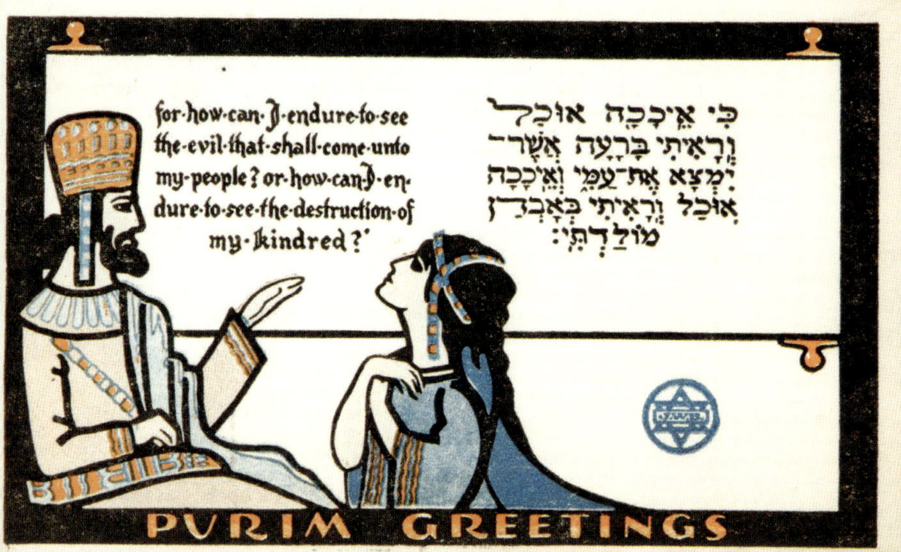

The Purim greeting card in the SMMJA collection was printed by USO with JWB insignia, and was sent to an Oklahoma City mother by a non-Jewish soldier on February 27, 1944. The National Jewish Welfare Board was founded in 1917 to provide support for soldiers in times of war. When America became involved in World War II, JWB sent chaplains to serve the needs of Jewish servicemen worldwide. One goal was to provide chaplains with the necessary supplies to meet the needs of Jewish soldiers. Enormous amounts of festival accessories, troop comforts, and kosher food were transported to chaplains overseas. By 1946, JWB had distributed tons of matzo , wine, kosher meat, salami, fish, macaroons, and other holiday delicacies to servicemen. Two million holiday leaflets and 8.5 million holiday greeting cards were produced and distributed by JWB, and circulation of religious accessories such as prayer books reached into the tens of thousands.

Jewish Welfare Board Purim Postcard
American, 1940–1945
3 x 5 in.
Dedicated by Museum Trustees in honor of Mildred Sanditen
93.40.32

BELOW: A custom of the Purim holiday is to give food. The tradition of sending gifts consisting of two types of food to friends on Purim is called *Mishloach Manot* and is prescribed in *Megillat Esther* (9:22). On this day, (and only during the day), men and women, young people and children, many in disguise, hurry through the streets with plates filled with choice goodies: fruits, wine, and cookies. *Matanot LaEvyonim* is Hebrew for "gifts to the poor." On Purim, every Jew is required to give a minimum of two gifts of food or money to two people in need. Often synagogues join together to raise money to give to the needy. Purim plates such as this might be used to take food to a friend, or to serve traditional Hamentaschen cookies.

Purim Plate
Israel, 20th century
Glazed Porcelain
8 in. diameter
Loan from Martha and Fred Strauss

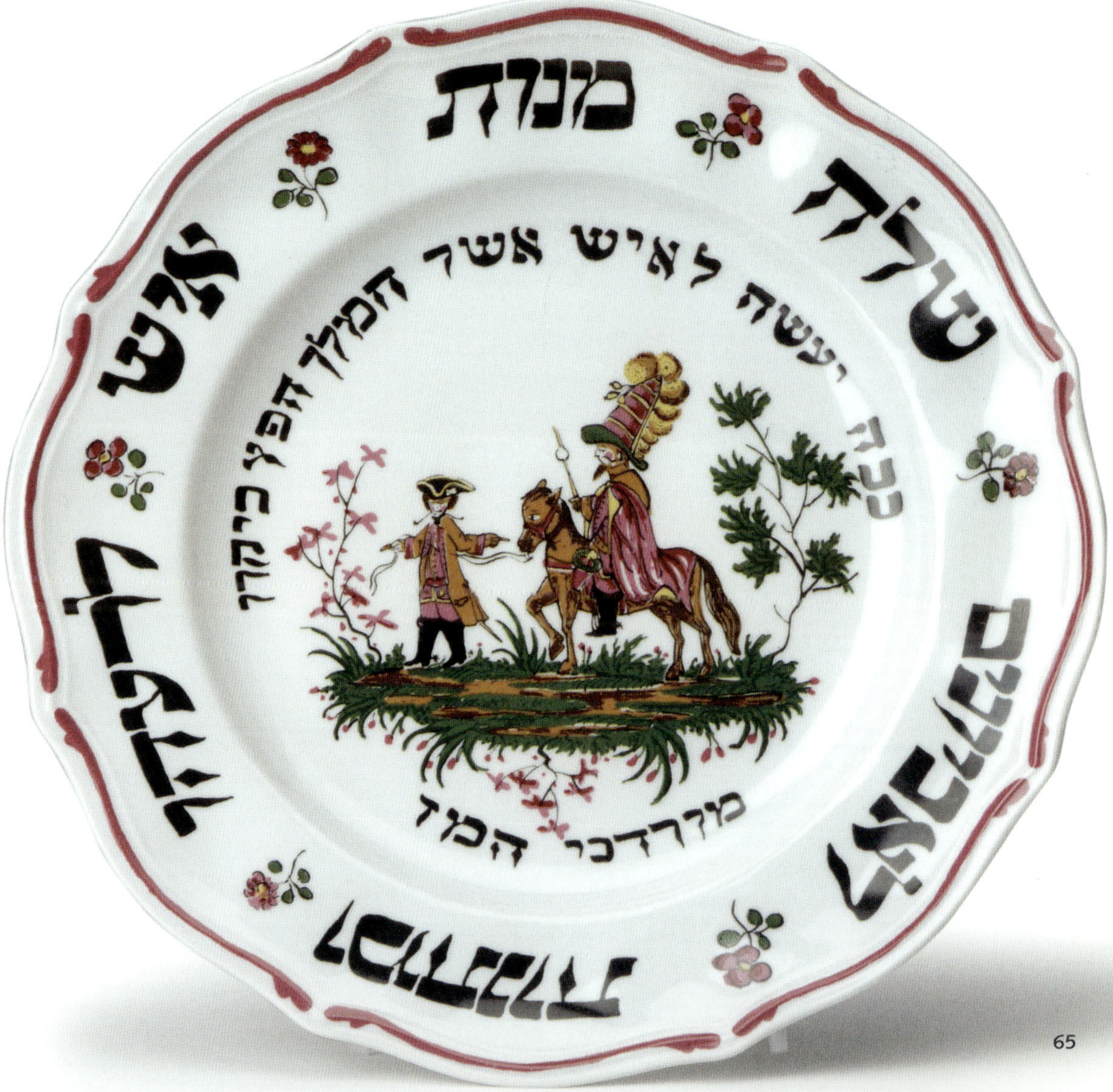

SAUL

For many years the prophet Samuel judged wisely over Israel, but finally the people asked him to choose a king. Samuel was reluctant, for he thought the people wanted the wrong kind of king: an aggressive warrior like other nations' kings.

G-d told Samuel to go ahead and find a king, and, one day, a young man named Saul came to the temple looking for a seer to help find his missing livestock.

When Samuel saw him he realized that the new king had come. And though Saul protested that he was from the weakest tribe in Israel, he was feasted and anointed with the sacred oil. Then Samuel gathered the people together in a great congregation, and announced Saul was the new king.

The story of Saul is from the Bible, 1 SAMUEL, 8 - 9.

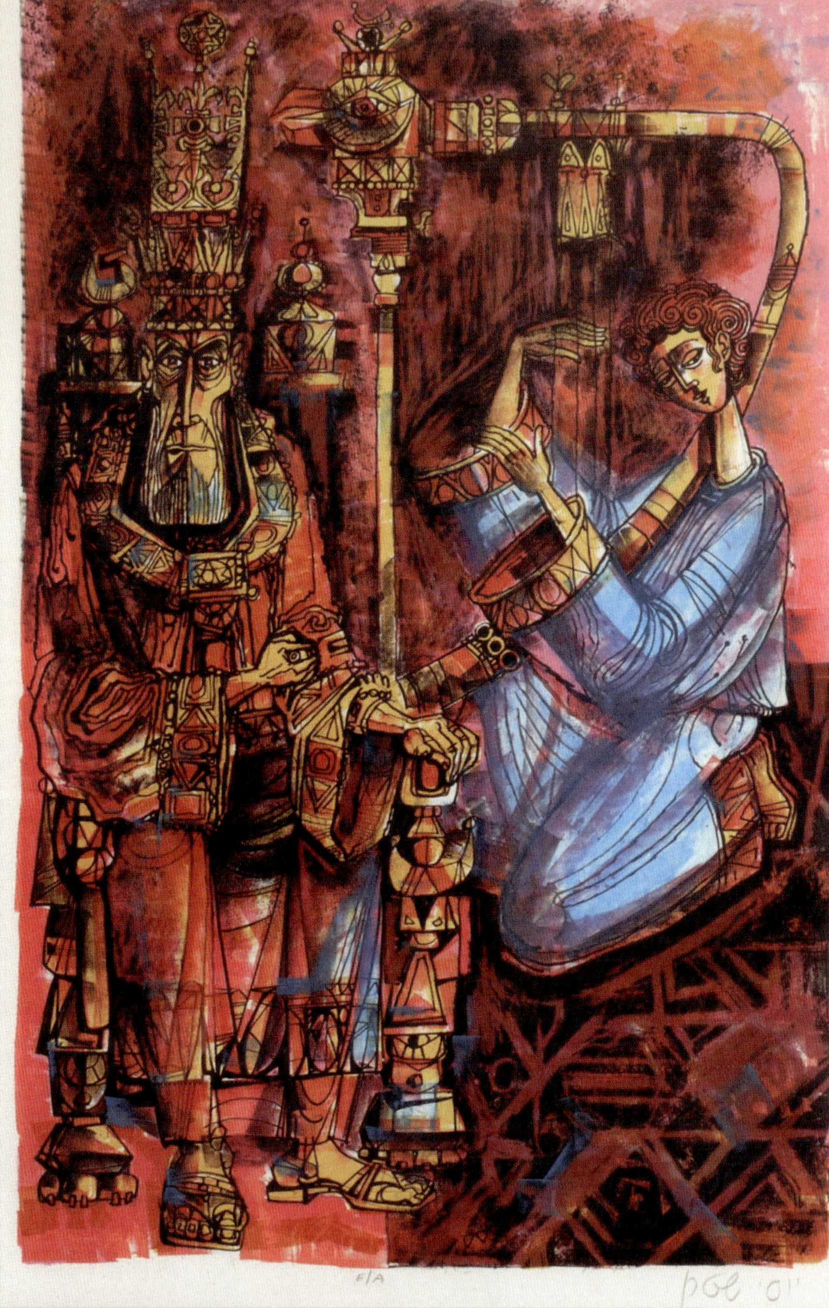

A tense King Saul gazes out from his angular golden throne as a youthful David, robed in blue, plays soothing music on his harp. The color and energy of this 20th century lithograph convey the beginnings of the relationship between the two kings.

SAUL, DAVID, AND THE HARP, 20th century
Lithograph, edition artiste
14 x 22½ in
Loan from Teddy Lachterman

DAVID

One day G-d commanded Samuel to take his horn of sacred oil and go to the house of Jesse, in Bethlehem, because one of his sons would be king after Saul.

Samuel met Jesse's seven sons, and chose Eliab, who was handsome, as Saul's successor "But the Lord said, do not choose him for his face or his stature, but for what is in his heart. So Samuel asked if Jesse had any other sons, and Jesse called David, his youngest, who had been watching the sheep. When David came to Samuel, the Lord said, "Anoint him, for this is he."

It chanced that in these days King Saul was troubled, and could not rest. His servants suggested a musician play soft music upon the harp for him, and when Saul asked for such a musician they answered, "There is a son of Jesse who plays skillfully upon the harp." So David came to the King and whenever the evil spirit fell upon Saul, David played his harp and sang, and Saul was soothed. Saul loved the lad and made him his armor-bearer, and kept him by his side. When Saul died, the elders of Israel came to David and asked him to be king. David became ruler at the age of thirty, and reigned for forty years.

One evening, David was relaxing on the roof of the palace, when he saw a beautiful woman bathing in a neighboring house. She was Bathsheba, the wife of Uriah, the Hittite. A strong temptation possessed David, who sent Uriah into the front lines of battle, where he would surely be killed. David commanded his captain to send his men into a danger zone close to Philistine archers, and Uriah was killed.

After Bathsheba had mourned her husband, David took her for his wife. G-d was not pleased and sent the prophet Nathan, to warn David of the consequences of his actions. "Once there lived in a city two men, one rich and one poor," said Nathan. "The rich man had many flocks, but the poor man had only one lamb, which was the family pet. Now the rich man prepared a Feast, and to save his own flocks, he seized the poor man's beloved lamb. David was outraged, and said, "Such a man deserves to die, for he has shown no pity." Nathan answered, "You are that man, for, though you had many wives, you destroyed Uriah so you could take his only wife." David knew he had sinned, and Nathan told him he would have many tragedies at home because of that sin. Bathsheba soon bore him a child, and it sickened and died. David bore G-d's punishment, sincerely repented and sought forgiveness. G-d then gave David and Bathsheba another child, a son, whom they called Solomon.

The story of David is from the Bible, 1 SAMUEL 16 – 2 SAMUEL 12.

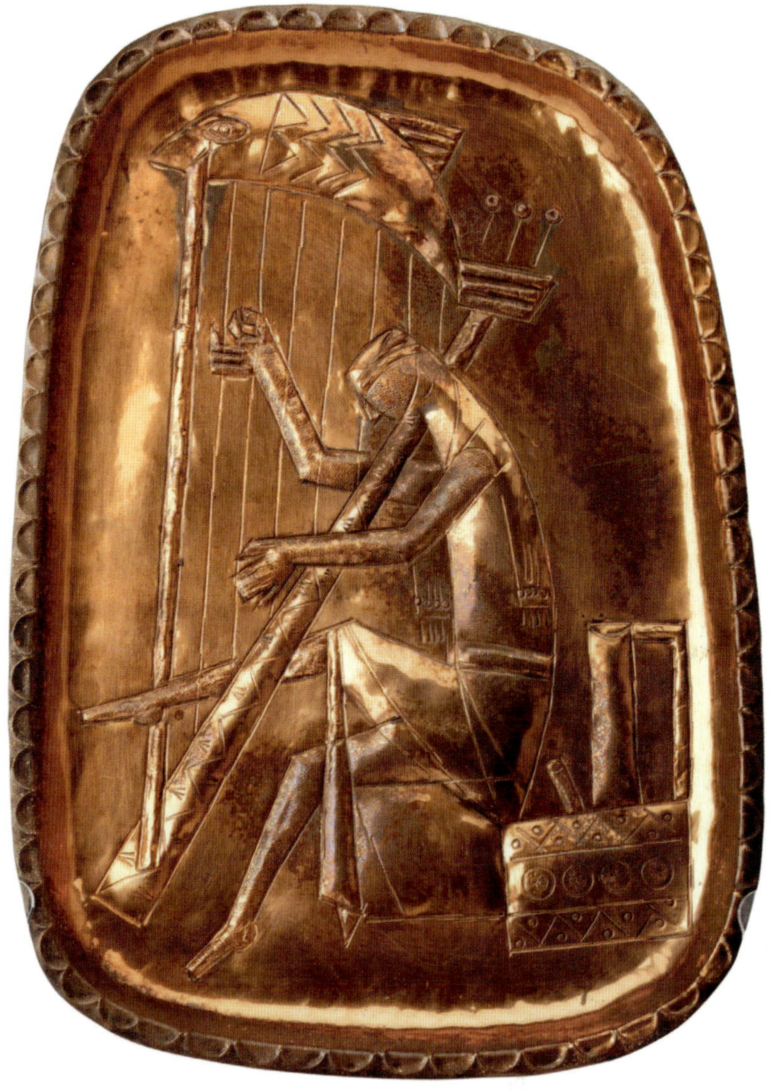

Throughout the near east copper hammered trays for decorative purposes have been made by local craftsmen and sold in the souks for hundreds of years. This asymmetrically shaped tray shows the influences felt by Israeli modernists during the 1950s and 1960s, a time when metal arts companies such as Pal-Bell were turning out modernist designs in metals with biblical themes and for Judaic purposes. This attractive tray pictures the young David at his harp, and was made in Israel for decorative use.

KING DAVID AND THE HARP
Copper hand-embossed tray
Israel, ca. 1955–1965
14 x 11 in.
Loan from Karen and Robert York

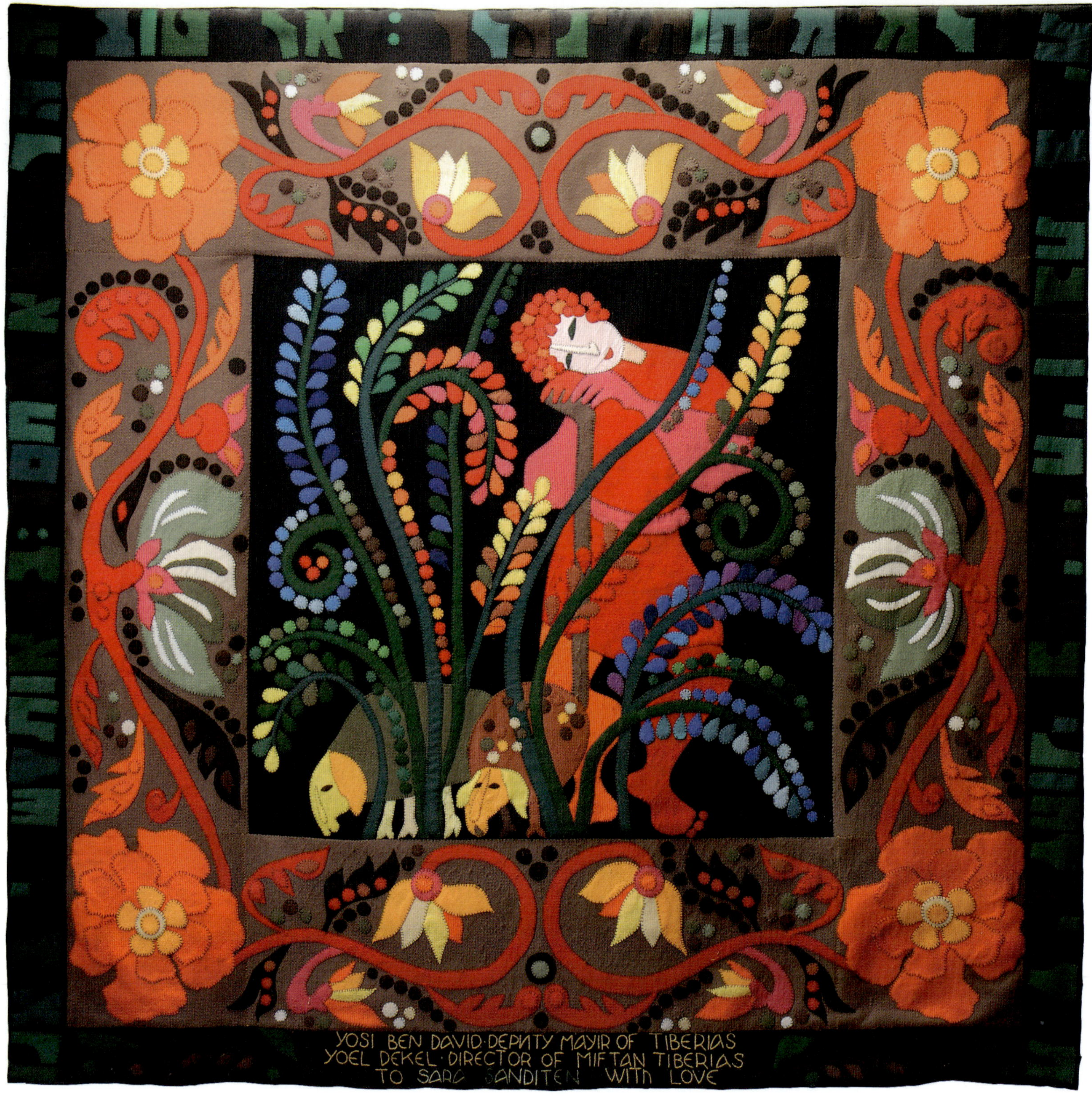

This colorful quilt was created by Julia Krimov, presumably in or near Tiberias Israel. It was presented by Yosi Ben-David, Deputy Mayor of Tiberias and Yoel Dekel, Director of Miftan, Tiberias to Sara Sanditen.

Young David the Shepherd, 20th century
Julia Krimov
Tiberias Quilt, Tiberias, Israel
Wool felt, 70 x 70 in.
Loan from The Flo and Morris Mizel Jewish Community Day School

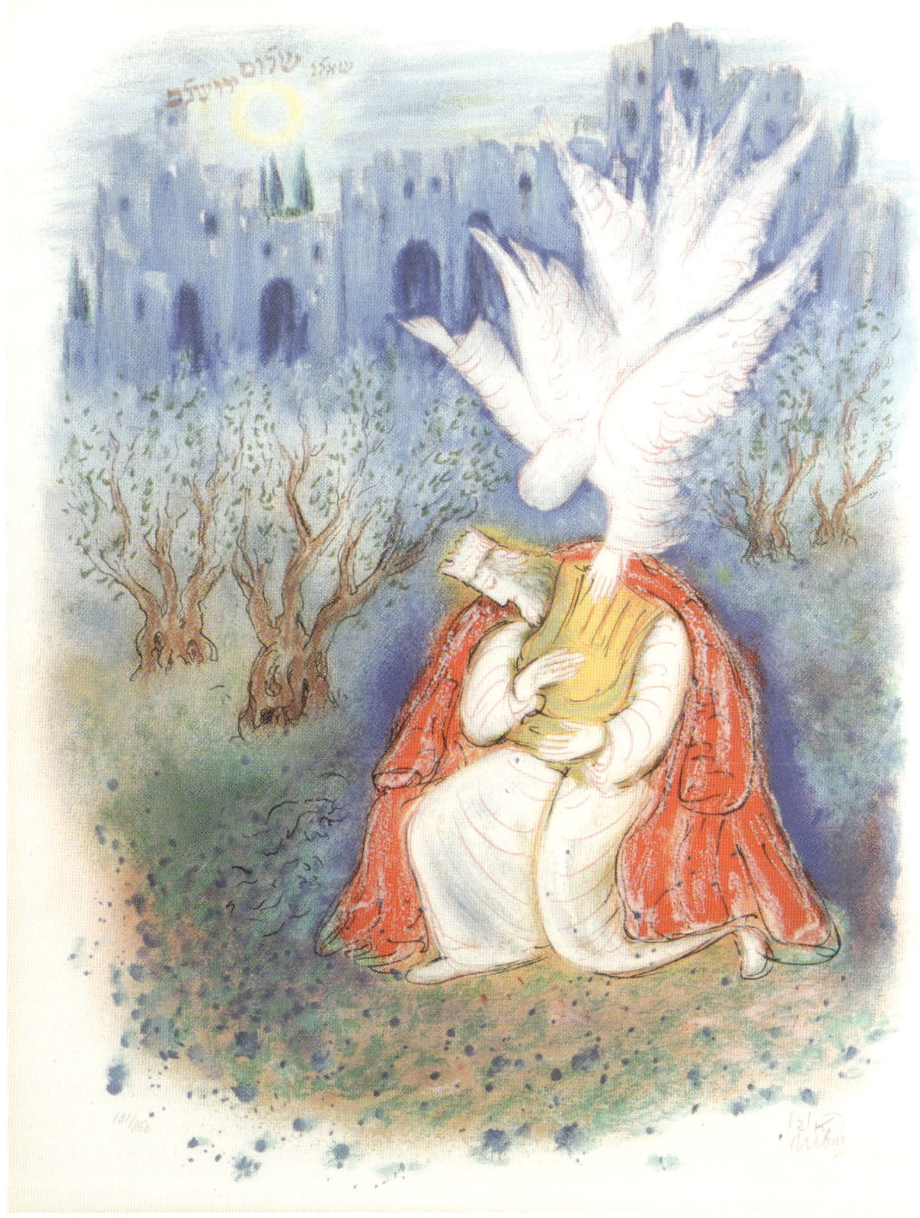

Born in Romania in 1893, as a young man Rubin visited Palestine to paint the ancient sites of Galilee and Judea. He studied painting in Paris at the École des Beaux-Arts, but returned to study briefly at the Bezalel School and then settled in Tel Aviv. Rubin, working to develop an indigenous style of art, began signing his paintings with his name, Rubin, in both Hebrew and English. Rubin's work remained focused on the Palestinian landscape, its folklore, and its population, but included in his search for an art connected to the ancient land of Israel were the recurring Biblical images and themes found in much of his later works. From Abraham to Moses, Rubin illustrated the stories of the Bible in paintings and lithographs. He first exhibited his work in New York, and since then, has exhibited many times in New York, Paris, Los Angeles, London, Venice, Geneva, Tel Aviv, and Jerusalem. Recognized as one of the most significant artists in the history of Israeli art, Rubin was a significant contributor to Israeli artistic culture.

King David, 1972
Reuven Rubin
Israeli, 1893–1974
Lithograph
29 x 23 in.
Loan from Estelle Finer

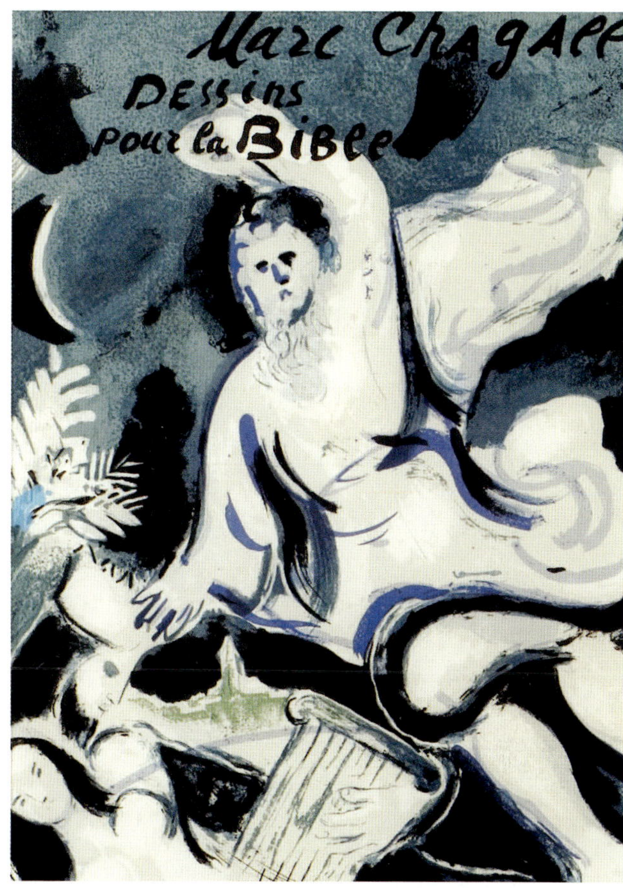

This lithograph depicting David, Bathsheba, and G-d served as the front cover for a special edition of Verve *Drawings for the Bible* in 1960.

In the 1930s Chagall traveled in the Near East, visiting the Holy Land, Syria, and Jerusalem. He was researching themes and local color for his *Drawings for the Bible*, a commission from long-time supporter and art dealer Ambroise Vollard. Chagall's illustrated Bible was finally published in 1956, 17 years after Vollard's death.

Drawings for the Bible, 1960
Marc Chagall
Russian, 1887–1985
Original color lithograph, (M. 230a)
6500 unsigned impressions
10¼ x 14 in.
Loan from Goldie Cash

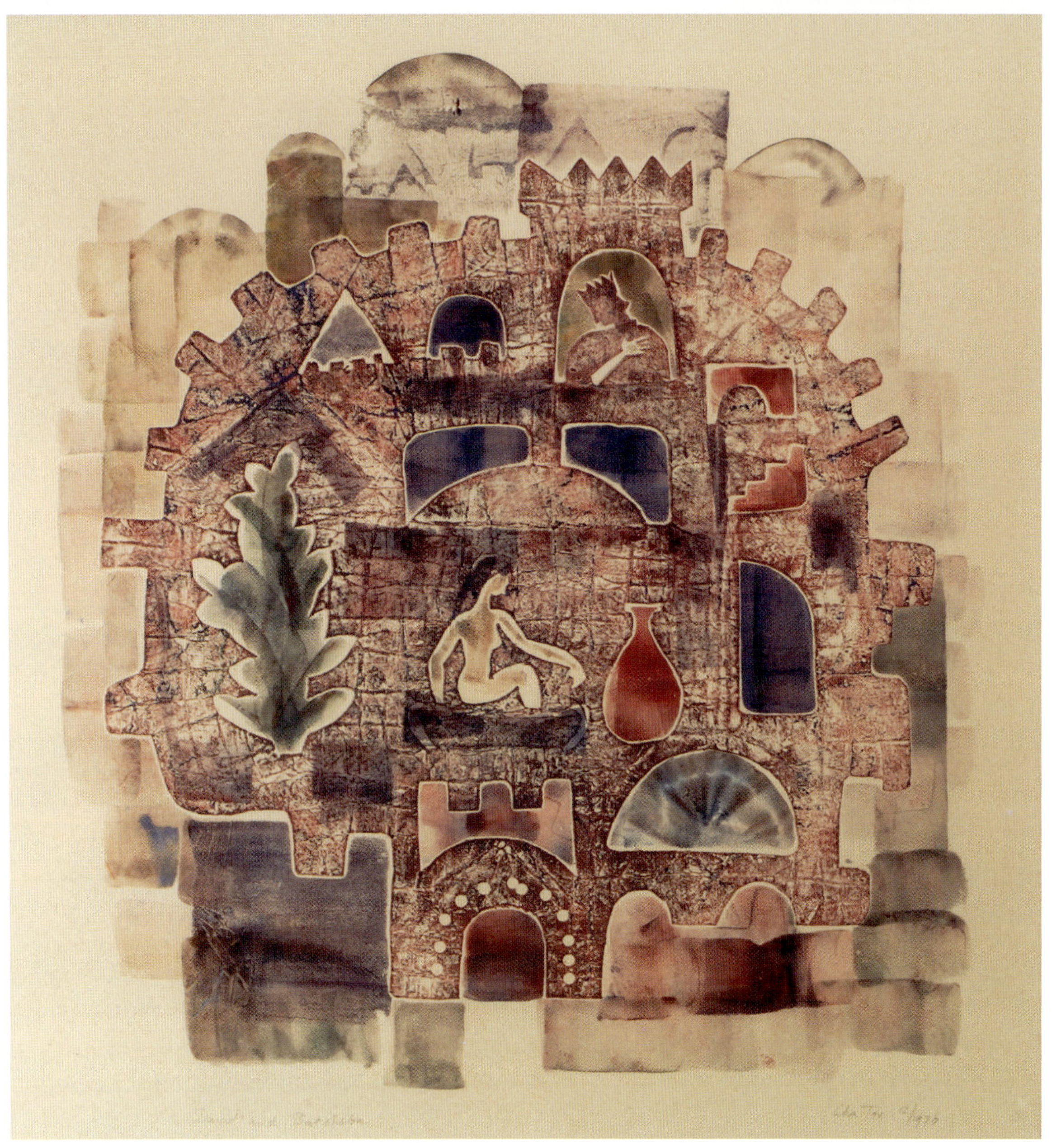

Lika Tov, currently living in Jerusalem, creates distinctive prints with Judaic imagery that illustrate Bible tales: *Creation, the Life of Moses, the Song of Songs,* and others. Her artistic creations are intricate, with cleverly embedded elements that invite discovery time and time again. She is well known in Israel both for her handmade prints, collographs, and illustrations of biblical stories created for Israeli television. Her life and work were featured in an article in *Hadassah Magazine* in 1998.

Tov grew up in the Netherlands and emigrated with her family to Israel in 1963. She met and later married Emanuel Tov, who became a noted biblical scholar and editor of the official Dead Sea Scrolls publication project.

David and Bathsheba, 1976
Lika Tov
Israeli, born Netherlands
Lithograph
29 x 31 in.
Loan from Susan Fenster

OPPOSITE: This work was engraved to illustrate the 1791 edition of *The Whole Genuine and Complete Works of Flavius Josephus, The Learned and Authentic Jewish Historian, Celebrated Warrior*, translated from the original in the Greek language and edited by George Henry Maynard and the Rev. Edward Kimpton. New York: William Durrell, 1792. It is embellished with 60 engraved plates, including two maps and a folding plan of Jerusalem.

This is one of the great illustrated books printed in the new United States of America during the 18th century. Almost by necessity, the roster of "American artists" responsible for these large engravings forms a Who's Who of early American craftsmen. Seven of these plates were executed by Alexander Andersen, who is generally considered America's first professional book illustrator. There are fourteen plates each by Amos Doolittle and Cornelius Thiebout. William Rollinson made six, J. Allen five, and two are the work of Benjamin Tanner.

Prophet Nathan & King David
USA, ca. 1750
Copperplate engraving, 10 x 8 in.
73.4

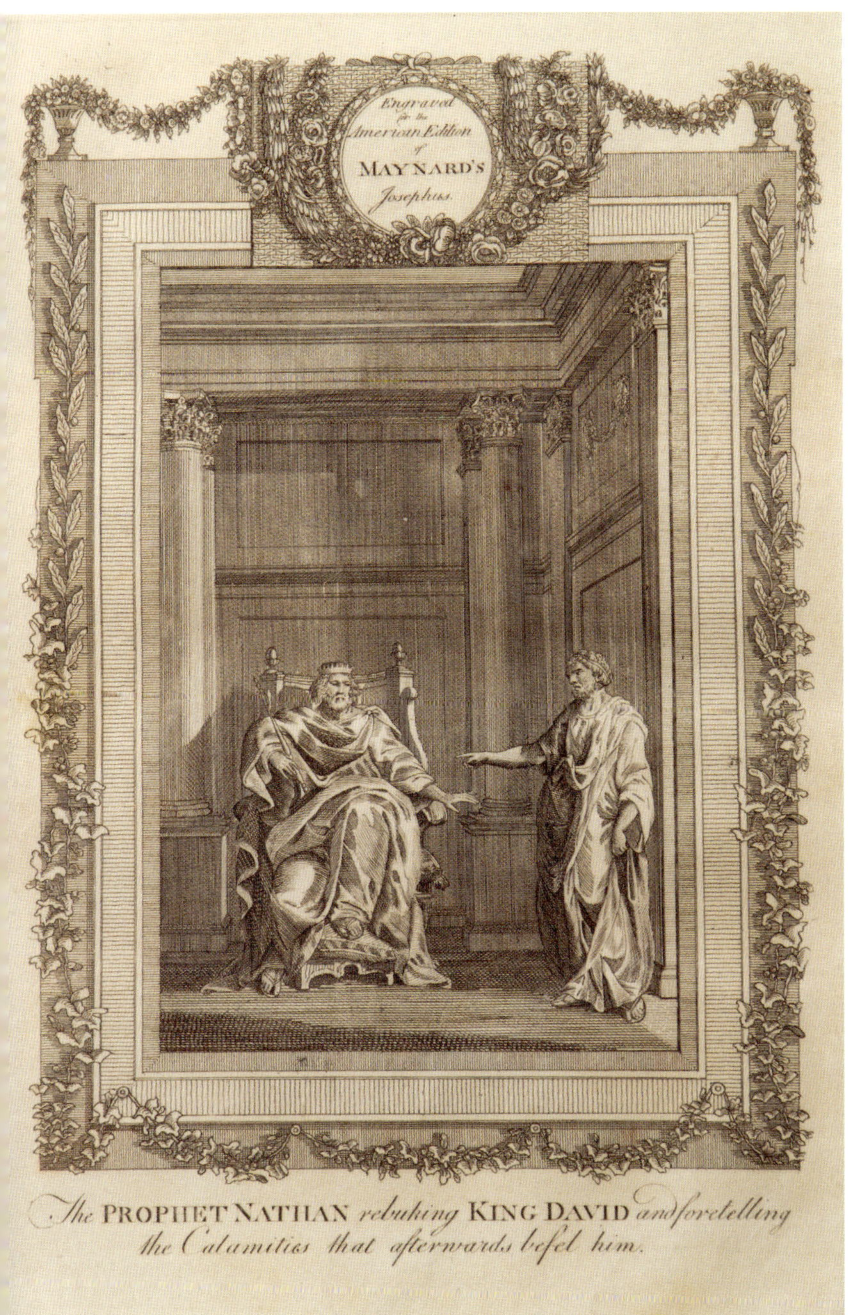

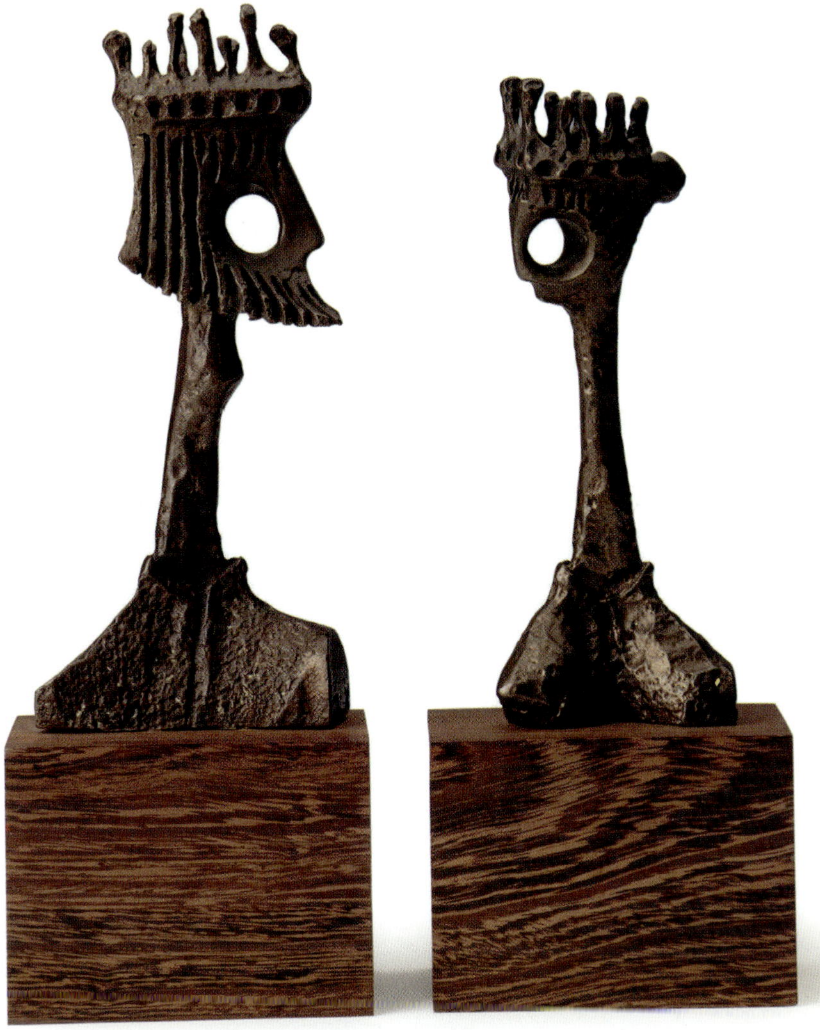

Born in Afghanistan as a son of a Kabbalist rabbi, Aharon Bezalel grew up on Bible stories. This small bronze, created in the 1970s, is an excellent example of Bezalel's move from wood to bronze sculpture. In this piece, he retained the simple subject, an episode from the story of a biblical character, while this work shows his trend toward related couples, begun in the late 1960s. The influence of ancient archeological figures is evident in the eye slits and two-dimensionality of these figures, while the tension and interdependence between two figures reveals the progression of Bezalel's sculptural language.

David and Bathsheba,
1971–1972
Aharon Bezalel
Israeli, born Afghanistan 1926
Bronze
9¼ x 3½ x 2 3/8 in.
Loan from Susan Fenster

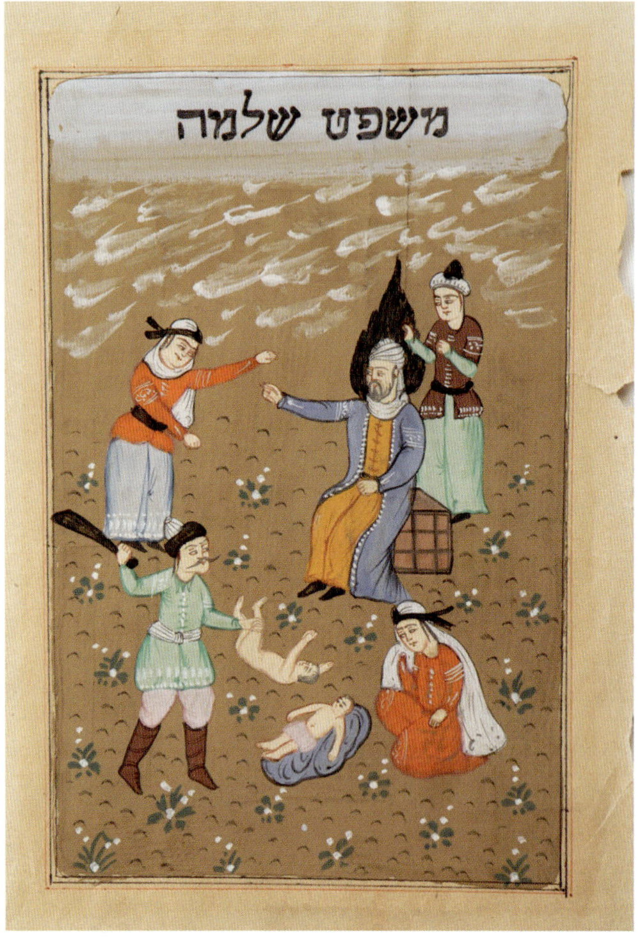

Persian miniature paintings are traditionally created to illustrate great literature, both religious and secular. This painting illustrates the Decision of Solomon at the moment when he told his servant to cut the child in two.

This illustration, from a Persian Bible study book, shows how Hebrew art follows the traditions of the area in which the object or painting is produced. Jews have resided in Persia since the dawn of the first Persian Empire, and biblical heroes such as Moses and Joseph have long been a part of Persian literature. It is believed that Persian translations of the Bible were achieved in cooperation with Jewish scholars, from the first translations in the sixteenth century.

The style of illuminated Hebrew manuscripts from the late 9th century to the present followed that of the host country in which Jews resided, so that the earliest illustrations from Muslim countries resembled Koran illumination. In the Middle East, manuscript illumination was a high art, and the hand-decorated book was appreciated into modern times.

Solomon's Decision
Persia, 20th century
Pigment on paper, 13 x 8 ½ in.
Gift of Family in honor of Jeanette Mann's 80th birthday, 76.7

SOLOMON

David's son Solomon became King of Israel after him. Solomon asked G-d for the understanding to govern the people and judge between good and evil.

This prayer of Solomon's greatly pleased G-d, and he gave Solomon a wise and understanding heart surpassing all before him, also that for which Solomon did not ask- both riches and honor and long life. So Solomon grew rich, powerful, and reigned for many years with justice and mercy and became, as G-d had promised, the wisest king of all times. Solomon held court to decide disputes between his people, and, one day, two women who were quarreling about a child were brought there. One woman said the child was hers, and that the other woman, who was her roommate, stole it after her child died. Then the other woman cried that the baby was hers and the other woman's child had died. They both fought for the child until King Solomon said "Fetch me a sword!" Then Solomon told servant to cut the child in half and give half to each woman. The first woman stopped him and offered to give up the child. But the other woman said to go ahead and cut the child in half. Solomon knew who the real mother was, the first woman, for she could not bear to see the child killed, so he gave her the child. And all the people saw that the wisdom of G-d was in Solomon.

When David was king he wanted to build a great temple on Mount Moriah, but G-d told him to wait, that his son Solomon would be the one to build the temple. In the fourth year of his reign, King Solomon began the project. Slowly it rose on Mount Moriah, where in years past G-d had appeared to David. It took thirteen years to complete, and when it was finished Solomon commanded the priests to place the ark with its two tablets of stone within the inner room of the temple, and Solomon prayed that G-d would hear the prayer of all who prayed for forgiveness there.

King Solomon was famed throughout the region for his great wisdom and judgment, his writing, his treasures from all over the world, his beautiful palaces, his ivory throne, his golden drinking cups, and his thousands of chariots and horsemen.

The Queen of Sheba came to Jerusalem with a great train of camels, laden with gifts, to visit with King Solomon. The Queen asked many hard questions throughout many days, and Solomon answered her wisely. The Queen of Sheba listened to his wisdom, and beheld all of his treasures, and she said, "I did not believe the tales that I heard of your Kingdom, but I see now that they are true, and more, for your wisdom and your prosperity are truly great." And after giving him many rare gifts, she returned to her own country to ponder the things she had learned.

The story of Solomon is from the Bible, 1 Kings, 3 - 10.

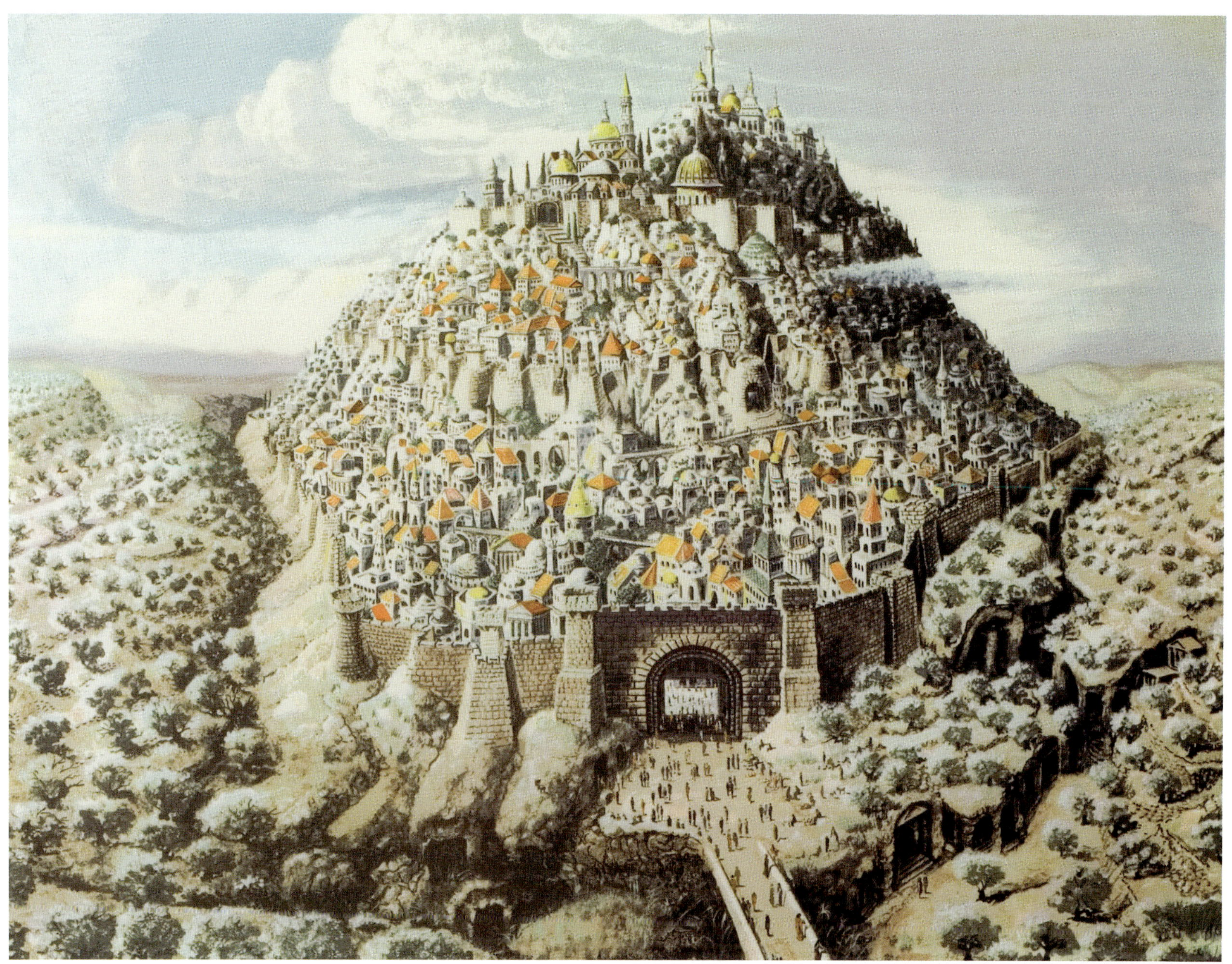

Jerusalem, a symbol for the Jewish people, is the city where David created a capital for the Israelites and where Solomon built the first Temple. Sometimes known as The City of David, its destruction by the Babylonians in 586 BCE only increased strong feelings about, and attachment to the city. The idea of rebuilding the Temple became a unifying force and the second Temple was, like the first, the focus of Jewish religious life.

The earliest habitation that has been identified is a walled settlement on the eastern hill that had a populace of around 2,000 people during the 2nd millennium BCE. This representation of early Jerusalem, which resembles those found in pilgrim's maps of the fourteenth and fifteenth centuries, must be an artist's conception of that settlement.

Unknown title (Biblical Jerusalem)
Unknown artist
Jerusalem, 20th century
Lithograph
Loan from Estelle Finer

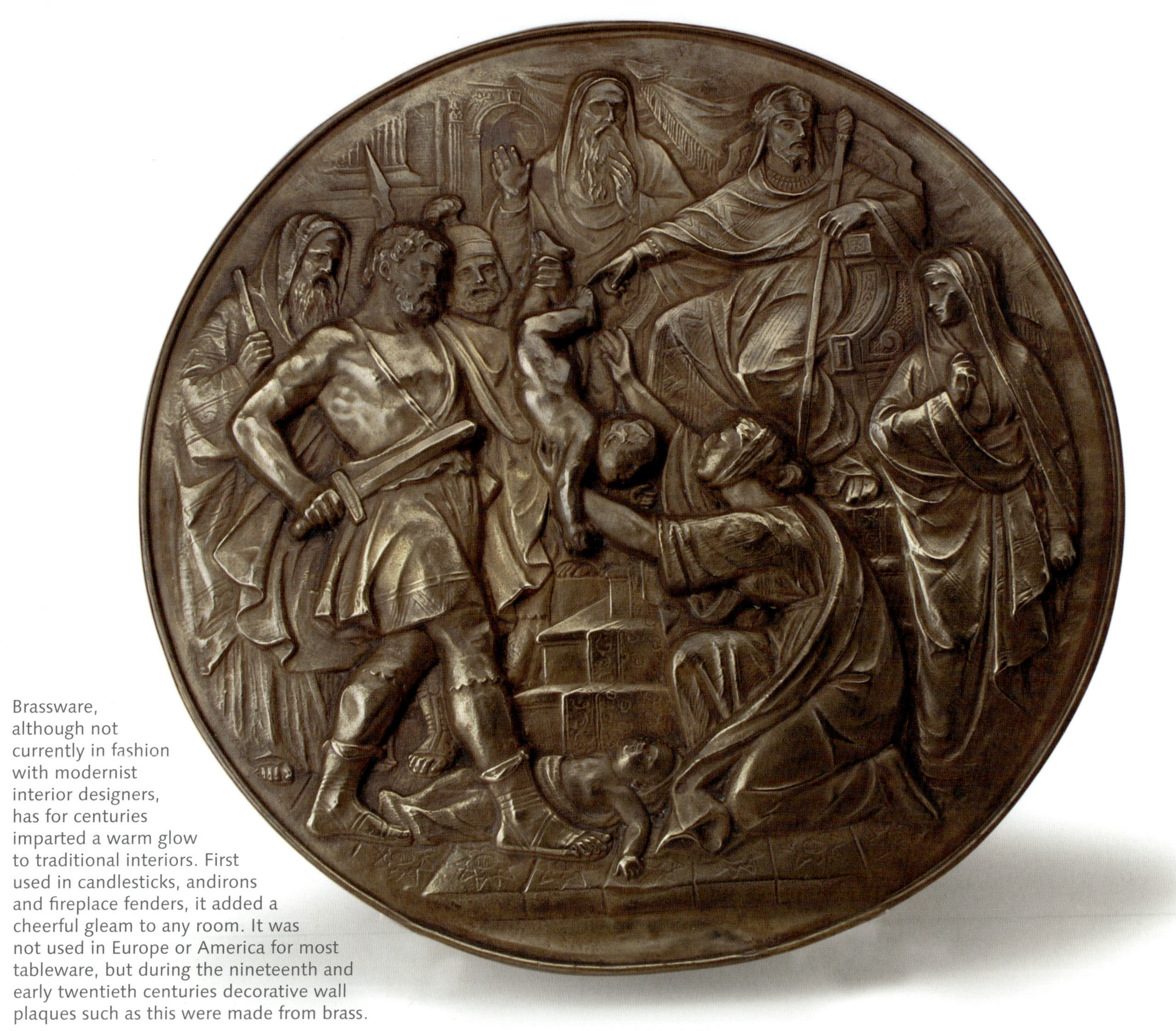

Brassware, although not currently in fashion with modernist interior designers, has for centuries imparted a warm glow to traditional interiors. First used in candlesticks, andirons and fireplace fenders, it added a cheerful gleam to any room. It was not used in Europe or America for most tableware, but during the nineteenth and early twentieth centuries decorative wall plaques such as this were made from brass.

The Judgment of Solomon
England, 19th century
Embossed brass , 22¾ in. diameter
Gift of Mr. and Mrs. Tom C. Stoffer
68.15

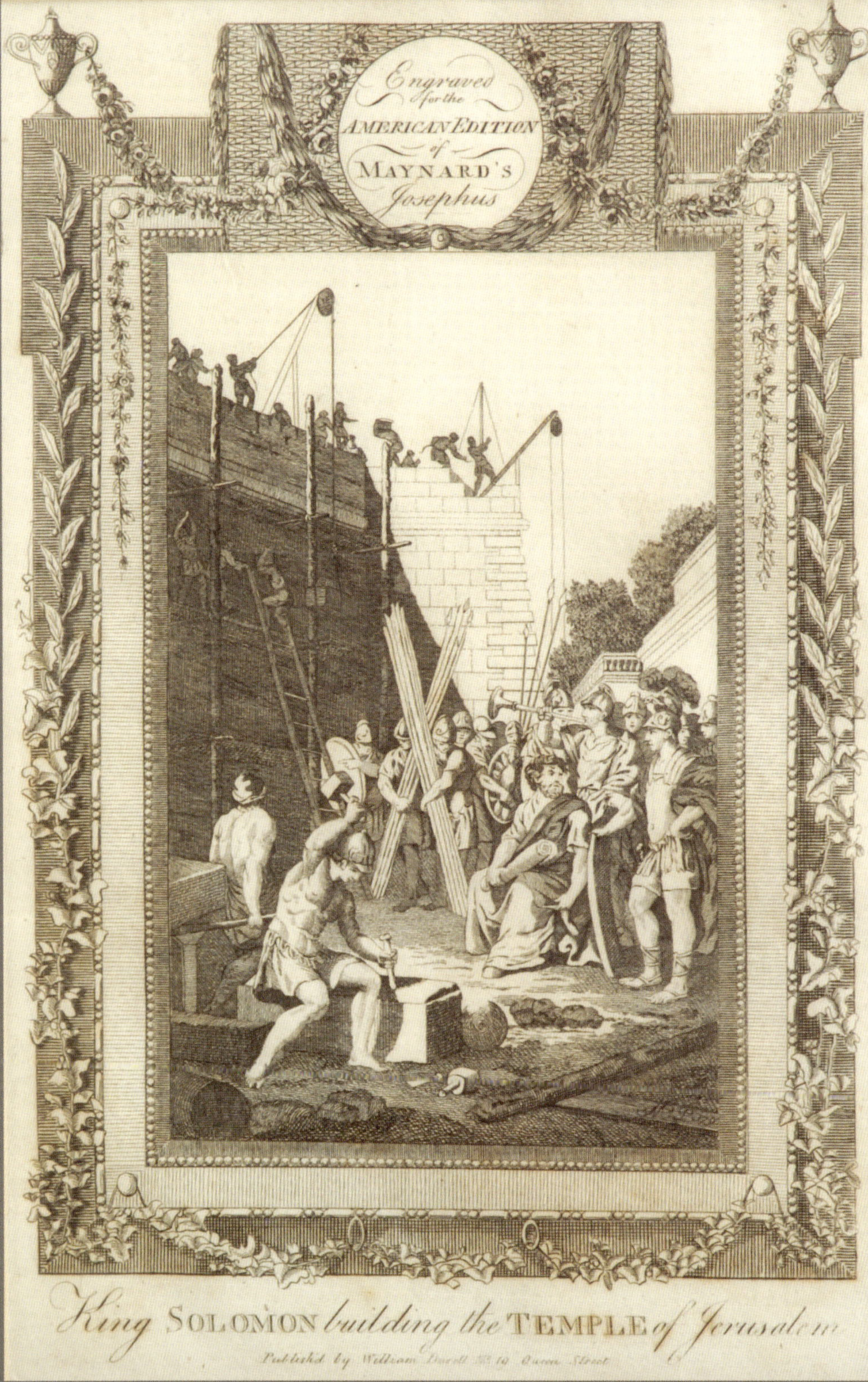

This work was engraved to illustrate the 1791 edition of *The Whole Genuine and Complete Works of Flavius Josephus, The Learned and Authentic Jewish Historian, Celebrated Warrior*, translated from the original in the Greek language and edited by George Henry Maynard and the Rev. Edward Kimpton. New York: William Durrell, 1792. It is embellished with 60 engraved plates, including two maps and a folding plan of Jerusalem.

This is one of the great illustrated books printed in the new United States of America during the 18th century. Almost by necessity, the roster of "American artists" responsible for these large engravings forms a Who's Who of early American craftsmen. Seven of these plates were executed by Alexander Andersen, who is generally considered America's first professional book illustrator. There are fourteen plates each by Amos Doolittle and Cornelius Thiebout. William Rollinson made six, J. Allen five, and two are the work of Benjamin Tanner.

Solomon Building the Temple, 1792
Copperplate engraving, 10 x 8 in.
Presented by Friends in Honor of Julius and Mildred Sanditen
1973.3

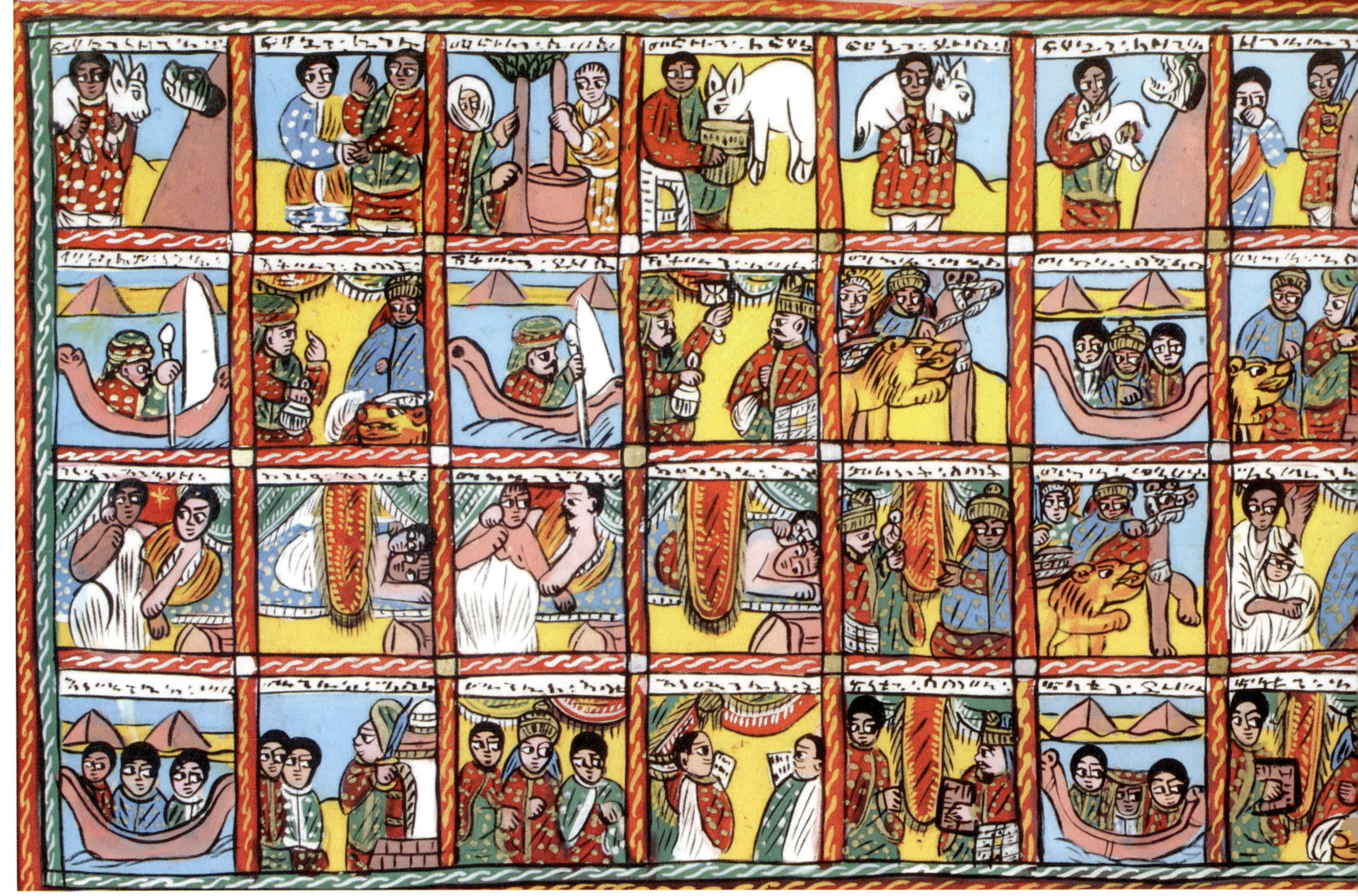

This mid-20th century folk painting was created in Ethiopia. Ethiopian narrative paintings, which are read from left to right and top to bottom, are a visual representation of a literary form, in a sense, like a comic book. For centuries these paintings have been created of the legend of King Solomon and Queen Makeda, also known as the Queen of Sheba. In Ethiopian tradition, the Queen of Sheba visits Solomon in Jerusalem and later gives birth to their son, Menelik, the first king of the Solomonic dynasty of Ethiopia.

These paintings are thought of as stories, and share common elements. Painted in the same style found in Ethiopian Orthodox church frescos, they follow traditional Ethiopian artistic rules: good characters are shown in full face with two eyes visible, while evil people are shown in profile, with one eye visible. The paintings show no perspective, but are drawn in charcoal, outlined in black ink, and filled in with flat colors. Each panel of the story is narrated in Amharic script called the *fidël*.

Story of Solomon & Sheba
Ethiopia, 20th century
Oil on canvas
18 x 48 in.
Gift of Stanley S. Slotkin
68.118

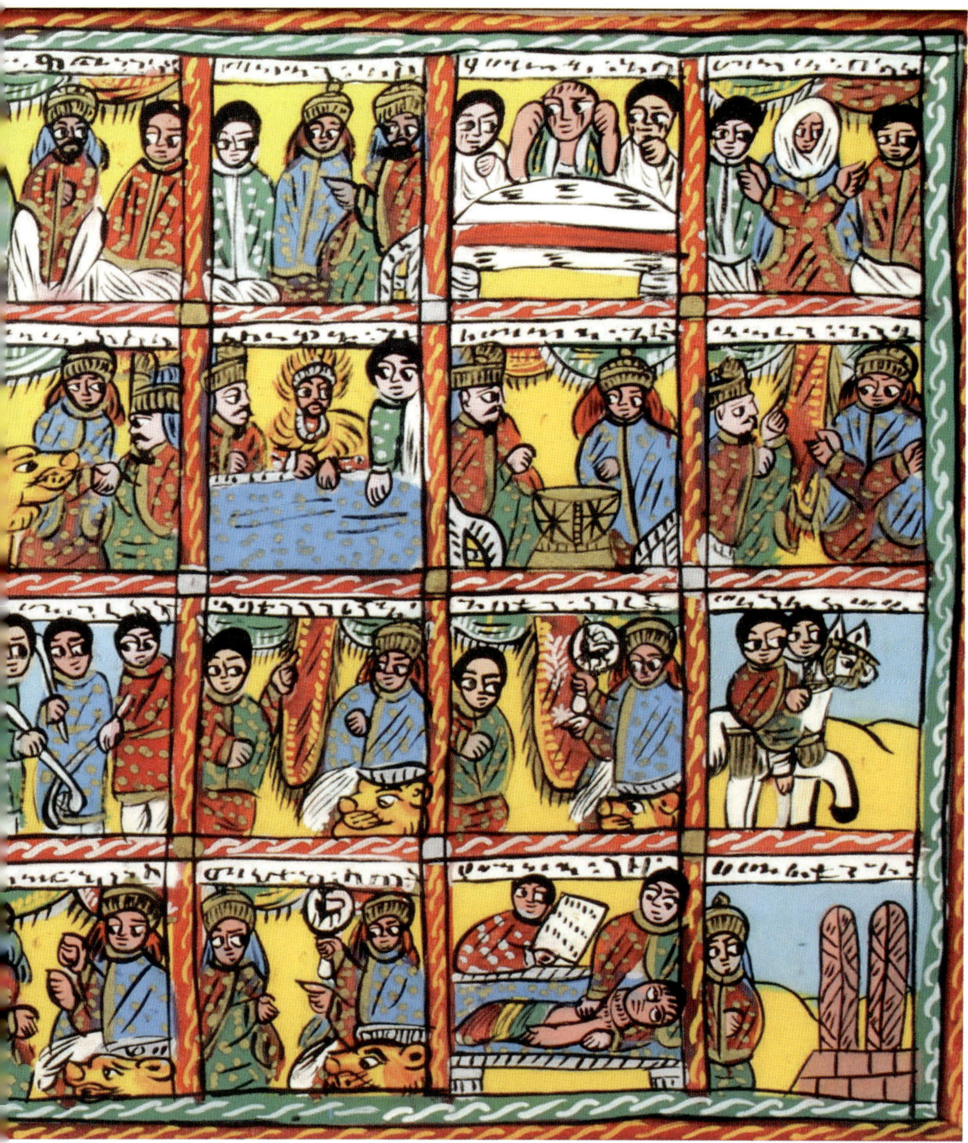

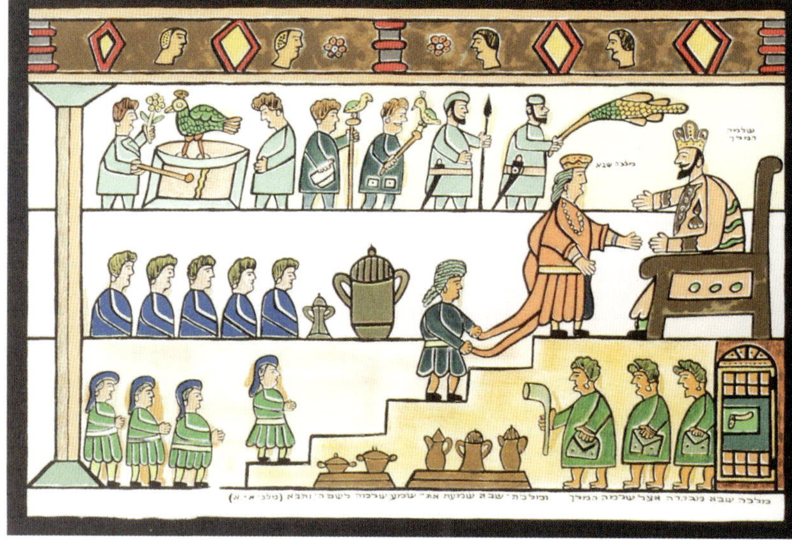

Born in the holy city of Safed in the hills of the Galilee, Shalom of Safed became the sole support of his family after the death of his parents. From his teens on he worked as a watchmaker and silversmith to support his family, then his wife and children. Shalom built colorful wooden toys for his grandchildren, and a friend who loved his work encouraged him to try painting. After much thought, Shalom painted what he knew; stories from the Bible he heard all his life in the holy city. His paintings are pictorial narratives of Bible stories. The form of narrative painting is taken from ancient murals at sites such as the synagogue of Dura-Europos; the action unfolds from right to left, the direction in which Hebrew is read. Shalom of Safed's art, unschooled in academic tradition, is a marriage of his Hassidic literary traditions and the color, light, and landscape of his native land, the Galilee.

Solomon and Sheba
Shalom of Safed
Israeli, 1895-1980
Lithograph
22½ x 27 in.
Loan from Rebecca and Jim Bednar

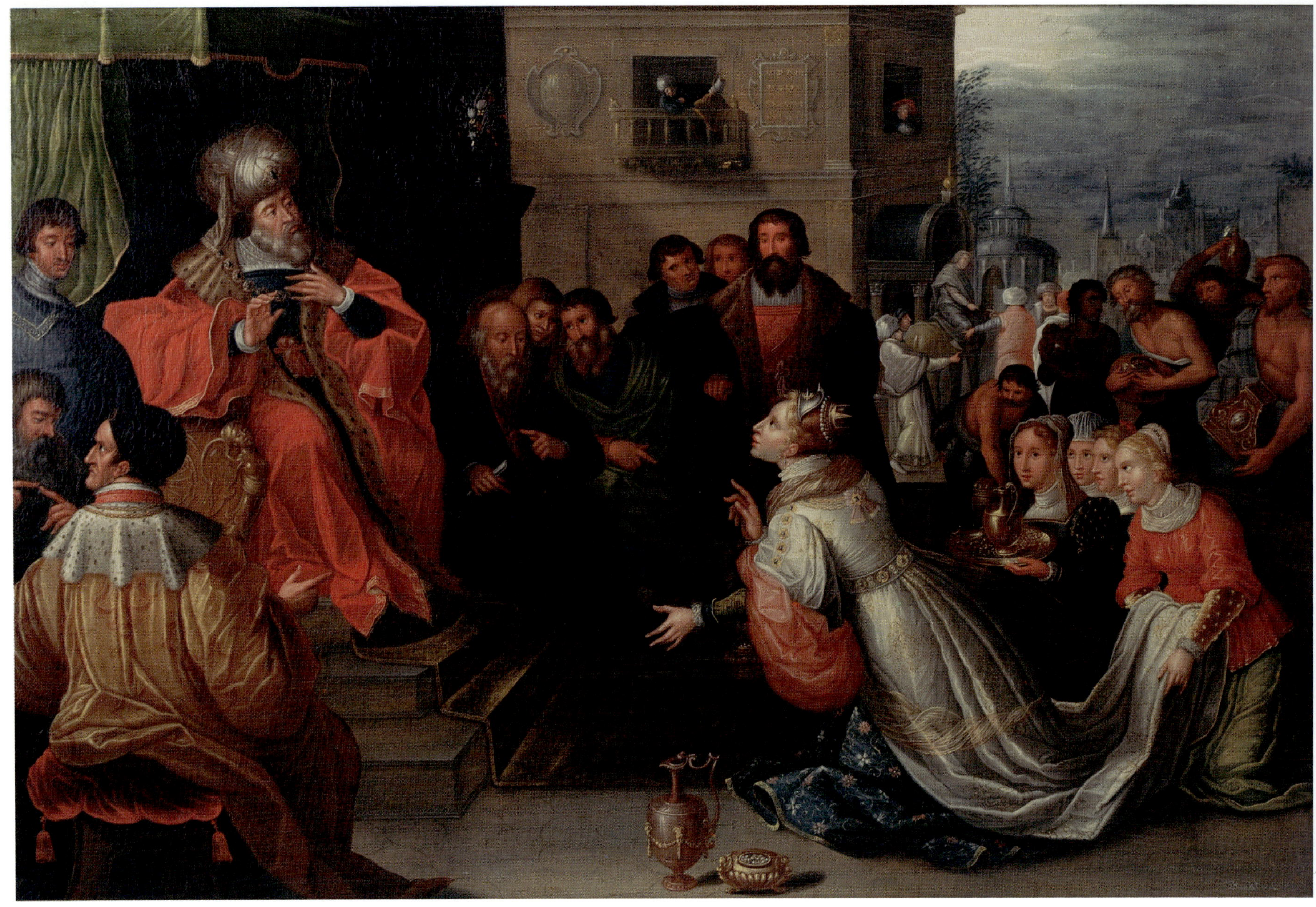

In this finely detailed panel painting by Cologne resident Franz Frantzen, we see the scene unfold as the Queen of Sheba approaches King Solomon at his court in Jerusalem. The scene is a combination of a fantasy landscape of Jerusalem, seen in the background, and courtiers dressed as German Gothic dignitaries. Solomon is orientalized by the addition of a turban, but Sheba and her attendants would be at home in any medieval German court. As was common with European history paintings, it is likely that many faces in this work are patrons of the painter.

Frantzen, a noted German painter, lived and worked in Cologne in the mid-nineteenth century. He specialized in this style of Old Master religious history painting, and unconfirmed information states he was a Jewish artist whose works were destroyed by the Nazis.

The Queen of Sheba Visits Solomon, ca. 1850
Franz Frantzen
German, 1819–1873
Oil on canvas, 23¼ x 32½ in.
Gift of Gerald Richards
75.15

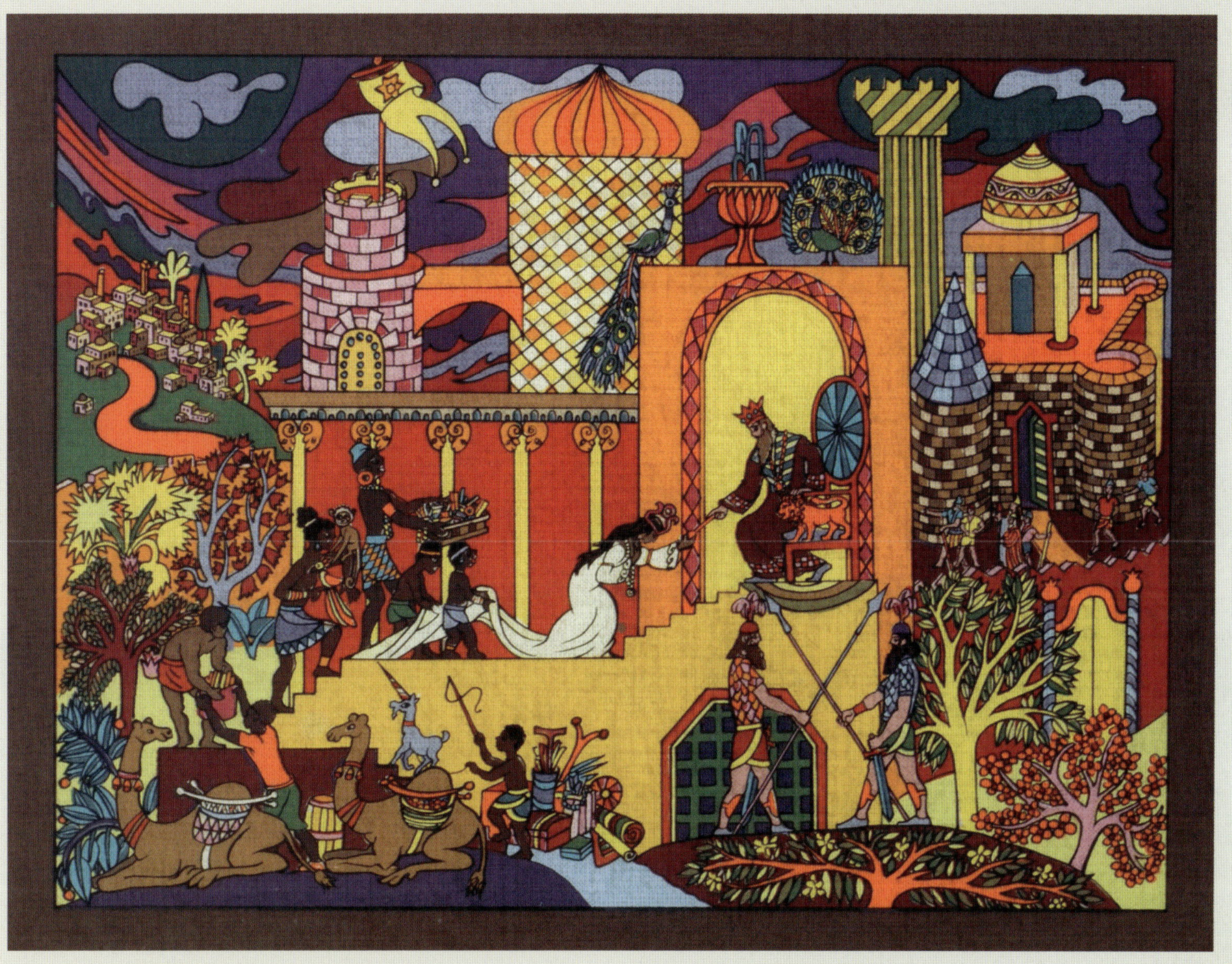

Born just before the Second World War in Lodz, Poland, Shlomo Katz immigrated to Israel in 1945. He studied art at the École de Beaux-Arts in Paris, and later developed his technique of oil painting on a gilded metal surface, evoking both oriental and medieval imagery. To successfully translate this coloration into works on paper, Katz experimented with metallic inks in golden tones. Katz's works are included in the collections of The Wolfson Museum of Judaica, Jerusalem; Biblical Museum, Tel Aviv; The Australian National Gallery, Canberra; Museum of Jewish Art, Paris; The Jewish Museum of Australia, Melbourne; The Jewish Museum of Hungary, Budapest; Judah L. Magnes Museum, Berkeley, and numerous synagogues and private collections throughout the world.

Solomon and Sheba, late 20th century
Shlomo Katz
Israeli, 1937–1992
Lithograph, 26 x 30¼ in.
Loan from Cynthia and Yohanan Zomer

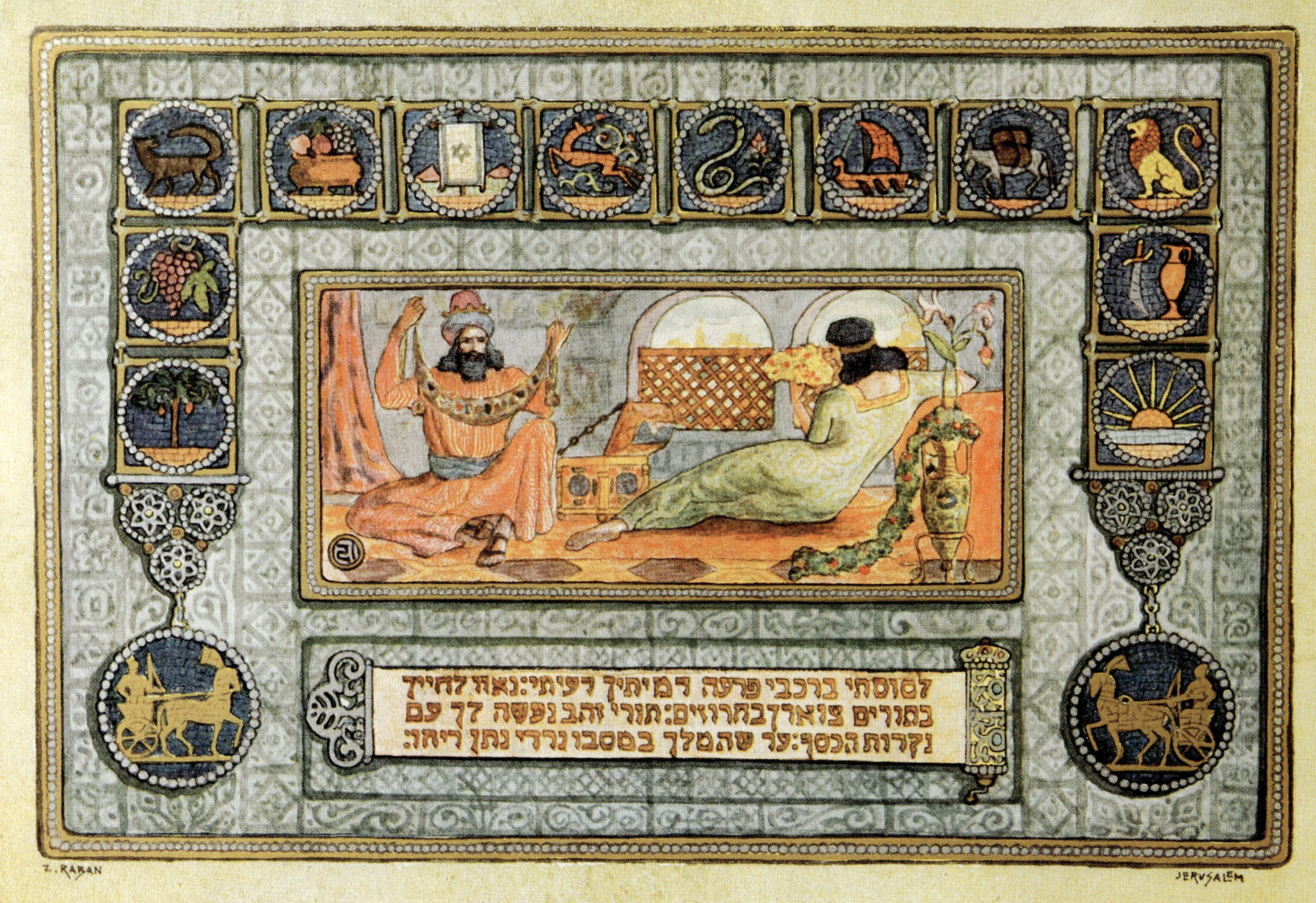

Ze'ev Raban, a native son of Lodz, Poland, studied art in many European academies before he met Boris Schatz in 1911. Schatz founded the Bezalel Academy to encourage a new Jewish art and craft tradition in Palestine, created by combining the best of European and Middle-Eastern arts. Raban was a major influence at the Bezalel, teaching metalwork, painting, and sculpture and then directing the Graphics Press and the Industrial Art Studio. By 1914 the majority of works produced in the Bezalel workshops were designed by Raban. Some of his most important contributions were the illustrations he made for Bezalel books—*The Song of Songs, the Book of Ruth, the Book of Esther, the Book of Job,* and the *Passover Haggadah*. These illustrations represent the pinnacle of the "Bezalel Style" combining Near Eastern art and the Art Nouveau influence of the *Jugendstil*.

Song of Songs
Ze'ev Raban
Israeli, 1890–1970
Bezalel School, Jerusalem, 1923
Book, leather & copper cover
Gift of Carl and Synah Lea Fishbein, 77.38

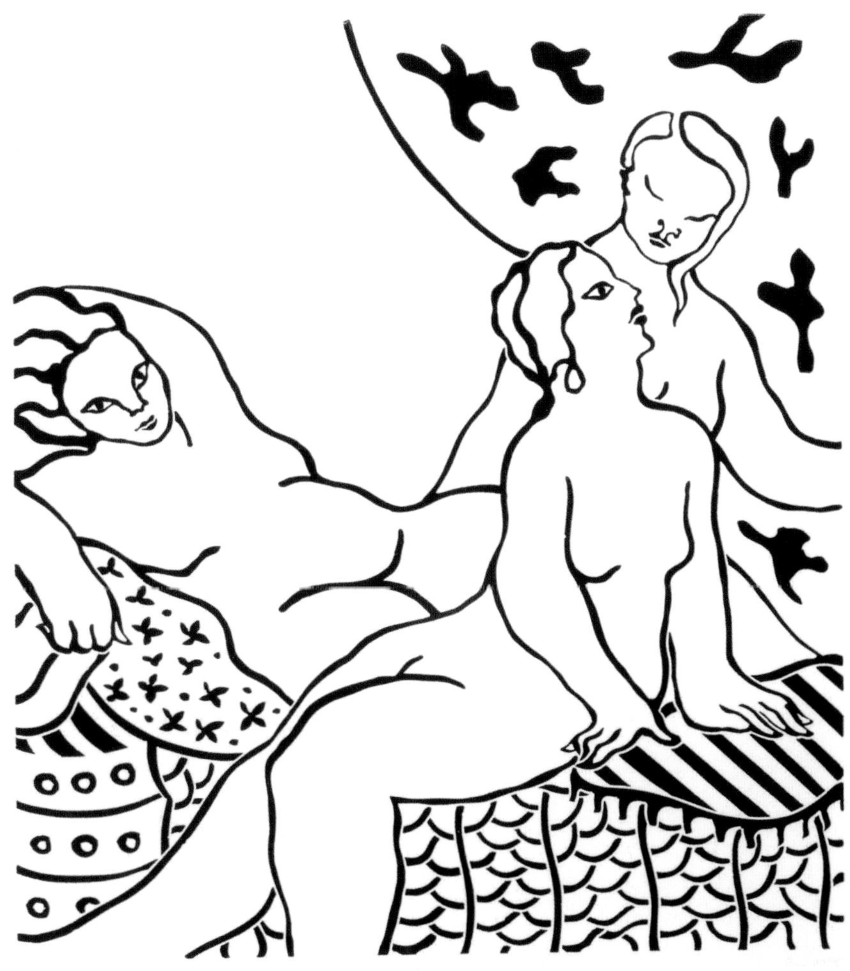

Born in Chicago in 1941, David Bennett studied literature at Harvard University. In 1973, after 10 years as a professional opera singer, he moved to Germany to begin a career in painting, but soon turned to printmaking. Bennett employs the linoleum cutting technique, a technique that enhances his highly decorative style with simplified forms expressed in bright, flat colors. The use of primary colors in his printing allows Bennett to explore ways to achieve greater depth and richness by overprinting and juxtaposing color and form.

"I'm always struck by the fact that Genesis is a fascinating story which runs the entire gamut of human emotions-love, hate, sexual feelings, jealousy, etc.—and does so with the simplicity and succinctness only to be found in the greatest works of art," said Bennett. David Bennett has had solo exhibitions in many cities in Germany and the United States. His works are held in such prestigious collections as the Lenbach Haus Municipal Art Museum, Munich, and the Jewish Museum, New York.

Solomon and His Wives, 1976
David Bennett
American, born 1941
Linoleum cuts, Edition Artiste, 17¼ x 16 in.
Loan from Laurel and Arthur M. Feldman

ISAIAH

One of the greatest of the Old Testament prophets, Isaiah's life spanned the turbulent period for the failing Israelites. Isaiah was the son of Amoz, lived in Jerusalem, married a prophetess, and had two children. He was called to prophesy to the Kingdom of Judah, which was threatened with destruction by Assyria and Egypt, but was spared because of G-d's mercy. Isaiah proclaimed a message of repentance from sin and hopeful expectation of G-d's deliverance in the future.

He announced that there were limits to what any earthly power, even Assyria, could do. A remnant, Isaiah predicted, would be spared to continue G-d's work, and, ultimately, a G-d-sent Deliverer would inaugurate a new age of justice and peace. Isaiah said, "And he shall judge among the nations, and shall rebuke many people; and they shall beat their swords into plowshares, and their spears into pruning hooks: nation shall not lift up sword against nation, neither shall they learn war anymore."

The story of Isaiah is from the Bible, ISAIAH 1 – 66.

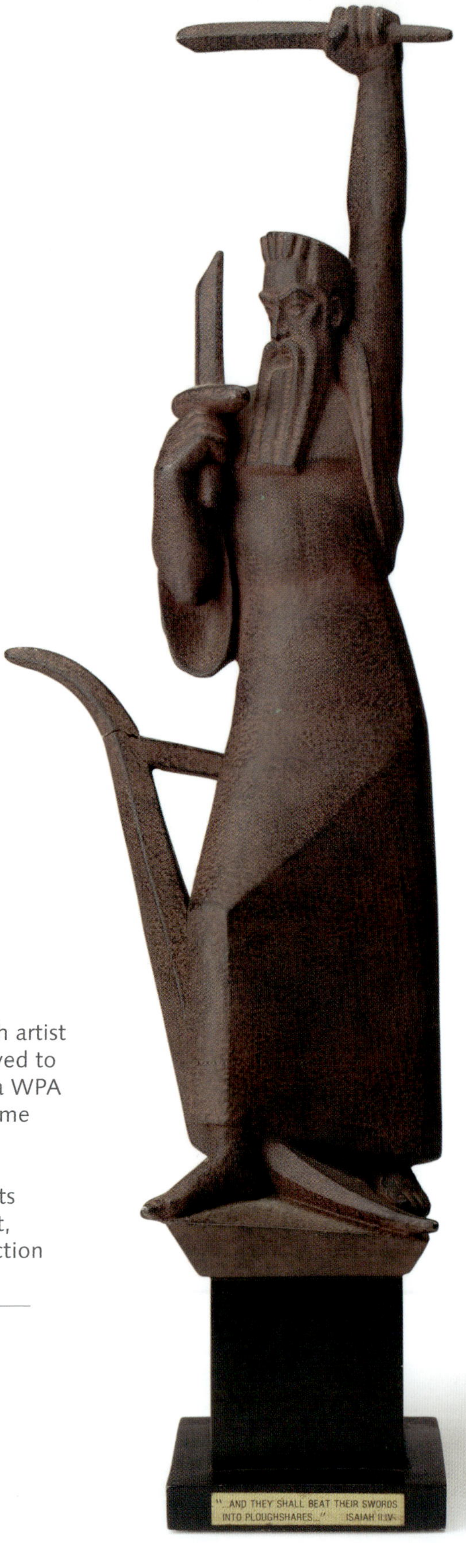

Moissaye Marans, a Romanian-American sculptor, was a Jewish artist who specialized in religious subjects. Born in Romania, he moved to the United States and settled in New York City. He worked as a WPA artist and won several prizes for his paintings but did not become widely known.

Alva Studios, a company in New York City, began to create reproductions of museum-owned sculpture in the 1950s. Artists at Alva Studios, working with the Metropolitan Museum of Art, The Smithsonian, and the Louvre, hand-finished each reproduction casting to match the material of the original sculpture.

ISAIAH, 1970
Moissaye Marans
Romanian-American, 1902–1977
Sculpture
Alva Museum Replicas, Inc.
24¼ x 7¾ x 5 in.
Loan from Susan Fenster

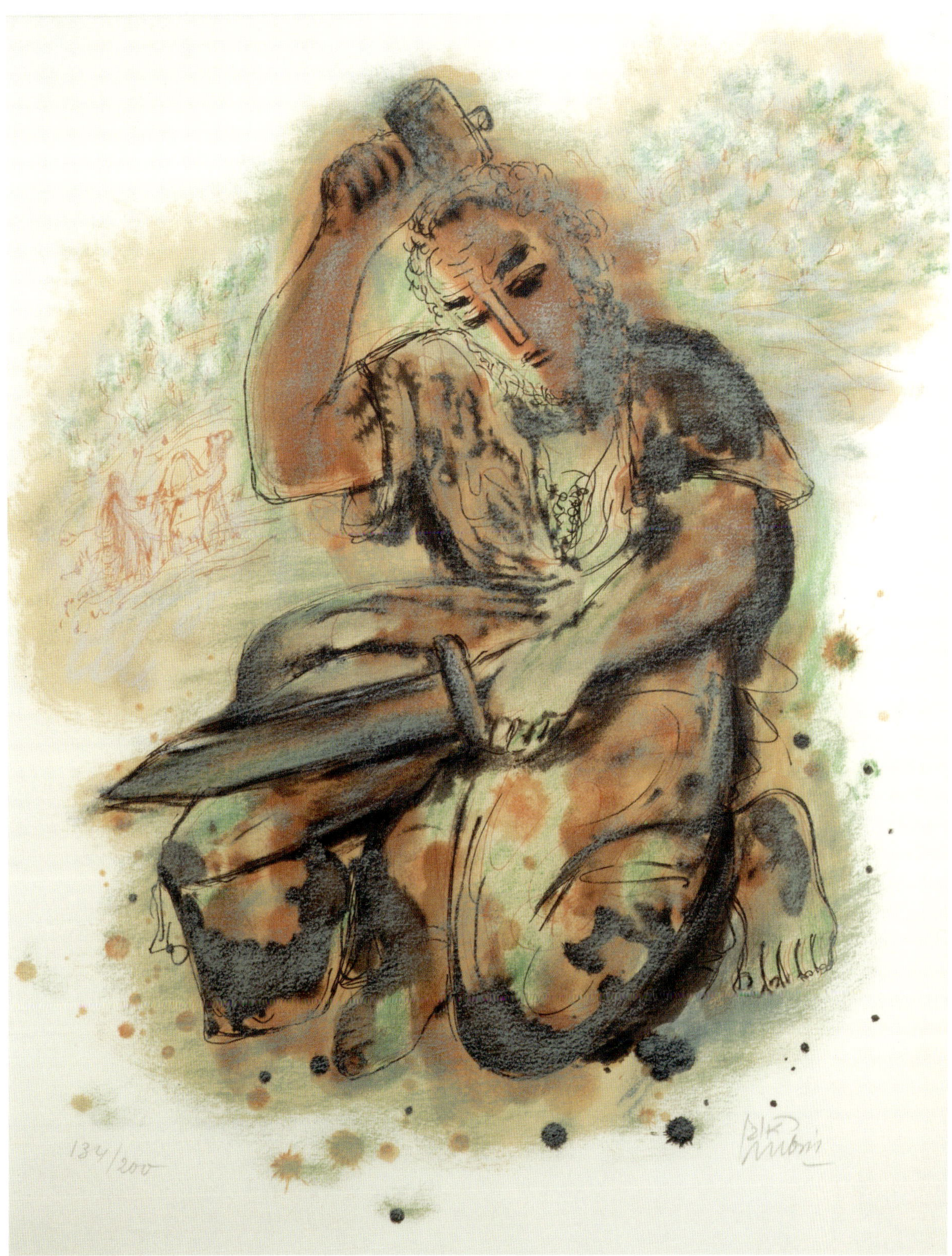

This 1973 original portfolio of *The Prophets* included a set of 12 lithographs signed and numbered IV/LXII by the artist in pencil, in an original red satin cover. Text was written by Dr. Haim Gamzu, Director of the Tel Aviv Museum. The ten prophets illustrated are: Moses, Joel, Elijah, Ezekiel, Jonah, Jeremiah, Zechariah, Isaiah, Micah, and Amos. "The prophets Isaiah and Jeremiah were given 'preferential treatment,' and Rubin allowed them two lithographs each, whereas he allowed only one for each of the other prophets," (Dr. Haim Gamzu, Director of the Tel Aviv Museum).

Isaiah, 1973
Reuven Rubin
Israeli, 1893–1974
Lithograph from *The Prophets Suite*, 134/200, 26 x 20 in.
Gift of Leona Glazer
2000.12.2

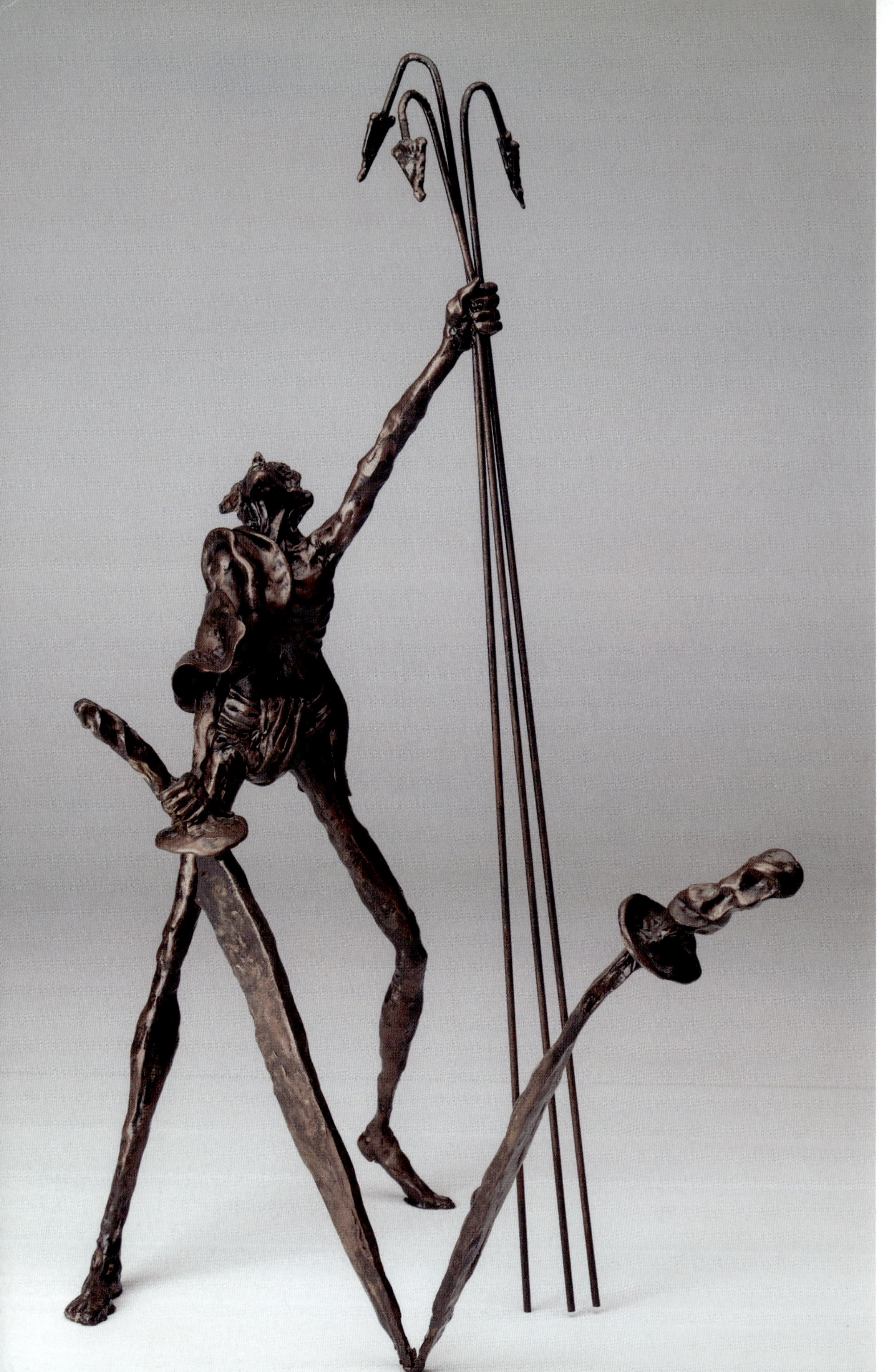

A multi-media artist and native of Washington, D.C., Phillip Ratner has spent many years working in sculpture, painting, etched glass, tapestry, drawing and the graphic arts. In 1984, he opened The Israel Bible Museum in Safad, Israel. Ratner also spent time in Israel using sculpture, painting and graphics to design more than 250 works of art relating to the Hebrew Bible. Ratner has degrees from Pratt Institute and American University, and for 23 years taught in Washington, D.C. area public schools. He continually builds his reputation as an international artist. His work is included in the permanent collections of the Smithsonian, the United States Supreme Court, the Library of Congress, the White House, The Statue of Liberty and Ellis Island.

Isaiah, Swords and Ploughshares, 20th century
Phillip Ratner
American, born 1938
Bronze
Loan from Estelle Finer

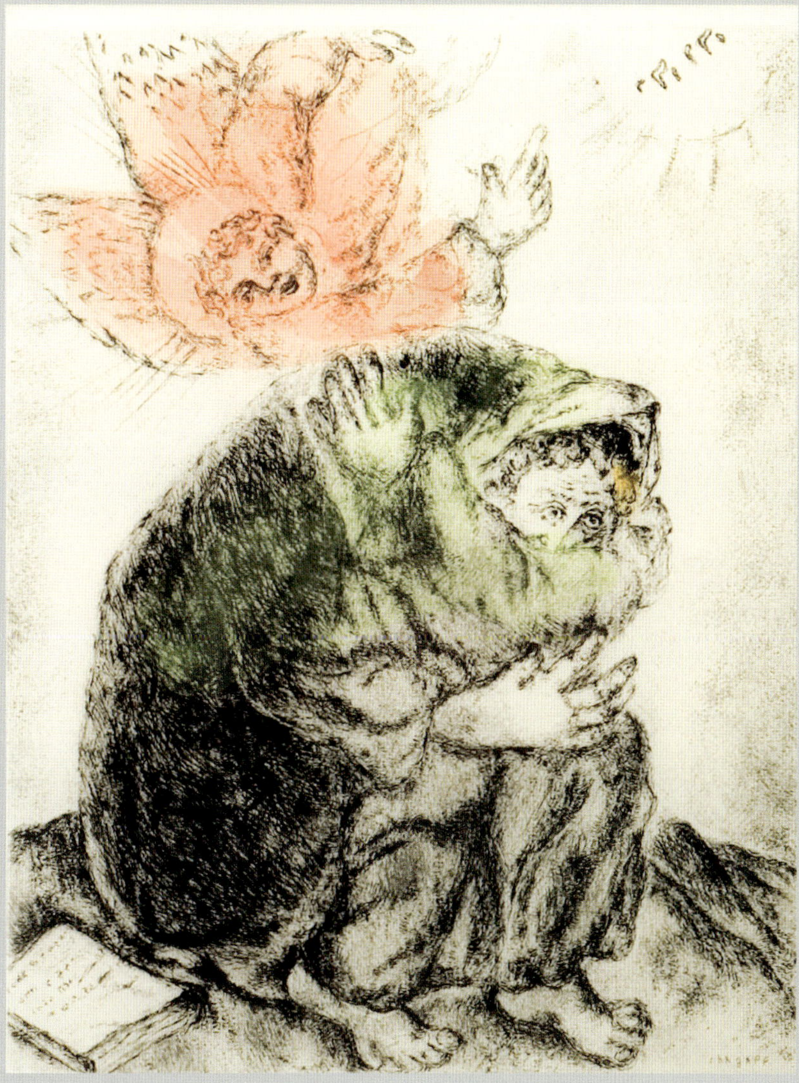

One of a series of 100 signed and numbered hand-colored proofs completed in the 1950s for the edition of 106 *Etchings from the Bible*; this image was included in the 1970 *Bibliotheque Nationale* show of Chagall's graphic works.

Marc Chagall, a Russian painter, printmaker, and stained-glass artist, was born in the ghetto of the village of Vitebsk, Russia, and grew up in the Jewish shtetl that would later provide imagery for many of his paintings. He persuaded his parents to let him study art, which eventually led him to St. Petersburg and Paris. Joining other expatriate artists of The School of Paris, Chagall developed his personal vision, influenced by the shtetl and modernized by Cubism. In the 1930s Chagall traveled in the Near East, visiting the Holy Land, Syria, and Jerusalem. He was researching themes and local color for his *Drawings for the Bible*, a commission from long-time supporter and art dealer Ambrose Vollard. Chagall's illustrated Bible was finally published in 1956, 17 years after Vollard's death.

Isaiah's Prayer, 1952–56
Marc Chagall
Russian, 1887–1985
Hand-colored etching, 9¾ x 12¾ in.
Loan from Bonnie and Gerald Polin

ELIJAH

When Elijah, a prophet of Israel, grew old, and tired from his life's work to stamp out the worship of Baal, he realized he was ready to leave this earth. He chose a successor, Elisha, who had become a close friend. Elisha loved his mentor and did not want to let him go, but Elijah was ready and began to say goodbye to his community. One day Elijah was out walking with Elisha and kept urging him to stay behind. But Elisha would not, knowing that Elijah was going to heaven that day.

As they approached the river Jordon, Elijah took off his cloak and smote the waters with it, and they parted, so that he and Elisha could cross on dry ground.

When they were on the other shore Elisha asked if G-d would allow a double portion of Elijah's spirit to remain with him. Elijah replied that he did not know if it was possible, but if it was, Elisha would be able to see Elijah as he was taken by G-d. Then, a chariot of fire drawn by horses of fire swept down and carried Elijah away in a whirlwind, and he was seen no more. But Elisha had witnessed the departure. Taking up Elijah's cloak which had fallen to the ground, he smote again the waters of the Jordon, and passed safely back to the other shore. And the sons of the Prophets knew that the spirit of Elijah rested with Elisha.

The story of Elijah is from the Bible, 1 KINGS, 12 – 2 KINGS 2.

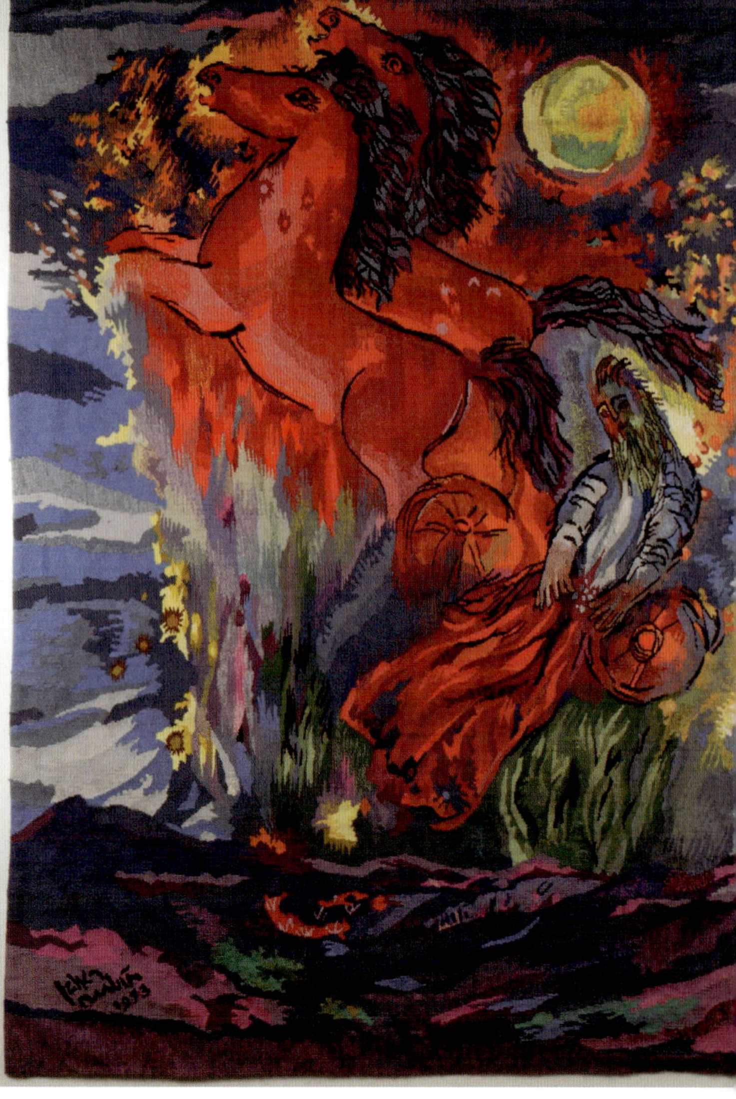

Made under the direction of artist Reuven Rubin by Tapestry of Jerusalem, Ltd, this wool tapestry is signed by the artist and numbered "4". Other Israeli artists such as Marc Chagall and Naftali Bezem supervised tapestries after their designs in the 1960s and 70s, at companies specializing in the construction of artists' tapestries.

ELIJAH IN THE CHARIOT OF FIRE, 1973
Reuven Rubin
Israeli, 1893 – 1974
Wool tapestry
67 ½ x 48 in.
Gift of Mr. & Mrs. Sam Zarrow, Mr. & Mrs. Jack Schlanger, Mr. & Mrs. Jack Satin, Mr. & Mrs. Julius Sanditen, Mr. & Mrs. Donald H. Newman, Mr. & Mrs. Cedric Marks, Mr. & Mrs. S. Carl Mark, Mr. & Mrs. Julius Livingston, Mr. & Mrs. Maurice Gimp, and Mr. & Mrs. A.E. Eichenberg, 1975.3

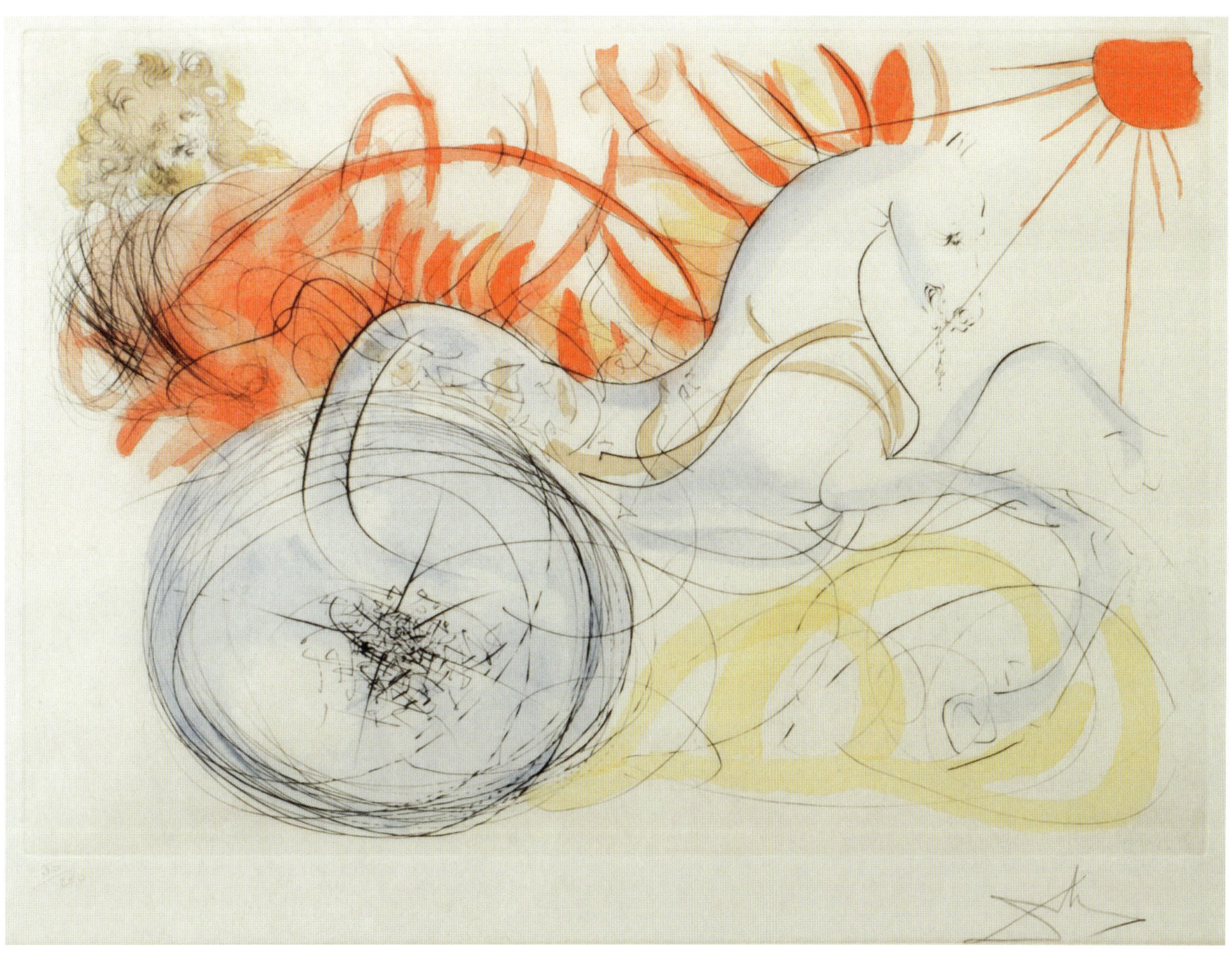

Born in Spain in 1904, Dali attended art schools in Madrid and Barcelona, where he learned to manipulate artistic styles and displayed unusual technical facility as a painter. By the late 1920s, he discovered both Sigmund Freud's writings on the erotic significance of subconscious imagery, and the Paris Surrealists, a group of artists and writers who sought to establish the "greater reality" of man's subconscious over his reason. From 1929 to 1937 he produced the paintings which made him the world's best-known Surrealist artist. By the 1940s Dali had become a master self-promoter. After 1950 Dali painted many works with religious themes, and increased his production of works on paper. Dali prints were created in different techniques: mostly etchings, but also engravings, woodcuts, lithographs and mixed-media. His graphic works were published either as individual sheets or as complete series or as portfolios or as illustrations in limited-edition books.

Elijah and the Chariot, 1975
Salvador Dali
Spanish, 1904–1989
Intaglio print, limited edition of 250
19 x 26 in.
Loan from Barbara and Ronald Winder

This 1973 original portfolio of *The Prophets* included a set of 12 lithographs signed and numbered IV/LXII by the artist in pencil, in an original red satin cover. Text was written by Dr. Haim Gamzu, Director of the Tel Aviv Museum.

The ten prophets illustrated are: Moses, Joel, Elijah, Ezekiel, Jonah, Jeremiah, Zechariah, Isaiah, Micah, and Amos. "The prophets Isaiah and Jeremiah were given 'preferential treatment,' and Rubin allowed them two lithographs each, whereas he allowed only one for each of the other prophets," (Dr. Haim Gamzu, Director of the Tel Aviv Museum).

Jeremiah, 1973
Reuven Rubin
Israeli, 1893–1974
Lithograph from *The Prophets Suite*, 134/200
20 x 26 in.
Gift of Leona Glazer
2000.12.1

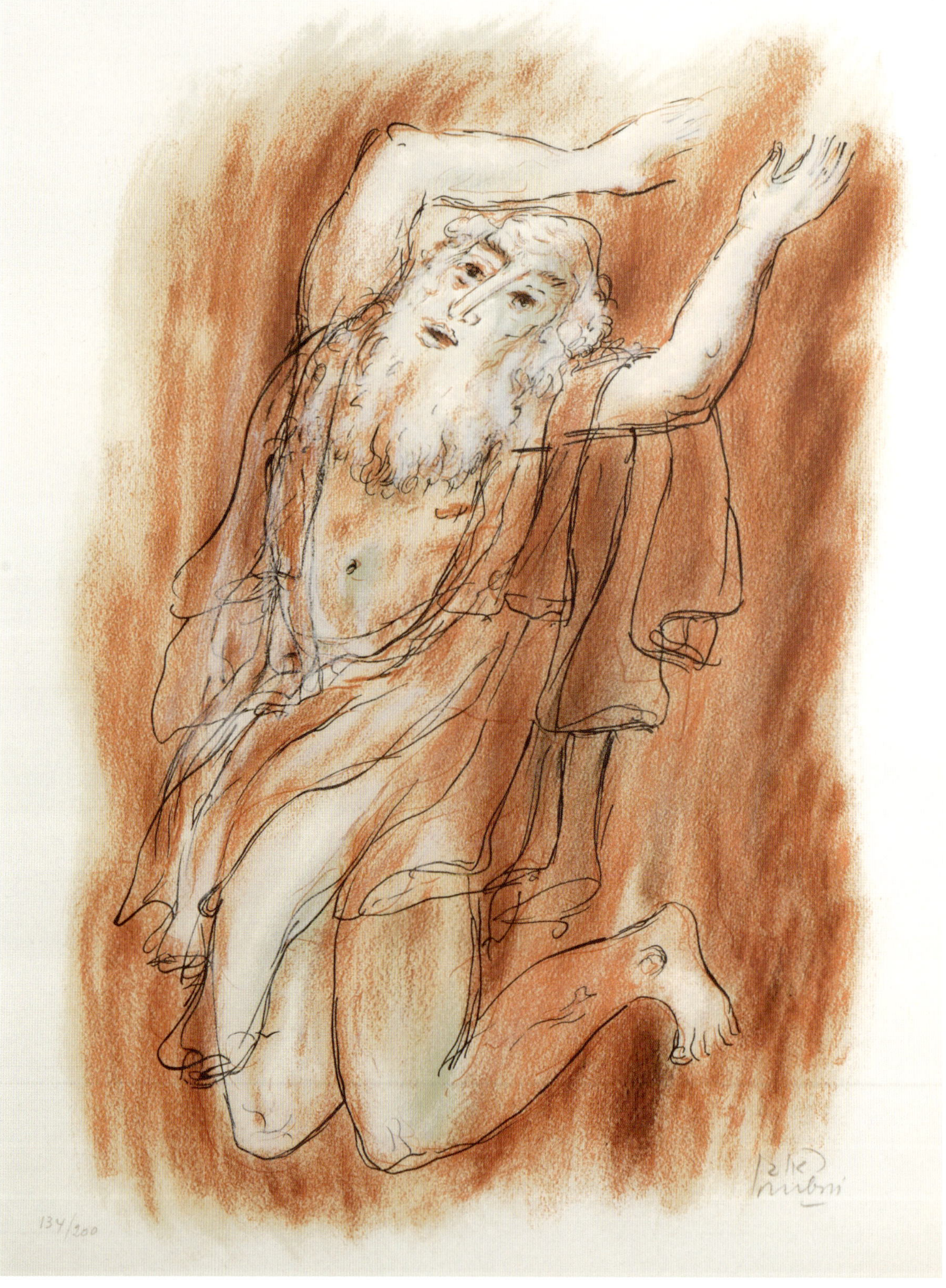

JEREMIAH

Jeremiah was a great prophet, from a distinguished line of priests of Anathoth, a village northeast of Jerusalem. Jeremiah had to speak for G-d during the final days of his beloved nation, Judah. Although he loved his nation, he opposed everything his king did, and was called a traitor. He was arrested, hounded, and threatened throughout his career for seeing the corruption in Judah and the political implications of the rise of Babylon. At one point he was left to die in an unused cistern, but was rescued by a friendly Ethiopian. As Jeremiah predicted, Jerusalem was captured and Judah's population deported. A misunderstood, lonely, sensitive man, Jeremiah is known as the Weeping Prophet because he watched his nation decline and finally fall under G-d's judgment.

Oh, that my head were waters, and mine eyes a fountain of tears, that I might weep day and night for the slain of the daughter of my people! —Jeremiah 9:1

The story of Jeremiah is from the Bible, JEREMIAH 1 - 52.

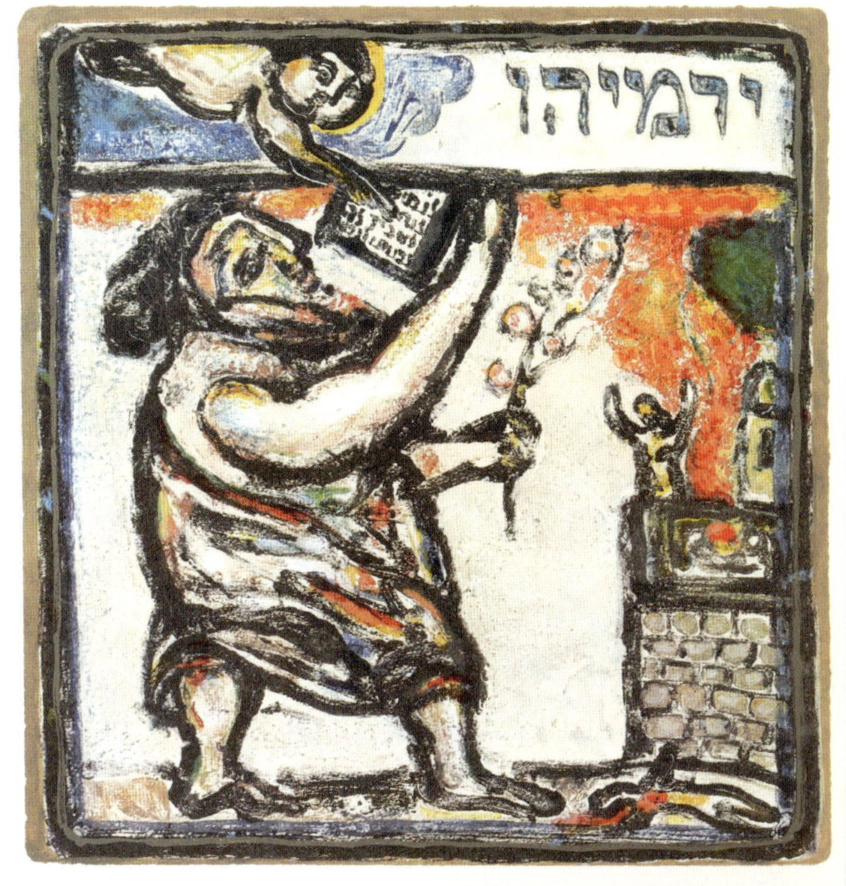

Shmuel Bonneh was born in Poland, 1930 and he immigrated to Israel in 1936. He studied with the painter Menachem Shemi, and the painter Abraham Yaskil. He was awarded the Hermann Struck prize of the Haifa Municipality in 1958. He lives in Haifa, where he has had one-man shows along with exhibitions in Jerusalem, Geneva, Paris, Frankfurt and the U.S.A. His works are found in the collections of the Israel Museum, The Museum of Modern Art in Haifa, the Tel-Aviv Museum, and in many private collections in Israel and abroad.

This lithograph portrays the prophet Jeremiah as he receives the word of G-d, saying he was ordained by G-d to be a prophet unto the nations.

THIRTY & EIGHT GATES TO THE BIBLE (38 she'arim la-Tanakh), 1983
Shmuel Bonneh
Israeli, born Poland, 1930 - 1999
Israel, 134/350
15½ x 12 in.
Loan from an anonymous lender

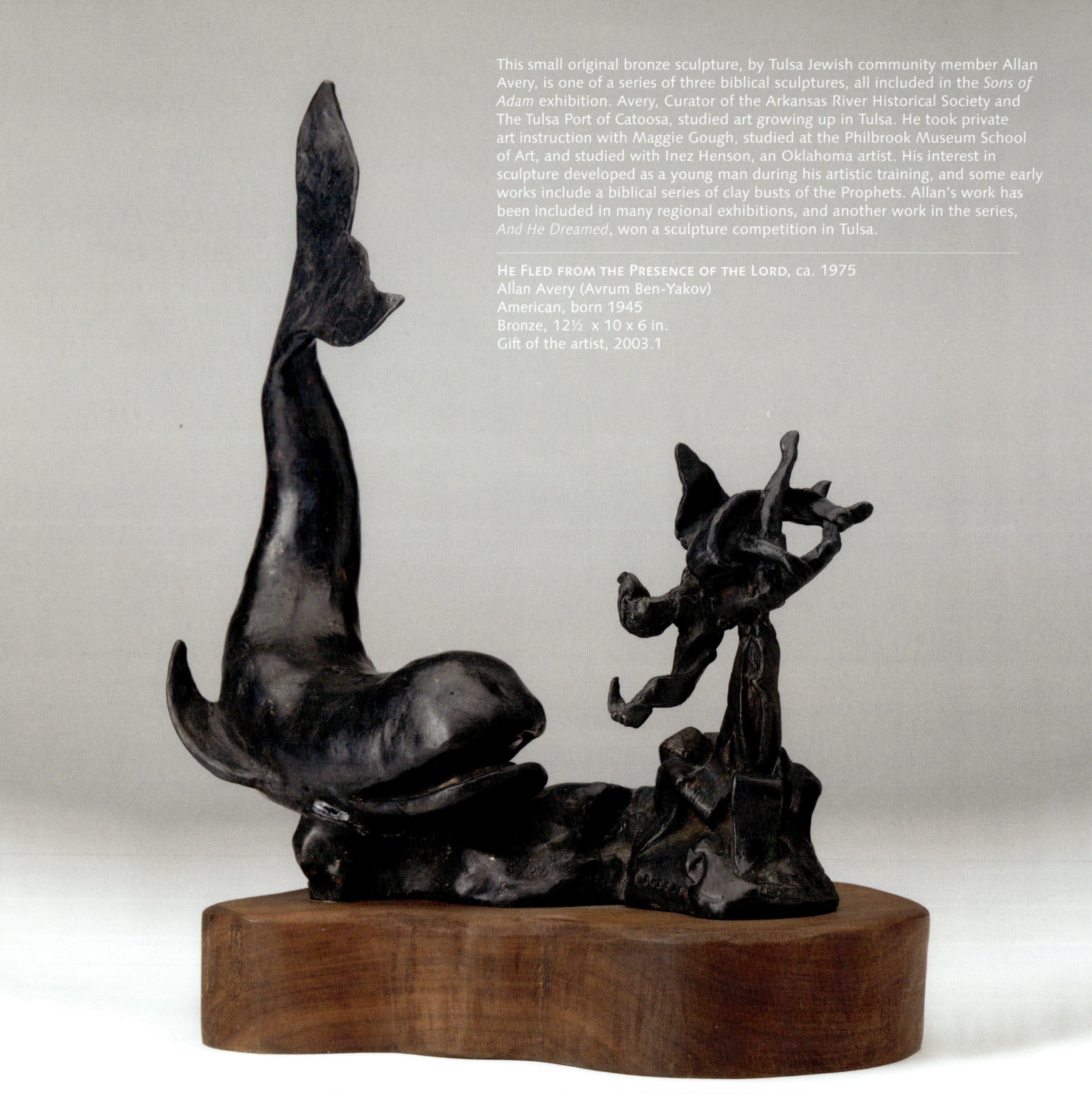

This small original bronze sculpture, by Tulsa Jewish community member Allan Avery, is one of a series of three biblical sculptures, all included in the *Sons of Adam* exhibition. Avery, Curator of the Arkansas River Historical Society and The Tulsa Port of Catoosa, studied art growing up in Tulsa. He took private art instruction with Maggie Gough, studied at the Philbrook Museum School of Art, and studied with Inez Henson, an Oklahoma artist. His interest in sculpture developed as a young man during his artistic training, and some early works include a biblical series of clay busts of the Prophets. Allan's work has been included in many regional exhibitions, and another work in the series, *And He Dreamed*, won a sculpture competition in Tulsa.

He Fled from the Presence of the Lord, ca. 1975
Allan Avery (Avrum Ben-Yakov)
American, born 1945
Bronze, 12½ x 10 x 6 in.
Gift of the artist, 2003.1

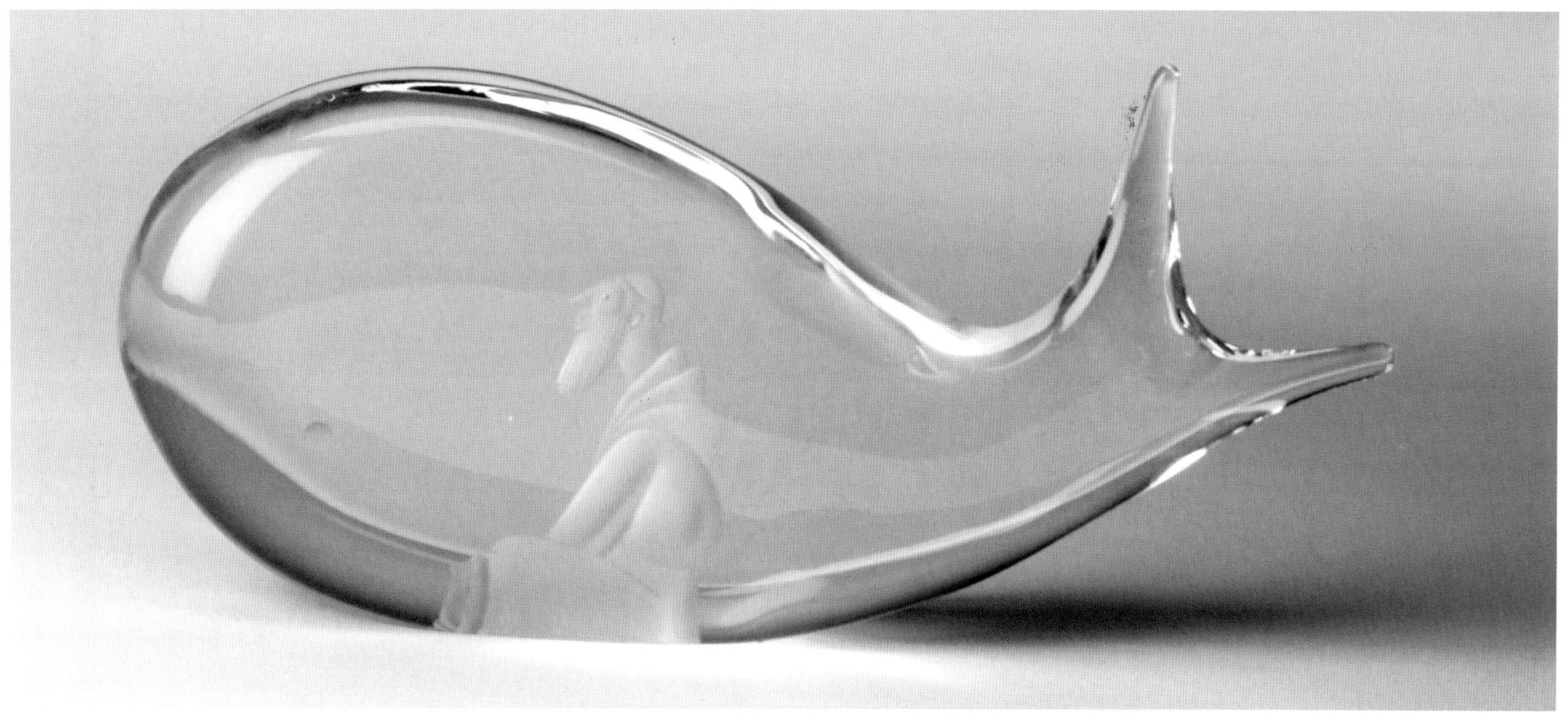

JONAH

Jonah, a prophet in the land of Judah, was chosen by G-d to go to Nineveh to tell the people of that city they would be destroyed for their wickedness. But Jonah did not want to go, so he boarded a ship heading in the opposite direction, to Tarshish. Jonah though he was safe, but G-d knew exactly what he was doing. As soon as the ship was away from land, a mighty storm arose. The sailors were afraid the ship would sink, and began to suspect that someone on board had displeased G-d. They decided to throw the guilty party overboard, and, to determine who was responsible, they cast lots. The lot fell to Jonah, who confessed, "I am the man who has brought this storm against the ship, for I have disobeyed the word of G-d." The sailors threw Jonah into the sea, and the storm ceased. But Jonah did not drown. A great whale swam near and swallowed him, and for three days and nights he remained in the whale's belly, repenting and praying. Then G-d commanded the whale to vomit Jonah up onto dry land, and this time he obeyed the voice of G-d and went to Nineveh. As soon as he had entered its gates, he declared that unless the people of that wicked city mended their ways and prayed for forgiveness, in forty days they would be destroyed. And they heeded Jonah's warning and escaped G-d's wrath.

The story of Jonah is from the Bible, JONAH 1 – 4.

Kosta, the parent glassworks of Kosta Boda and the oldest glassworks in Sweden that is still in operation, has a fascinating history that forms a valuable part of Swedish cultural heritage. The glassworks was founded in 1742 near Dåfvedshult, and continues today with three main workshops in Sweden. Kosta Boda artist Vicke Lindstrand created this charming sculpture of Jonah inside the Whale.

JONAH AND THE WHALE
Kosta Boda, Sweden
Glass
3 x 6½ x 1 in.
Loan from Susan Fenster

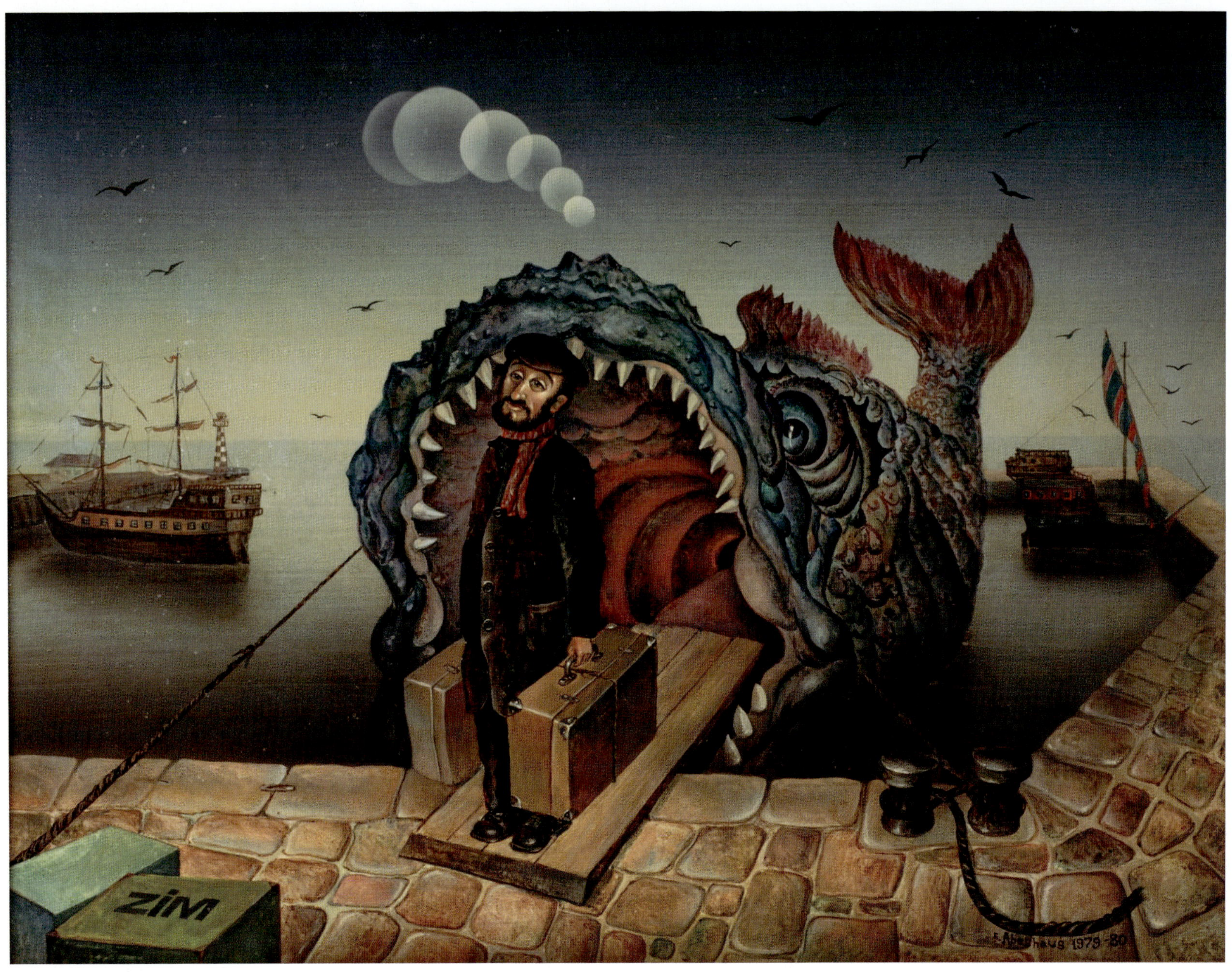

Eugene Abeshaus, born in Leningrad (now St. Petersburg) in 1939, graduated from the V. Mukhina Institute of Arts and Industrial Design in that city. Founder of Aleph, a Jewish artist collective in the mid-1970s, Eugene Abeshaus and Aleph caused a stir exhibiting Judaic works in Leningrad, and many members of the group emigrated to Israel or the United States to continue creating their work in a more supportive atmosphere. After 20 years of life in Israel, Abeshaus' artistic language is a humorous fusion of western post-modernism, Near Eastern decorative arts, and Russian sensibilities.

Jonah at Haifa Port, 1980
Eugene Abeshaus
Israeli, born Leningrad, 1939
Acrylic on Masonite, 22¾ x 28 in.
Gift of Deana Maloney and Sama Abend in honor of the 80th birthday of their mother Mildred Sanditen
1993.15

RACHEL

The stories of Rachel's marriage to Jacob and their two children are told in the Bible (Genesis, chapters 29-31). Rachel died in childbirth during a journey, outside Bethlehem. Jacob buried her by the roadside there, rather than at the family burial plot in Hebron, because he foresaw that his descendents would pass the site during their forced exile to Babylon. So Jacob set up a monument where exiled Jews could pray and be comforted as they were led into captivity. Ancient writings describe the grave marker as twelve stones that represented the Twelve Tribes of Israel, with one large stone that symbolized Jacob.

Of all the Matriarchs, Rachel is most remembered as a loving mother of her children. The Midrash (rabbinic commentary on Biblical verse) relates how, at the destruction of the first Temple, the Patriarchs pleaded before the Heavenly court to show mercy to the wayward Jews. The ears of Heaven remained deaf until Rachel entreated on their behalf, "Master of the Universe! Be as forbearing as me. You know how much Jacob loved me and how hard he worked to marry me. Yet on the wedding night my father switched me with Leah. I did everything in my power to help her so that she would not be discovered and ashamed forever. Now, Oh merciful King, though my children have sinned, and have been exiled and punished, stop and have mercy on them." Immediately, G-d said, "For you, Rachel, I shall return them from exile." So the verse says, "Thus says the L-rd, A voice was heard in Ramah, lamentation and bitter weeping, Rachel weeping for her children; she refused to be comforted for her children, because they are not" (Jeremiah 31:14).

The story of Rachel is from the Bible, Genesis 29-31, *and* Jeremiah 31:14.

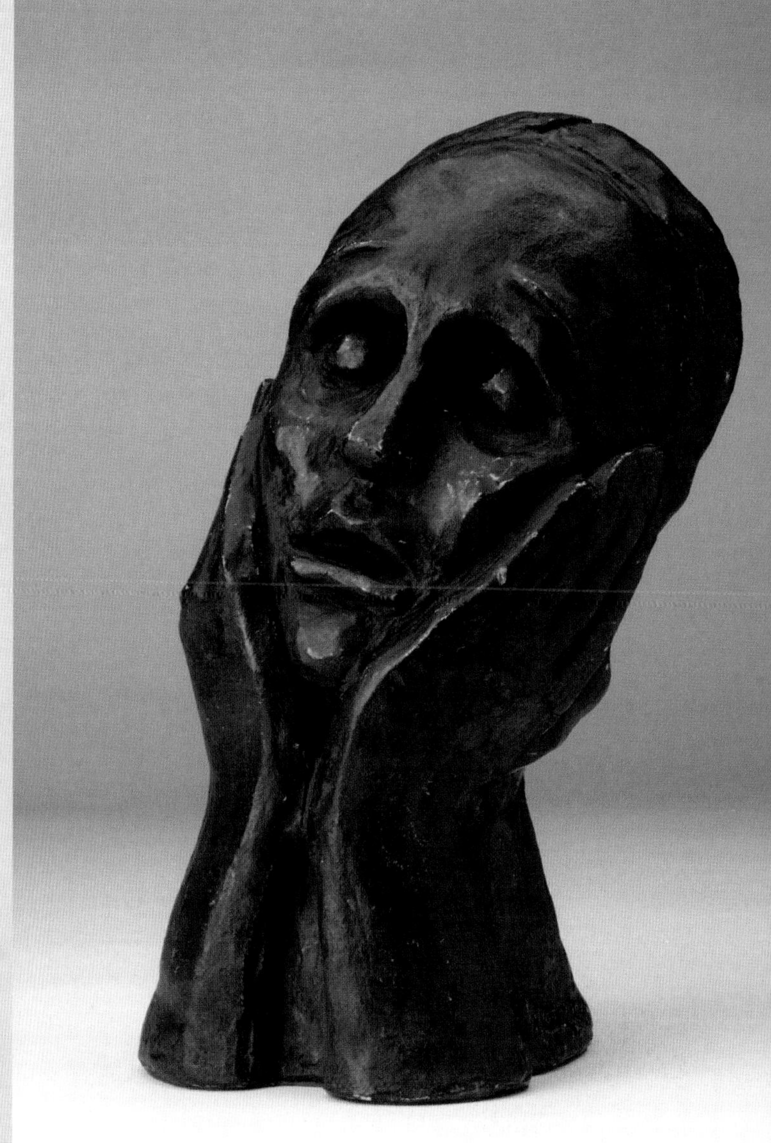

Max Band, a Lithuanian painter and sculptor, studied at the Berlin Academy and authored a "History of Contemporary Art" in 1935. Band emigrated to America and spent time in New York at the beginning of WWII, but moved on to California where he worked until his death in 1974.

Rachel Weeping for her Children, 1959
Max Band
American, born Lithuania, 1900 –1974
Plaster of Paris, bronze finish, 8½ x 6 in.
Gift of Alan Livingston on behalf of his mother, Mrs. Gertrude Livingston, 2004.13.1

LENDERS TO THE EXHIBITION

Anonymous lenders
Sue and Rick Arlan
Rebecca and Jim Bednar
Zella Borg
Sanford Cardin
Goldie Cash
Congregation B'nai Emunah
Rosalind Cook
Joe Degen
Shirley and Robert Dormont
Jennifer and Bruce Fadem
Laurel and Arthur M. Feldman
Susan Fenster
Irene and Irving Fenster
Estelle Finer
Irvin Frank
Gilcrease Museum of Art
Rebecca Kantor
Carolyn and Ron Kriegsman
Teddy Lachterman
Rita and Dr. Simon Levit
Sallye and Donald Mann
Rosalee Minsky
The Flo and Morris Mizel Jewish Community Day School
Rita Moskowitz
Drs. Bonnie and Gerald Polin
Gail and Kip Richards in care of the Tulsa Jewish Retirement Center
Phyllis and Howard Raskin
Isabel Sanditen
Mary Sanditen-Schwartz
Marge Singer and Kenneth Renberg
Martha and Fred Strauss
Temple Israel
Eva Unterman
Barbara and Dr. Ronald Winder
Dr. Karen and Robert York
Maxine and Jack Zarrow
Cynthia and Dr. Yohanan Zomer

THE SHERWIN MILLER MUSEUM OF JEWISH ART

2007 BOARD OF TRUSTEES